Advance Praise for
*A Roman Commentary on
St. Paul's Letter to the Philippians*

Richard Cassidy makes a convincing case for interpreting Paul's letter to the Philippians against the background of the Roman Empire with its emperor cult and its reliance on a system of slave labor. He lucidly explains how crucial it is to recognize, first, that Paul wrote the letter from Rome as a prisoner of the Roman state and, second, that Philippi was a Roman colony where Latin was the official language on coins and inscriptions. The author makes judicious use of an impressive range of literary, inscriptional, numismatic, and archaeological evidence to make his case. This concise "Roman commentary" from an expert with unsurpassed insight into the relevance of the Roman context for understanding early Christianity is an eye-opener, with many remarkably fresh and illuminating insights into Paul's letter.

Martinus C. de Boer
Vrije Universiteit of Amsterdam

A carefully executed counter-imperial reading of Philippians informed by masterly use of well selected Greek and Roman sources that brings to life and illuminates Paul's subtle but sustained critique of Roman imperial culture, thus the title *A Roman Commentary*; bristling with fresh exegetical suggestions combined with rich, theologically insightful exposition such as the twenty-page treatment of Paul's "Christ Drama" (2:6–11).

Carl R. Holladay
C. H. Candler Professor Emeritus of New Testament
Emory University

Professor Richard Cassidy's *Roman Commentary on Philippians* is an extremely useful book for specialized scholars, students, and a general audience interested in St. Paul and his world. The book is characterized by its author's profound knowledge of the Greco-Roman world of the New Testament, as well as by his comprehensive and in-depth grasp of the relevant vast scholarly discourse. In a detailed introduction, Professor Cassidy presents the Roman character of Philippi, Paul's ministry at the city, and its newly founded Christian community. Furthermore, he addresses all critical introductory questions on the Epistle to the Philippians. He then proceeds to a detailed interpretation of its text in a comprehensive but at the same time concise manner. While no questions remain unanswered, Professor Cassidy adroitly avoids extensive notes or addenda, thus making for fascinating reading.

Christos Karakolis
Professor of New Testament
National and Kapodistrian University of Athens, Greece

This is a commentary that challenges us to read a very familiar text in quite a fresh way. Through Cassidy's sensitive reading, we hear Paul's emphasis on the Roman qualities of the city Philippi and of Paul's own situation, and, through Cassidy's analysis of the letter's dramatic qualities, we discover some surprisingly subversive implications.

Wayne A. Meeks
Woolsey Professor Emeritus of Religious Studies
Yale University

Richard Cassidy's new commentary on the Epistle to the Philippians not only focuses in on a refreshing and detailed analysis of the text, examining the breathtaking vocabulary and images used by Saint Paul in his challenging presentation of Christ and his message to a community of believers threatened with persecution. It also brings alive the ancient world of Philippi and Rome, the dynamic context of empire and slavery, in which the Epistle was composed. It is an important contribution to our understanding of an ancient text and its contemporary significance.

Rev. David M. Neuhaus, SJ
Pontifical Biblical Institute, Jerusalem

The title (*A Roman Commentary on St. Paul`s Letter to the Philippians*) already shows the focus of the book: The letter was written in Rome and has a substantial attitude toward the dangerous situation of both St. Paul and the Philippians. Therefore the extended Introduction is very interesting, which deals especially with this situation, for example, the military history of Philippi, the Roman character of the city, the emperor cult, slavery, persecution, the position of Philippi`s magistrates. Cassidy clearly offers his positions with a lot of arguments and without forgetting other positions. The book is to be read fluently and sophisticatedly, as it describes the questions of the epistle. A very fine book, even if the reader cannot accept all of its details.

Wilhelm Pratscher
University of Vienna

This commentary brings together an empire critical reading of Acts and Paul's letter to the Philippians. Writing as Nero's prisoner in Rome, Paul, the former troublemaker at Philippi, tries to comfort, strengthen and encourage his now persecuted fellow-Christians in this Roman provincial city. For Richard Cassidy, Philippians is fundamentally a letter about Christ. In chains, Paul composed the drama of Christ's descent to a Roman cross and later cosmic exaltation in order to challenge Roman claims of power and slave-based society. A well-written commentary, based on a nuanced reading of the Greek text, deeply engaged in critical scholarship and with a distinctive, unique thesis.

Prof. Dr. Angela Standhartinger
University of Marburg, Germany

A Roman Commentary on St. Paul`s Letter to the Philippians needs to be explained from its Roman socio-historic context in order to better understand it. Richard Cassidy has managed to do this superbly. His commentary is one of the few that helps readers visualize the specific situation of Paul and the community of Philippi at the time that the letter was written from prison. Through his exegetical-hermeneutical analysis of the text, and bearing in mind the background of the Roman Empire—detailed in the Introduction—it is possible to understand Paul's sufferings as a prisoner, as well as the hardships of his recipients' discrimination and persecution. His commentary is a great contribution to the recent studies of Philippians.

Elsa Tamez
Emerita Professor of the
Latin American Biblical University, Costa Rica

COVER PHOTO ACKNOWLEDGMENT

This photo beautifully depicts the contemporary ruins of Philippi's forum and its surroundings. Mrs. Liza Evert of Athens originally took this photo for the cover of her own book, *Paulos ho Apostolos tōn Hellēnōn*. She has graciously authorized its use for the cover of this commentary.

A ROMAN COMMENTARY ON

ST. PAUL'S LETTER TO

THE PHILIPPIANS

A ROMAN COMMENTARY ON ST. PAUL'S LETTER TO THE PHILIPPIANS

by
Richard J. Cassidy

A Herder & Herder Book
The Crossroad Publishing Company
New York

A Herder & Herder Book
The Crossroad Publishing Company
www.crossroadpublishing.com

© 2020 by Richard J. Cassidy

Crossroad, Herder & Herder, and the crossed C logo/colophon are registered trademarks of The Crossroad Publishing Company.

All rights reserved. No part of this book may be copied, scanned, reproduced in any way, or stored in a retrieval system, or transmitted, in any form or by any means, electronic, mechanical, photocopying, recording, or otherwise, without the written permission of The Crossroad Publishing Company. For permission please write to rights@crossroadpublishing.com.

In continuation of our 200-year tradition of independent publishing, The Crossroad Publishing Company proudly offers a variety of books with strong, original voices and diverse perspectives. The viewpoints expressed in our books are not necessarily those of The Crossroad Publishing Company, any of its imprints or of its employees, executives, or owners. Although the author and publisher have made every effort to ensure that the information in this book was correct at press time, the author and publisher do not assume and hereby disclaim any liability to any party for any loss, damage, or disruption caused by errors or omissions, whether such errors or omissions result from negligence, accident, or any other cause. No claims are made or responsibility assumed for any health or other benefits.

Book design by The HK Scriptorium
Cover design by Sophie Appel

Library of Congress Cataloging-in-Publication Data
available upon request from the Library of Congress.

ISBN 9780824501648 paperback
ISBN 9780824501631 cloth
ISBN 9780824501679 ePub
ISBN 9780824501686 mobi

Books published by The Crossroad Publishing Company may be purchased at special quantity discount rates for classes and institutional use. For information, please e-mail sales@crossroadpublishing.com.

DEDICATION

Chief Judge Michael J. Talbot, Ret.
Michigan Court of Appeals

REFLECTION

The words of Hebrews 12:1 that "we are surrounded by so great a cloud of witnesses" are words that I embrace as I reflect regarding the unfolding stages of this commentary. I can identify so many assisting friends within my mind's eye. I am filled with a deep and abiding gratitude and motivated to pray the more. St. Paul, show the way for all such prayers in honor of the name of Jesus.

Contents

INTRODUCTION ... 1

1. Titles of Exaltation in the Eastern Provinces ... 1
2. Maiestas ... 3
3. The Character of Augustus's Rule ... 5
4. The Military History of Philippi ... 6
5. The Roman Character of Philippi ... 7
6. Roman Citizenship at Philippi ... 11
7. The Emperor Cult at Philippi ... 12
8. Slavery in the Roman Empire ... 16
9. Paul's Ministry at Philippi according to Acts ... 20
10. Christian Slaves at Philippi ... 21
11. The Christian Community of Philippi and Its Persecution ... 23
12. The Perspectives and Responses of Philippi's Magistrates ... 27
13. Philippians Authored from Rome ... 29
14. The Date of Philippians ... 32
15. The Unity of Philippians ... 34
16. Philippians as a Prison Letter ... 34
17. Paul's Purposes in Philippians ... 38
18. The "Narrative" Embedded in Philippians ... 42
19. Philippians' Subversiveness When Performed ... 43

COMMENTARY ... 45
Outline of Philippians ... 45
  I. Opening of the Letter (1:1-11) ... 46
    A. Address and Salutation (1:1-2) ... 47
    B. Thanksgiving (1:3-11) ... 54

II.	Overview of Paul's Situation (1:12-26)	61
	A. Paul's Chains Advance the Gospel (1:12-13)	63
	B. Paul's Chains Engender Division (1:14-18)	65
	C. Paul's Potential for Death or Life (1:19-26)	70
III.	The Same Conflict at Philippi and Rome (1:27-30)	74
IV.	Harmony and Unselfishness (2:1-5)	78
V.	Drama Depicting Christ's Descent to a Roman Cross Followed by Cosmic Exaltation (2:6-11)	81
VI.	Further Encouragement for the Philippians (2:12-16)	99
VII.	Paul again Envisions His Death (2:17-18)	102
VIII.	The Mission of Timothy (2:19-24)	104
IX.	The Mission of Epaphroditus (2:25–3:1)	108
X.	Paul's Response to a Threat from "the Circumcisers" (3:2-7)	113
XI.	Paul's Communion with Christ in Life and Death (3:8-16)	115
XII.	Paul's Response to a Threat from "the Enemies of the Cross of Christ" (3:17–4:1)	121
XIII.	Entreaty to Euodia and Synteche (4:2-3)	131
XIV.	Encouragement to Rejoice and Be Grounded in Christ (4:4-9)	134
XV.	Response to the Philippians' Gift (4:10-20)	137
XVI.	Concluding Greeting and Benediction (4:21-23)	144

Appendix I: Cartography	148
Appendix II: Roman Provincial and Imperial Coins	160
Appendix III: Images of Slaves	166
Appendix IV: Later Images of Paul as an Imperial Prisoner	170
Appendix V: Material Factors in the Production of This Commentary	172
Bibliography	174
Index of Passages	202
Index of Authors and Contributors	208
Index of Subjects	212

Introduction

THE EXPLOSIVE POWER OF PHILIPPIANS is twofold. First, in a social setting in which Roman propaganda insists that Nero is lord and savior, Paul counters that Jesus *alone* is Lord. Second, in a social system in which slaves are exploited unto "social death," Paul proclaims that Jesus consciously embraced the form of a slave and underwent the slave's form of death.

In the setting of his custody in Rome, Paul has gained critical new insights regarding the status path followed by Jesus Christ and regarding the implications of this path for fundamental features of the Roman imperial order. In this letter to his beloved Philippians Paul counsels and encourages them with specific reference to their discipleship. He effectively challenges the cult of the Roman emperors. He also implicitly challenges the slave-based foundation of the empire.

Nineteen sections comprise this Introduction. The need for this extended setting of the stage arises from the complexity of the situations at Philippi and at Rome. Each location has a prehistory that must be grasped in order to appreciate the story world of the letter, a story world in which Paul and the Philippians are both experiencing Roman persecution.

1. Titles of Exaltation in the Eastern Provinces

The emperor cult initiated by Augustus and practiced by his successors is a complex phenomenon. In the present section the focus is on three titles—god, lord, and savior—that were central to this cult. These titles will be considered in greater detail within the commentary proper. In the next section, the related phenomenon of *maiestas* will be considered.

Because of the way these titles function in Philippians, it is useful to establish that the Julio-Claudian emperors from Augustus to Nero all enjoyed acclaim as "god," "lord," and "savior." Paul may not have had personal knowledge of all of the mechanisms by which these titles were attributed to a given emperor. Nevertheless, these titles were extensively proclaimed in the cities and regions in which Paul traveled. The examples that follow indicate that these forms of acclaim were accorded to all of the emperors who ruled during Paul's lifetime.

Augustus. An Egyptian papyrus from AD 1 (Deissmann 1978, 353) refers to Augustus as "god and lord emperor" (*hyper tou theou kai kyrious autōkratoros*). An Egyptian inscription from 24 BC (Deissmann 1978, 345) references him as "god of god" (*theon ek theou*). The powerful combination of "god" (*theos*) and "savior" (*sōtēr*) appears in an inscription for Augustus at Olympia (Deissmann 1978, 344).

Tiberius. An inscription from a monument in Athens (Vanderpool 1959, 87) refers to Tiberius as "the august god" (*theos sebastos*). An inscription from Abila in Syria before AD 20 (Deissmann 1978, 353) describes Tiberius and his mother, Livia, as "the lords augusti" (*tōn kyriōn sebastōn*). An inscription from Myra in Lycia (Ehrenberg and Jones 1976, 75) identifies Tiberius as "the benefactor and savior of the whole world" (*ton euergetēn kai sōtēra tou synpantos kosmou*).

Gaius. In *Embassy to Gaius* 353, Philo notes Gaius's self-adulation as a "god": "Are you the god-haters who do not believe me to be a god (*theon*), a god acknowledged among all the other nations. . . ." In *Epitome de Caesaribus* 3, 7 Aurelius Victor reports Gaius's order that he be addressed as "lord" (*dominus*). A sestercius minted at Rome (Braund 1985, 77; Smallwood 1967, 40) describes Gaius as father of his country "for citizens *saved*" (*ob cives servatos*).

Claudius. A votive inscription from Magnesia between AD 50 and 54 (Deissmann 1978, 347) refers to Nero's sonship to "the greatest of the gods, Tiberius Claudius" (*tou megistou theōn Tiberiou Klaudiou*). A papyrus document from AD 49 and an ostracon from AD 54 both call Claudius "the lord" (ibid., 353). An inscription from Aezani (Tellbe 2001, 253) describes him as "god savior and benefactor" (*theos sōtēr kai euergetēs*).

Nero. A votive inscription at Cos in AD 53 (Deissmann 1978, 345) refers to Nero as "the good god" (*agathō theō*). Nero is mentioned as "lord" (*kyrios*) in various inscriptions and papyrus documents. (See the listing and discussion in the commentary at 2:11.) Nero is also frequently called "savior" (*sōtēr*). An inscription from Cyprus in AD 60–61 designates him with this unadorned title (Smallwood 1967, 52, no. 142). According to Deissmann (1978, 364) Nero was acclaimed in the eastern provinces as "savior of the world" (*sōtēr tou kosmou*) from the time of his accession. Nero was so enamored of this designation that he coined for himself (ibid., 365) the adjective "world saving" (*sosikosmios*).

2. Maiestas

Because the concept of *maiestas* ("treason") was probably decisive in Paul's case, an overview of the various meanings of this term during the Julio-Claudian era is useful.

Just as the Julio-Claudian emperors utilized the emperor cult as a means of *enhancing* their status, so they utilized prosecutions on the grounds of *maiestas* as a means of *defending* their status. The crime of *maiestas* originally involved "the diminution of the majesty of the Roman people" (Lintott and Balsdon 1996, 913). Nevertheless, *maiestas* proved to be "a plastic and expandable concept" (Levick 1976, 184). In the hands of the Julio-Claudians, various alleged offenses were prosecuted under the cover of *maiestas*.

In treating the reports of Tacitus, Suetonius, and Dio Cassius, bias and exaggeration must be considered (Elsner and Masters 1994, passim). Nevertheless, the following reports suffice to establish that the charge of *maiestas* was extensively used by the Julio-Claudian emperors.

According to Suetonius (*Domitian* 21), Domitian observed that "the only time that anybody believed an emperor's statement that he had detected a conspiracy was when the conspiracy succeeded and he was dead." Such an articulation expresses the perceived threat under which each emperor lived. It partially explains why Augustus and those who succeeded him in the Julio-Claudian line preemptively invoked *maiestas*.

A kind of "imperial solidarity" came to be associated with *maiestas* (Baumann 1974, 225). For example, it became an offense against *maiestas* to diminish the memory of the emperors who had been deified by the senate. It also became an offense against *maiestas* to dishonor the image of a ruling emperor.

Augustus, in his most recognized use of this charge, employed it to prosecute his own daughter and five senators with whom she had had liaisons. In addition to the fact that Julia's conduct engendered scandal against his own reputation, Augustus may have suspected that some of his daughter's paramours were actually plotting against him (Syme 1960, 427).

Tiberius employed *maiestas* in several ways. Dio Cassius's summarizing assessment is as follows: "Among the other ways in which his rule became cruel, he pushed to the bitter end the trials for *maiestas*, in cases where complaint was made against anyone for committing any improper act, or uttering any improper speech, not only against Augustus but also against Tiberius himself and against his mother" (*Roman History* 57.19).

Soon after succeeding Tiberius, Gaius announced that he was putting an end to Tiberius's wanton use of *maiestas*. Yet Gaius himself soon began to condemn many on this charge. Tacitus points to a parallel between Gaius's reversal regarding *maiestas* and his reversal on the matter of accepting sacrifices made to him. Initially Gaius published a decree forbidding sacrifices to his name. Later he "ordered temples to be erected and sacrifices to be offered to himself as a god" (*Roman History* 59.4).

After his ascension, Claudius abolished *maiestas*. Over the course of his reign, the use of this charge was reduced. Yet seemingly in the case of Lucius Vitellius, and perhaps in other cases as well, Claudius did authorize *maiestas* (Cassidy 2001b, 60-61).

As a consequence of his extreme youth, Nero was cautious about utilizing *maiestas* during his first years as emperor. After he perpetrated the murder of his mother, Agrippina, however, Nero began to engage openly in many forms of aberrant conduct.

In his reports for AD 62 Tacitus indicates that *maiestas* proceedings were undertaken against the praetor Antistius on the grounds that he had composed verses satirizing Nero (*Annals* 14.48-49). Another bizarre case is reported by Suetonius and Dio Cassius: Nero had the procurator of Egypt recalled and then banished because he had the effrontery to bathe in the imperial bath, which was being constructed for a forthcoming visit by Nero (Suetonius, *Nero* 35.5; Dio Cassius, *Roman History* 62.18).

Two additional episodes illustrate Nero's megalomania regarding his majesty. The senator Thraesa had been boycotting Nero's performances and was in turn forbidden from joining in welcoming Nero back to Rome from Campania. When Thraesa inquired regarding the particulars of the charge against him, his offense was specified as a violation of Nero's *maiestas* (Tacitus, *Annals* 16.22.1, 21.1): Thraesa had failed to render appropriate homage to Nero's "celestial voice" (*caelestis vox*).

Another "violation" of Nero's *maiestas* led to death. Dio Cassius reports that, after Nero won contrived victories at the Phythian games in Greece in the year 67, throngs of Romans were turned out to welcome him with the chorus "Hail Pythian Victor." Nero so prized this title of acclaim that he ordered Sulpicius Comerinus *Pythicus* to abandon the use of his own name lest Nero's *maiestas* be diminished! In the appraisal of Richard Bauman (1974, 156–57) when Sulpicius Comerinus and his son continued to sign their own full names, they were in effect signing their death warrants!

3. The Character of Augustus's Rule

Julius Caesar and the five emperors who succeeded him (Augustus, Tiberius, Gaius, Claudius, and Nero) constitute the Julio-Claudian dynasty. Of these six rulers, Augustus and Nero are arguably the most important for the interpretation of Philippians. Augustus developed the political framework that enabled him and the other Julio-Claudians to wield sovereign power. Nero's importance arises from what Philippians implies regarding his embrace of practices that rendered him an "enemy" of Christ.

After his defeat of Mark Antony, Augustus's power was unrivaled. Virgil's *Aeneid* heralded him as the ruler of an empire without end (*imperium sine fine*). Nevertheless, Augustus needed a strategy that would protect him from assassination by senators and others who remained committed to the Roman Republic. The strategy that Augustus formulated was to rule not as a dictator but rather as the *princeps*, as "the leading citizen."

Under this strategy, Augustus created an arrangement that was, in effect, a "disguised monarchy" (Garnsey and Saller 1987, 1–3). A full description of his constitutional and military initiatives is beyond the scope of this study. In terms of longevity, Augustus ruled a vast empire for forty-five years. Further, during his reign, he established the principle that each succeeding *princeps* was to be sought within the imperial family (Syme 1960, 438–39; Levick 1976, 31–67).

4. The Military History of Philippi

Philippi takes its name from Philip of Macedon, who gained control of the city of Crenides and its surrounding territory circa 356 BC. In 168 BC, the Roman general Aemilius Paullus defeated King Perseus at Pynda and placed all of Macedonia under Roman control (Gill 1994, 400–402). The eventual result was that Philippi became a city within the Roman province of Macedonia. It continued as such until the Battle of Philippi in 42 BC. In this battle, Mark Antony and Octavian (later acclaimed by the senate as "Augustus") defeated the forces of Brutus and Cassius.

More successful in the battle than Octavian, Antony took steps to establish Philippi as a Roman military "colony" (*colonia*), providing land there for the victorious veterans who had completed their term of service. Coins issued by Antony at this time (Collart 1937, 225) feature his head with the initials A I C V P. The last three letters stand for "Colonia Victrix Philippensium" (Colony of the Victory of Philippi). The letters A I indicate that the coins were issued by Antony's authority (Grant 1969, 274).

Twelve years later, in 30 BC, Octavian (Augustus) defeated Antony and Cleopatra at the Battle of Actium, a site not far from Philippi. Augustus himself then used Philippi as a settlement location for military veterans, especially for a contingent from his own praetorian guard.

Acting now with unrivaled power, Augustus formally refounded Philippi as *his* colony (Williams 1995, 281). To advertise his own role, Augustus proceeded to issue new coins that effectively minimized Antony's earlier achievements. These coins proclaimed that Augustus was the authentic founder of the colony. Augustus's head appears on the obverse of these coins with four abbreviated Latin words: *Colonia Iulia Augusta Philippensis*.

The abbreviation *Iussu Aug* ("ordered by Augustus") also appears on these coins, indicating that they were explicitly authorized by Augustus. By making reference to *Iulia* (Julia), Augustus publicized his alignment with the Julian family into which he had been adopted. In effect he was acting demonstratively as the heir of Julius Caesar.

One additional coin pertaining to Augustus's role as the decisive founder of the colony should be considered. The obverse of this coin features the figure of Victory carrying a wreath and a palm branch. On the left of this figure, the abbreviation VIC (Victory) appears. On the right, the abbreviation AUG (Augustus) is found.

The reverse of this coin depicts three sets of praetorian standards and the abbreviation COHOR PRAE PHIL (Praetorian Cohort at Philippi). The coin thus commemorates the decision of Augustus to settle a cohort of his praetorian guards at Philippi.

Coins of this type can also be dated to the regimes of Claudius and Nero. The minting of such coins decades after Augustus settled his praetorians is testimony to the continuing importance of Augustus's initiatives at Philippi.

The impact of Roman military personnel twice receiving land grants at Philippi should be underscored. Antony settled legionary veterans after the Battle of Philippi in 42 BC, and Augustus settled praetorian veterans (and probably some veterans from Italy) after the Battle of Actium in 30 BC. DeVos (1999, 236) cites scholars who hold that approximately five hundred colonists were settled by Antony after 42 BC and five hundred by Augustus after Actium in 30 BC. DeVos's own conjecture is that two to three thousand veterans may have been settled after each battle.

How did these military settlements impact the total population of Philippi? Estimates need to take account of the population of the city proper and that of its surrounding villages and farming lands. Oakes (2007, 45) initially estimates the population of the town proper at 10,000 with an additional 5,000 inhabitants for the suburbs. He then observes that a much higher figure of 46,000 could be appropriate if it were judged that the land area that the colony encompassed was actually much larger (ibid., 46). DeVos (1999, 239) conjectures that the population of the town proper would have been between 9,000 and 11,500, a figure in the same range as Oakes's first projection.

5. The Roman Character of Philippi

In its governance and in its daily life, Philippi was highly Romanized and Latinized (Reumann 2008, 3). Apart from Rome itself Philippi was easily the most "Roman" city that Paul encountered. In various ways, the term "minor Rome" is apt for Philippi.

Legally, Philippi possessed the *Ius Italicum*. This privilege conferred various rights, principally the right that landed property in Philippi was exempt from taxation just as it was in Italy (Vincent 1902, xvi–xvii). Latin was universally used for the civic inscriptions at Philippi, as well as for the colony's coins. The architectural style of Rome was replicated in many of the colony's buildings and roads. The toga and other forms of Roman dress were frequently worn in public.

The Roman emperors and the local magistrates embellished the city with architecture designed "to advertise the glory of the emperor and the power of Rome" (Koukouli-Chrysanthaki 2011, 448). Claudius and Nero, the emperors who ruled during the first decades of Paul's ministry, continued their predecessors' promotion of Philippi and Macedonia. The colony's first forum was built during the reign of Claudius (ibid). Claudius also extended the Via Egnatia from Neapolis to Byzantium via Thrace. In AD 61 Nero ordered inns to be erected along this new segment of the road (Peterlin 1995, 162).

Augustus's land grants to praetorians and other veterans are an indication that Philippi possessed a significant amount of land suited to agriculture. Roman traders also sought their livelihood in Macedonia and settled in Philippi as merchants. The mercantile life of the city flourished in shops along the thoroughfares and in the bulding complex at the *agora* (Koukouli-Chrysanthaki 2011, 449–50).

As a result, Philippi, along with its port Neapolis, became a flourishing urban center. Vendors and traders, among them some Jews, traveled to the city from the eastern provinces of the empire (ibid). The imperial coins minted at Philippi (Kremydi 2011, 177; Koukouli-Chrysanthaki 2011, 451; Levick 1967, 61) undoubtedly proved beneficial for Philippi's trade and commerce.

The governance structure of Philippi reflected established Roman patterns. Collart (1937, 262) identifies inscriptions listing the following political officeholders: *duumviri iure dicundo* (literally, "two men for the administration of justice"); *quaestores*, *aediles*, *quinquennales*, *irenarchae* (literally "officers of the peace"), and *decuriones* (senate members).

As the two chief magistrates of the city, the *duumviri iure dicundo* exercised significant power over the political, religious, and cultural life of the city. They were both the chief executive and chief judicial officers of the colony (Saddington 1996, 2430). They were, in effect, "shadows" of the consuls at Rome (Fuhrmann 2012, 58).

The *duumviri* presided over meetings of the colony's senate and, upon the completion of their terms of service as magistrates, they were themselves eligible for election to the colony's senate as decurions (see below). Because of their jurisdiction over both civic and religious observances (Stevenson 1949, 172), the *duumviri* played a significant role in the functioning of the emperor cult at Philippi. Unlike the consuls at Rome (who possessed the highest form of *imperium*), the *duumviri* of Philippi could not impose death sentences, and they could not raise armies (Fuhrmann 2012, 58).

The *quaestors* and *aediles* were subordinate to the *duumviri*. The *quaestors* were generally responsible for municipal finances. The *aediles* had responsibility for public buildings, streets, and aqueducts. As a general rule, the term of office for these latter magistracies was a single year; however, as their name indicates, the *duumviri quinquennales* served for a five-year term (Tellbe 2001, 219). The *duumviri* and other magistrates of Philippi annually professed an oath of allegiance to the reigning emperor, probably at a city-wide observance of an imperial anniversary.

A concrete example of the Philippian magistrates' wide influence can be seen in their oversight of the theater-arena at Philippi. This theater was originally constructed by Philip of Macedon. Under Roman auspices it was reconstructed as an arena while retaining its properties as a theater (Koukouli-Chrysanthaki 2011, 249). This impressive facility served as a venue for mime actors and for competitions by gladiators and by hunters who contested against wild beasts (ibid., 451). Significantly, the theater also served as a site for rituals and religious spectacles promoting the emperor cult and the cults of other deities.

For the purpose of promoting these dramas and spectacles, Philippi's magistrates funded a residential troup of actors. A "chief mime" (*archimimus*) was delegated to oversee these productions and to represent the interests of the actors in their dealings with the magistrates (Collart 1937, 272–73).

Other offices pertaining to the actors' troupe are also known from inscriptions. (The Latin names for these personnel are another indication of the Roman character of the colony.) A *choragiarius* was responsible for the oversight of the chorus and for providing the supplies necessary for its performances (ibid., 233). A *locator scaenicorum* was responsible for the stages and the sets (ibid., 272). The role of a *muneriarus,* who provided funds for individual performances or spectacles, is also attested (ibid., 383).

Former magistrates were eligible for election to the colony's senate or consilium as *decuriones,* serving for life. Sherwin-White comments regarding the general influence of *decuriones* in Roman territories (1996, 477): "They controlled the public life of the community, its administration, and finances, incuding the voting of decrees and statutes. They had charge of its external relations, including the sending of embassies and petitions to the emperor or provincial governor."

The "authorities for ensuring peace" (*irenarchs*) were the chief police officers of the colony. Fuhrmann (2012, 67) cites *The Digest*'s definition of them as those "who are in charge of public discipline and correcting behavior." At least two other groups within the colony, lictors and "market police," also fulfilled police functions.

Collart follows Lecrivain's view that the *duumviri* were each entitled to have two lictors attend them (1937, 272). The lictors of a provincial governor carried *fasces,* five-foot-high bundles of rods bound with a red cord. Because provincial governors were authorized to impose the death penalty, lictors who attended provincial governors carried an axe within their *fasces.* The lictors who attended the *duumviri* at Philippi probably carried *bacillae,* a term for *fasces* without the axe. Nevertheless, the rods themselves were potent enough to inflict a severe flogging (Fuhrmann 2012, 63–64, 186).

Some slaves functioned in police roles. It was common practice for "public slaves" (slaves owned by the municipality) to accompany magistrates to help them make arrests and otherwise oversee public safety (ibid., 64). Similarly, public slaves could also be assigned as jailers and torturers (ibid., 65).

The "market police" (*agoranomoi*) supervised Philippi's commerce. In doing so they played a significant role in the daily life of the colony. The *agoranomoi* were tasked with preventing fraud, ensuring honest weights and measures, and guaranteeing that applicable fees were paid (ibid., 59). They might be assisted in these tasks by public slaves.

The Romans were not the initiators of the practice of using public slaves in the role of police. Centuries earlier, in 477 BC, Athens established an armed police force consisting of more than three hundred Scythian slaves. These slaves were owned by the state. They were initially housed in tents in the agora and subsequently on the acropolis (Finley 1968, 172; Westermann 1964, 7).

6. Roman Citizenship at Philippi

The influence of Roman veterans and their descendants at Philippi was a key factor contributing to the *romanitas* of the colony. Fully apart from any other extension of citizenship, the heritage of these veterans would have sufficed to make Philippi the most Romanized city that Paul visited prior to his incarceration in Rome.

Nevertheless, Augustus may actually have extended citizenship broadly at Philippi. Such a step would have been consistent with his initiatives regarding colonies he established elsewhere. Basing his conclusion on reports by Tertullian (*De pallio* i) and Appian (*Punic Wars* 136), Sherwin-White (1980, 227) asserts that Augustus conferred Roman citizenship widely at Carthage. In that African setting Augustus integrated the existing Punic city-state (*civitas*) into a new colony to form a unified entity of Roman citizens. The new emperor followed a similar practice in Cisalpine Gaul (ibid., 248). When he settled three thousand of his praetorians at that location, Augustus also bestowed citizenship on the members of the Salassi tribe and incorporated them into the new Augustan colony.

According to Susan Alcock (1993, 137) Augustus followed a comparable policy for a colony he founded at Patrae in Achaea. Augustus named this colony *Colonia Aroe Augusta Patrensis*. Because Patrae had suffered a decline in population, Augustus brought Greeks from the surrounding towns to the site of his new colony. According to Pausanias (*Description of Greece* 7.18.7), Augustus "granted freedom to the Patraeans, and to no other Achaeans; and he granted also all the other privileges that the Romans are accustomed to bestow on their colonists."

Barbara Levick (1976, 70) identifies Emporion in Spain as another place where Augustus accorded the native inhabitants (in this case both Spanish and Greek) the same Roman citizenship enjoyed by the veterans originally settled by Julius Caesar. In this instance the inhabitants of a *municipium* rather than a colony received the citizenship (Keay 1996, 524).

Were these four specific instances indicative of a more general policy that Augustus and other emperors followed with respect to prominent colonies? Stevenson (1949, 129) responds affirmatively: "In a military 'colonia' many of the original settlers were as ex-legionaries already citizens, but the practice seems to have involved the enfranchisement of a large number of natives." Levick and Breeze (1996, 364) give a similar assessment: "the original communities would often receive citizenship and coalesce with the colony."

If Augustus (or his successors) followed such a practice for Philippi, the Thracians and Greeks resident at Philippi at the time of its colonization received grants of Roman citizenship. In such a scenario Philippi eventually became a city consisting basically of Roman citizens—*apart from their slaves.*

7. The Emperor Cult at Philippi

The emperor cult at Philippi was multifaceted and permeated the life of the colony. This cult was practiced at temples and altars dedicated to the Julio-Claudian emperors and their family members. It was practiced at worship sites for various authorized deities. It was also practiced in the colony's civic buildings and in public spaces such as the forum and the theater.

Collart's study of the primarily Latin inscriptions in Philippi has established that there were various types of Roman-authorized hierophants at Philippi. Markers indicate the existence of *flamines* for Augustus and Claudius and women *sacerdotes* for Livia (1937, 412). Collart concludes from other inscriptions that a college of *pontifices* existed in the colony (ibid., 265). Still another inscription mentions an *augur* (ibid.). The priests who conducted sacrificial rites traditionally assumed some financial responsibility for the banquets that followed these events (Price 1984a, 113).

The *augustales*, a membership of former slaves inaugurated by Augustus, played an important role in the promotion of the cult of Augustus and that of his successors. As ex-slaves, the *augustales* were barred from the magistracy and priesthood. However, as designated promoters of the name of Augustus, these former slaves wore special insignia and fulfilled particular tasks, thereby acquiring a modicum of status and honor (Rives 1996, 215).

That the *augustales* gained prominence and honor through their benefactions at Philippi is indicated by the survival of eleven inscriptions honoring them (Pilhofer 1995, 41). Inscriptions on two stone blocks from the theater at Philippi reveal that the *augustales* had the privilege of reserved seating (Collart 1937, 269; Bormann 1995, 46).

Additional archaeological evidence that pertains at least indirectly to the emperor cult at Philippi has come from the recent discovery of two temples at two corners of Philippi's forum. One of these temples apparently housed the curia of the colony (Koukouli-Chrysanthaki and Bakirtzis 1995, 39–41). The location of these temples at a prominent civic site suggests that they functioned in the preeminent cult of the colony, that is, the emperor cult, as opposed to the service of one of the pagan deities. Even if these temples were formally dedicated to the cults of Cybele, Silvanus, and other deities, rituals pertaining to the emperor cult could still easily be celebrated in their sanctuaries. (See below on syncretism.)

Another monument in the colony's forum indicates that the emperor cult flourished at that central location. Dedicated to Livia, the wife of Augustus and the mother of Tiberius, this large monument features seven women priests as presiding figures in a cult focused on Livia. This monument may not have been constructed until the second half of the first century AD (ibid., 18) and may not have been viewed by Paul. Yet already in AD 44, Livia had been proclaimed *diva* ("divine") by Claudius.

In addition to altars associated with the forum temples and with the monument to Livia, two other altars situated on the great plain of Philippi adjacent to the town also served the emperor cult. According to Suetonius, these two altars had been consecrated by the victors' legions in the aftermath of the Battle of Philippi (*Tiberius* 14.3).

In 20 BC, when the young Tiberius was on a military assignment given him by Augustus, he approached Philippi and was startled by the spontaneous brilliant flames blazing from these two altars (Suetonius, *Tiberius* 14.3; Dio Cassius, *Roman History* 44.6). In Barbara Levick's view (1976, 27), these reports signal that the priests associated with these imperial altars staged a spectacle in order to win the favor and future patronage of Tiberius.

Coins minted at Philippi also attest to the existence of these altars. The reverses of coins honoring Augustus, Claudius, and Nero all depict a scene featuring these altars. On these coins both Julius Caesar and Augustus are standing upon a *cippus*, and Caesar is crowning Augustus. The inscription over their heads reads, "the divine Augustus, son of the divine Julius." In the estimation of Michael Grant (1969, 275), the coins indicate "that Julius and Augustus became the tutelary deities of the colony."

Because of syncretism, sanctuaries dedicated to pagan deities were also potential sites for the celebration of the emperor cult. Price (1984a, 109) has shown with respect to the province of Asia that the emperor cult was effectively promoted at sanctuaries dedicated to pagan deities. The imperial festivals for the province of Lycia were held in the sanctuary of the goddess Leto at Xanthus. The so-called festival of the savior (*sebastoi*) was held in the sanctuary of Asclepius at Pergamum.

At Philippi, archaeologists have identified the sanctuary of Artemis, the sanctuary of Silvanus, the Three Niches sanctuary, the sanctuary of Cybele, and the sanctuary of the Egyptian deities Isis and Sarapis (Koukouli-Chrysanthaki and Bakirtzis 1995, 21). Collart also mentions a large *cippus* commemorating *Isis Regina* (1937, 467). The gladiators and arena hunters affiliated with Philippi's theater participated in the cults of such deities as Nemesis, Ares, and Nike (Koukouli-Chrysanthaki 2011, 451–52).

These sanctuaries were potential sites for the emperor cult. The support and active involvement of Philippi's magistrates were crucial for the continued existence of these sanctuaries. Among the inscriptions for Isis and Sarapis referenced by Collart (1937, 447), one indicates that an official of the colony (who served as *duumvir, irenarch, decurion*) sponsored a tribute to Isis and Sarapis within the precincts of Philippi's forum.

Not only did Philippi's magistrates offer support to the cults of deities, they also served directly as *pontifices* and *flamines* within the emperor cult. For example, a *duumvir quinquennalis* served as an *augur*; the *patronus* of the colony served as a *flamen*; a *duumvir* and *decurion* served as a *pontifex* and *flamen* (ibid., 265).

Collart has also identified an inscription mentioning that a member of the *augustales* was simultaneously a *dendrophorus* (ibid., 412, 456). Since the *dendrophoroi* (literally "branch bearers") were officials for the cult of the forest god Silvanus, the inscription establishes that the person commemorated was simultaneously a promoter of the emperor cult and the cult of Silvanus. Such involvement in two cults (presumably not limited to this one individual), combined with the magistrates' authority over *any* pagan sanctuary, argues that the sanctuaries of all other cults could be easily appropriated for services related to the dominant emperor cult.

Before considering the *civic* sites at Philippi that were suited to the celebration of the emperor cult, it is useful to note the various ways in which the emperor cult was celebrated at public venues within the provinces of Asia Minor. In this province, the emperor cult was celebrated in the imperial temples and in the sanctuaries of pagan deities. However, it was also celebrated in all the major edifices of a city, including theaters, gymnasia, and baths. Price states regarding gymnasia (1984a, 110), "Gymnasia were certainly the location of imperial sacrifices and banquets and some even contained special rooms for the imperial cult."

A city's streets and public squares could easily be appropriated for the emperor cult. Festivals honoring the emperor often became city-wide celebrations (ibid., 111–12). The local magistrates frequently joined the priests in a procession that included musicians, choirs, and costumed dancers as well as the garlanded animals that would be sacrificed at the city forum. Those dwelling along the route of the procession might offer sacrifice on their own household altars as the procession passed; special libation bowls containing an imperial image could be used at this time.

Price emphasizes that observances of the imperial cult in Asia Minor were designed to engage the entire populace of a city (ibid., 112). In some instances, the involvement of the city's residents was explicitly decreed. An edict for an "emperor day" from the city of Messene in the Peloponnese indicates that the Roman magistrate "instructed all to wear crowns and to sacrifice, keeping themselves free from work" (ibid., 112, referencing an inscription published by von Gonzenbach).

Depending on the imperial anniversary being celebrated (the emperor's date of birth, the anniversary of his accession to the throne, the dates of his significant military victories, etc.) the animal sacrifices might be followed by banquets and theatrical and sporting events at the town's theater. Artistic and athletic competitions were central parts of these imperial festivals. Prizes were awarded in music, drama, poetry, and mime.

In some cities of Asia Minor prizes were also awarded for the best compositions praising the emperor (Price 1984b, 89-90). Paid "god speakers" (*theologoi*) also honored the emperor with their prose compositions. Solemn oaths to the emperor might be sworn by the populace on such occasions.

In the archaeological situation of ancient Philippi (see Plate V in Bakirtzis and Koester 1998), the following public sites have the potential for serving as sites for the emperor cult: the theater of Philippi; the public baths; the palaestra; the forum (*agora*); the commercial forum (*macellum*); settings along the two primary east–west roads. The colony's gymnasium, which was discovered beneath the ruins of a later church basilica (ibid., 38) also functioned in this capacity.

Like the magistrates of Asia Minor, Philippi's magistrates might have readily decreed city-wide observances for important emperor-related events. Such celebrations could be mandated for the aforementioned public sites as well as at various temples, shrines, and sanctuaries. The following events might have been celebrated city-wide: the emperor's date of birth, his date of accession, dates relevant for prominent members of the imperial family, the dates of significant military triumphs; the date of the foundation of the colony. Certainly the anniversaries of the Battle of Philippi and the Battle of Actium would have been key dates for the celebration of the emperor cult at Philippi.

In summary, the emperor cult dominated the public life of Philippi and is a factor to be reckoned with in any assessment of Paul's perspectives in Philippians. In his visits to the colony, Paul would have encountered the emperor cult at every turn. The expectations of the Philippian magistrates regarding the participation of *all* Philippians in this cult would have been a paramount issue both for Paul and for his converts.

8. Slavery in the Roman Empire

Slavery, in various grades of cruelty, was institutionalized throughout the Roman Empire. One estimate of the slave population of the empire projects ten million slaves, between 16 percent and 20 percent of the total population of fifty million (Harris 1980, 118). More recently, the slave population has been estimated at six million, approximately 10 percent of a total population of sixty million (Morley 2011, 267). In Roman Italy, slaves numbered 1 to 1.5 million out of a population of 5 to 6 million, about 20 to 30 percent of the total population (Joshel 2010, 8, following Scheidel).

Slaves were disproportionately concentrated in cities but were also extensively deployed in agricultural settings. In addition to privately owned domestic slaves and agricultural slaves, there were also "public slaves" (*servi publici*), who were owned by municipalities. Public slaves performed a variety of tasks, including service as record keepers and accountants for the civic administration (Fuhrmann 2012, 64). Such slaves also functioned in various police capacities.

Public slaves served also as wardens for temples dedicated to various pagan deities. Collart (1937, 274) indicates that public slaves provided assistance for the cult of Silvanus at Philippi. Also in Philippi, there is an inscription commemorating the public slaves who constructed and maintained the colony's aqueducts (Lenski 2006, 345).

It is beyond the scope of this overview to provide a detailed analysis of Roman slavery and the means by which the continued demands for various types of slaves were fulfilled. A significant percentage of the slaves utilized for Rome's economy resulted from military conquest. Roman generals routinely enslaved soldiers of conquered armies as well as large segments of the conquered populations. Professional slave merchants followed in the wake of the Roman armies to purchase and transport these new slaves. Under Roman law all captives of war automatically became slaves (George 2011, 392, 400).

Abandoned infants and children represented yet another source of slaves. The childen born to those who were already enslaved were probably the principal source of new slaves (Scheidel 2011, 293).

Within the world in which Paul lived and traveled, slaves were treated as property to be owned and used. Slaves were casually bought and sold. On the seller's platform (*catasta*), they could be demeaningly inspected and evaluated as though cattle. *Servus* was the customary Latin term for male slaves. *Ancilla* was commonly used for adult female slaves (Westermann 1955, 58).

Slaves had no legal protection. Their daily life was completely governed by the wishes of their masters. Slaves could be insulted capriciously, punished harshly, and exploited sexually by their owners. They could be tortured and cast into chains. The ultimate punishment that could be visited upon slaves has particular significance for Philippians 2:6-8—slaves could be crucified according to the wishes of their "lords."

Marriage between slaves was prohibited. Those who entered into quasi-spousal relationships were regarded only as *contubernales* ("tent-mates"), and any offspring from such a union (*vernae*) belonged to the slaves' owners. The owner might compel the mother to raise these newborn slaves or else decree that they be taken from their mothers and auctioned as property (Joshel 2010, 40).

The "natal alienation" that slaves suffered was a major aspect of the degradation they experienced (ibid., 94). This term refers to the slave's loss of any ties to their parents and to their places of origin. Slaves had no parent-conferred name but were rather named by the slaveowners. Behavior-oriented names such as *Hilarus* ("cheerful"), *Felix* ("happy"), *Fides* ("faithful"), *Epaphroditus* ("charming"), and *Tychicus* ("lucky") were among the common names for slaves. The simple name "boy" (*puer*) might be affixed to any male slave (Westermann 1955, 58).

Given the patriarchal character of Roman society, it was especially significant that slaves had no socially acknowledged father. The stigma of having no recognized father endured even if a slave were fortunate enough to gain emancipation. Freed slaves who acquired great wealth and influence were still subject to being shamed by the jibe of illegitimacy (Joshel 2010, 43).

Slaves were consigned to labor for the duration of their lives. A slave might be ordered to undertake a specific agricultural task or a specific domestic task for decades. Alternately, the slave might be shifted from task to task or shifted from domestic work to agricultural work on a moment's notice.

If the threat of punishment was the social whip by which slaves were controlled, the hope of manumission was the positive incentive for compliant behavior. If slavery was "social death," manumission was a kind of "social rebirth," although hardly a complete one (ibid., 42).

Formal manumission might occur in one of three ways: (1) the slave-owner could declare a slave free before the censor when a census was taken; (2) the owner could set the slave free in his will; (3) the owner could appear before an appropriate magistrate with the slave and a third party who, by collusive arrangement, would declare to the official that the slave was really a free person wrongfully held in slavery (Bradley 1994, 155). Informal manumission occurred when the owner freed a slave by a letter to the slave or by proclaiming the slave's freedom orally in the presence of friends who acted as witnesses.

When a citizen-owner freed a slave by any of these means, the freed person automatically gained Roman citizenship with its attendant rights, such as the right of marriage and rights concerning property (Joshel 2010, 42). These freed slaves, however, might be very limited economically. In many instances the terms of their manumission might still require them to render economic service to their former owners, especially if the slave had not monetarily compensated the owner at the time of manumission (Bradley 1994, 159).

Even if the slave were able to negotiate terms for purchasing freedom (some slaves were able to so from their *peculium*, a sum of money under their own control), other ongoing obligations (*obsequium*) toward the former owner might still have to be fulfilled. As a result many ex-slaves remained subservient to their former owners and did not achieve economic prosperity (Joshel 2010, 44-47).

Nevertheless, a significant number of ex-slaves made their mark on Roman life as a result of their economic success and political influence. In some instances, the wealth acquired by *libertini* (former slaves) exceeded that held by the richest members of the Roman elite (Morley 2011, 283). As previously noted, *libertini* who prospered economically might become members of the *augustales*, a special membership instituted by Augustus to confer status upon freed persons.

Slaves who received manumission in conjunction with their bureaucratic service in the emperor's "household" (*familia caesaris*) often continued in important positions within the *familia caesaris* as freed persons. In certain cases, these *libertini* came to exercise power that rivaled or surpassed the power of those in the equestrian or senatorial orders.

9. Paul's Ministry at Philippi according to Acts

Luke's extended descriptions of Paul's endeavors in Acts 16 provide important insights for the analysis of Philippians. In addition, Luke indicates in Acts 20:1-6 that Paul returned to Philippi at least once and possibly twice after his first visit. Martin (1976, 7), followed by O'Brien (1991, 5), places Paul's initial arrival at Philippi between AD 49 and 52. Riesner (1998, 322) posits that Paul's mission in Macedonia began in AD 49.

Various commentators on Acts have challenged the reliability of Luke's imaging of Paul in Acts on the grounds that Luke presents a "political apologetic" in an effort to gain the favor of the empire's officials for the Christian movement. According to this interpretation Luke is striving to show these officials that Christianity poses no threat to the empire.

Proponents of the political apologetic theory hold that Luke intentionally portrays Paul as favorable to, and compatible with, the Roman imperial system. Yet as argued in Cassidy (2014, 148–53), Luke does *not* portray Paul in such a manner.

An analysis of Luke's *Paulusbild*, Luke's full portrayal of Paul, is beyond the scope of the present study. Nevertheless, in Acts 16, Luke portrays Paul as someone subversive of the values and patterns of imperial Rome. Further, Luke portrays the Roman magistrates of Philippi in an unfavorable light in this passage, especially when he depicts them acquiescing publicly to Paul's demand for conciliation.

Roman officials happening to reading Acts 16 would have considered at least three aspects of Paul's ministry to be troubling. Paul's outreach to slaves, his reserve regarding his Roman citizenship, and his refusal to cooperate with the magistrates of the colony.

In Acts 16:15 and 16:34, Luke implies that Paul baptized the slaves of Lydia and the slaves of the town jailer. Slaves as well as family members are referenced in the phrases "with her household" and "with all his household." Paul's third initiative regarding slaves consisted in freeing a young slave girl from an oppressive spirit (Acts 16:18). Slaveowning Roman officials would not have failed to note these three "pro-slave" endeavors by Paul at Philippi.

Paul's "reserve" toward his Roman citizenship would also have troubled Roman officials who regarded their citizenship as an unsurpassed honor. Paul did not publicly disclose his citizenship, even though doing so would have enabled him to avoid a beating in the town center of Philippi (Acts 16:19-39). He only disclosed his elite status in the semiprivate setting of his jail surroundings when he informed the magistrates' lictors as to the violations that occurred. Later, in Acts 22:24-29, Luke portrays Paul following a comparable approach to his Roman citizenship.

On the question of Paul's conformity with the Roman imperial system, it is significant that Luke's Paul publicly confronts the colony's Roman magistrates. He demands that the magistrates repair their offense to his honor by coming personally to the jail to reconcile with him. He boldly reprimands the magistrates for beating him "publicly" (*dēmousia*) without a hearing (Acts 16:37) and then for attempting to force him to leave the town "secretly" (*lathra*).

In the end, the powerful magistrates of Philippi capitulated to Paul! The "sit in" (Williams 1995, 291) that Paul enacted so shamed the magistrates that they came to his side to remedy the dishonor they had visited upon him (Rapske 1994, 305).

In summary, Luke's reports in Acts 16 can easily convey to Roman readers that Paul is a troublemaker who presents a danger for the established Roman order at Philippi and elsewhere. Luke's reports also portray the colony's magistrates publicly capitulating to the very missionary that they themselves had beaten and consigned to jail.

If Luke's objective were political apologetic, it would have been counterproductive for him to have depicted Paul in such a manner and to have portrayed the magistrates of Philippi in this way. The alternative view is that Luke was attempting to provide his readers with a reliable overview of Paul's ministry as it unfolded at Philippi. Luke was by no means trying to foist a "political apologetic" upon his readers (Cassidy 2014, 145–55).

10. Christian Slaves at Philippi

In the discussion above concerning the population of Philippi, reference was made to Peter Oakes's estimate that the population of the town and suburbs of Philippi might have totaled 46,000. If the percentage of slaves at Philippi approximated the 10 percent for slaves in the empire as a whole (Morley 2011, 267), the number of slaves at Philippi was about 4,600. However, if the total population of slaves at Philippi and its suburbs was lower than the figure estimated by Oakes, the number of slaves would have been correspondingly lower.

Because Philippi was proximate to Amphipolis, a hub for slave traders merchandising Thracian slaves (Harris 1980, 126), slaves might have been purchased at Amphipolis and transported to Philippi over the Via Egnatia. Slaves suited to agriculture would have been especially prized by veterans who received grants of land at Philippi. Roman veterans may have directly acquired slaves as a result of the conquests in which they participated.

As discussed in the preceding section, three passages from Acts 16 indicate the presence of slaves at Philippi. Some members of Lydia's household were probably slaves. The colony's jailer and some members of his household were also likely slaves. Certainly the girl possessed by an evil spirit was a slave.

Lydia, a dealer in purple goods from Thyatira, is Paul's first (and only named) convert at Philippi (16:14-15, 40). Because freed slaves sometimes took as their personal name the location at which they had gained freedom, Lydia may herself have once been a slave in the region of Lydia in Asia Minor (Parsons 2008, 230, citing Strabo). Luke indicates that Lydia was baptized "with her household" (*kai ho oikos autēs*) and probably understands that slaves from Lydia's household and business were among those baptized (Glancey 2011, 462; Haenchen 1971, 499).

In Acts 16:23-34 the jailer consigning Paul to the inner prison was probably a public slave. At 16:33b Luke probably envisions slaves as well as family members when he writes that the jailer was baptized "with all his household" (*kai hoi autou pantes*). As Rapske notes (1994, 353), "There is no difficulty in a highly-placed public slave possessing slaves of his own."

The clairvoyant girl portrayed in Acts 16:16-21 was almost certainly a slave. Luke uses the term for a young female slave (*paidiskēn*) in identifying her (LSJ 1968, 1287; Longenecker 1995, 258). The entire scene highlights the "lordship" of her masters (*kyrioi*) over her.

11. The Christian Community at Philippi and Its Persecution

As Reumann's overview makes clear (2008, 84–86), it is notoriously difficult to estimate the number of Christians at Philippi. Most efforts to do so attempt to project the number of house churches and the number of members per church. Peterlin conjectures regarding the social composition of the Christian community at Philippi that its membership included landowners, agricultural day laborers, tradespeople, small merchants, veterans, and slaves. Without providing an empirical basis for his assessment, he concludes (1995, 169): "the Philippian church was fairly large in size."

Because external reports concerning the size of the population are lacking and because data from within the colony (for example, grave markers, other instances of Christian iconograpahy) are lacking, projections regarding the size of the Christian population are highly tentative. Nevertheless, when several reports from Acts and various references from Philippians and Paul's other letters are considered against the backdrop of Pliny's reports (*Letters* 10.96.9) concerning the rapid growth of the Christian population in Bithynia-Pontus, it can be argued that the Christian community of Philippi experienced intense growth.

Such rapid growth is here posited to have occurred between Paul's initial visit to the colony (circa AD 49) and the time when he composed his letter in the mid to late 60s.

In one of his letters to Trajan, Pliny, the imperial governor for Bithynia-Pontus, remarks that a "contagion" (*contagio*) involving the Christian "cult" has occurred in the province (*Letters* 10.96.9; cf. Meeks 2003, 27). Pliny delineates this contagion with reference to the classes of people and the geographical regions now infected by this cult.

Regarding population, Pliny indicates that the cult involves "a great many individuals of every age and class, both men and women" (*multi enim omnis aetatis omnis ordinis, utriusque sexus etiam*). Slaves are undoubtedly among the population groups Pliny is identifying here. For earlier in the letter he has indicated that he tortured two Christian slave women who served as ministers in their community (*Letters* 10.96.8). Pliny indicates, moreover, that the cult infected "not only the towns, but the villages and rural districts too" (*neque civitates tantum, sed vicos etiam atque agros*).

Nothing in Pliny's letter identifies the person or persons animating the Christian contagion in Bithynia-Pontus. However, as regards Philippi, reports from the Acts of the Apostles, from Philippians itself, and from Paul's other letters suggest that "a contagion of Christ" was promoted by none other than Paul himself.

Luke's reports in Acts 16 suggest that, within a compressed interval of time, the name of Paul, the proclaimer of Christ, became extensively known at Philippi. Two highly public episodes were central to this process.

The owners of a clairvoyant slave girl took the initiative in denouncing Paul and Silas to the magistrates. The magistrates, however, acting in their official capacities, tore the clothes off the two missionaries and then had them beaten (Acts 16:19-22). Since these events took place in the marketplace (*agora*) of the city, it can be presumed that news of this episode spread rapidly throughout the colony.

As discussed above, the next day, the magistrates interacted with Paul in another public episode (Acts 16:37-39). At Paul's insistence the magistrates came to the jail and "conciliated" (BDAG 2000, 765) with Paul and Silas.

These two magistrates (*strategoi = duumviri*) were the most prominent persons at Philippi. Their every move was spotlighted. At their orders, Paul was beaten with "many blows" before the gathered crowd. Then, when they learned that Paul was actually a Roman citizen, they came publicly to the prison to appease him. In combination, these two episodes had the potential for making the name of Paul (and Paul's Lord) known throughout the colony and its environs.

Further, Paul is portrayed with an aura of noble dedication in these scenes. His exact motivations may not have been fully clear to those who witnessed or heard of these events. Yet Paul endured brutal treatment because he did not want his Roman citizenship to becloud his proclamation regarding the sovereignty of Jesus.

Before departing the colony (Acts 16:40), Paul took a potentially consequential step for the growth of the nascent Christian community. He returned to Lydia's household and encouraged the sisters and brothers who were now "in Christ" under Lydia's patronage. In effect, Paul buttressed Lydia's household as the first Christian "cell" at Philippi.

Prima facie, Paul does not refer to Lydia within Philippians. However, Elsa Tamez (2017, 105–6) proposes that Lydia is in Paul's view in 4:3a when he opaquely refers to a "genuine companion" (*gnēsie syzyge*).

Philippians 4:15 suggests that Paul kept in close contact with the community at Philippi during much of the time between his initial visit and the writing of his letter. (As noted, Acts 20:6 indicates a second visit, and Acts 20:1 may imply a third visit.) In Philippians 4:16, when speaking of the gift that Epaphroditus has now brought to him, Paul affirms that the Philippian church has benefited him "time and again" (*kai hapax kai dis*).

Paul's wording at 2 Corinthians 11:9 suggests that Corinth was one of the locations at which the Philippians provided for Paul's ministry (Meeks 2003, 27, 31). Whatever the precise time and place of these gifts, the very fact of recurring monetary gifts testifies to the growing numerical strength and robustness of the Philippian community.

The significant participation by the Philippian church in the Jerusalem collection may also be taken as an indication of the strength of the congregation (2 Cor 8:2-4; 9:2-4; Rom 15:25-27). If Paul's comment in 2 Corinthians 8:2 regarding "the depth of their poverty" (*hē kata bathous ptōcheia*) is an indication that many of the Philippians were financially deprived, a relatively large number of contributions would be needed to ensure that a significant gift could be collected.

The existence of "bishops and deacons" (*episkopoi kai diaconoi* in 1:1) at the time of Paul's letter also suggests a numerically significant community. Paul's use of the plural forms probably indicates the functioning of at least two persons in the area of "oversight" and two persons in the area of "service." (Further analysis is provided at 1:1 in the commentary proper.) If only a few pockets of Christians constituted the community at Philippi, formally designated ministries would not have been needed.

Paul's characterization of Epaphroditus as the Philippians' "apostle" (*apostolon*) to Paul's need in 2:25 is significant as another reference to a designated ministry at Philippi. Such "apostles" may have represented the community on external matters such as the transmission of letters or, as in this case, the transmission of a financial gift. Meeks uses the phrase "apostles of churches" to distinguish such emissaries from itinerant charismatic apostles like Paul (ibid., 133).

Paul's bold assertion in Rom 15:23 may also reflect rapid growth at Philippi. Writing from Corinth, Paul provides perspective for his projected journey to Rome and then to Spain. His extravagant claim is that "I no longer have any room for work in these regions. . . ." A numerically robust church at Philippi and well-established churches elsewhere in Macedonia and Achaia may be Paul's basis for making such a claim.

Two additional aspects pertaining to the growth of the Christian community at Philippi also deserve attention. The locations at which the community gathered is the first aspect. The second aspect is that this community was suffering persecution from the magistrates of the colony.

Three or more locations may have served as venues for the Philippian Christian community. According to Acts 16:13, there was a place for prayer outside the city's gates. There a group of women customarily gathered, Lydia among them. This open-air location, or others like it, may have subsequently been utilized by the growing Christian community.

Lydia may have also featured in the second type of site at which Philippi's Christians gathered. Her residence and/or her place of business might have been large enough for Christian gatherings. Peterlin (1997, 158) follows Ramsay in inferring that her house was "rather commodious." She was apparently able to accommodate Paul, Silas, Timothy, and Luke in a suitable fashion.

The town jailer's domestic quarters may also have served as a Christian gathering place, even though these quarters were more easily subject to the magistrates' oversight. Christians who owned large tracts of land outside of the town's gates might also have been able to accommodate members of the community.

Christians might also have met at *leschai* if such edifices existed in Philippi during the middle decades of the first Christian century. *Leschai* were small neighborhood buildings constructed for gatherings and furnished with seats. A building at Philippi located within a recently identified second-century residential complex might have functioned as such a *lesche* (Koukouli-Chrysanthaki 2011, 449). In other Greek cities *leschai* were common (LSJ, 1040). At Athens there were 360 of them (Smith 1870, 681).

Whatever the numerical strength of the Christian community at Philippi and whatever the locations at which it gathered, this community was *under persecution*. Paul states at 1:30 that he and the Philippians were "engaged in the same conflict which you saw and now hear to be mine."

Vincent (1902, 36) provides an effective summary concerning the three instances of persecution that Paul alludes to in this verse: "The reference here is to his experience in his first visit to Philippi, and to his latest experience in Rome. Their conflict is the same. . . . They too have suffered persecutions, and for the same reason, and from the same adversaries." Expanded comments regarding the character of the magistrates' persecution will be given in the following section and in the commentary proper.

12. The Perspectives and Responses of Philippi's Magistrates

As a result of their encompassing powers, the magistrates of Philippi must be the agents of the persecution that Paul references in 1:30. The magistrates control the colony's economic, religious, and political life, and it is within the framework of their rule that Paul's Christians are growing in an epidemic-like fashion.

The analysis set forth in the following paragraphs posits a correspondence between the phenomenon of the Christian contagion at Bithynia-Pontus and the phenomenon of a presumed Christian contagion at Philippi. This analysis also posits that the Philippian magistrates' response to the contagion at Philippi was comparable to the harsh response that the governor Pliny gave, approximately fifty years later, to the Christian superstition that was troubling his province.

In his letter to Trajan (*Letters* 10.96.1-10) Pliny characterized the principal effects of the Christian contagion. The rapid growth of Christianity within the province led to temples being almost entirely deserted (*iam desolata templa*). A further consequence was that scarcely anyone could be found to buy the flesh of the sacrificial victims (*cuius adhuc rarissimus emptor inveniebatur*).

When faced with these disruptions to the order and peace of the province, Trajan and Pliny responded decisively by treating the Christian community as a *hetaeria*. In his rescript to one of Pliny's previous letters, Trajan had directed Pliny to prevent any *hetaeriae* (societies, guilds, even associations of firefighters) from becoming established in the province (*Letters* 10.96.7; 10.34.1). *Hetaeriae* dated from pre-Roman Greece and were associations that combined a religious purpose with a political purpose (Cornell and Rhodes 1996, 702). Trajan was presumably following the lead of his Julio-Claudian predecessors in proscribing *hetaeriae*.

Acting now in the light of Trajan's earlier rescript, Pliny issued a decree (*edictum*) banning the Christian community as an illicit *hetaeria*, and he began harsh measures to eradicate it. Using information that he gained from an informer (*ab indice*), Pliny constructed a test in which suspected Christians were pressured to venerate the image of the emperor and curse the name of Christ. Pliny tortured two women slaves (*ancillae*) who were ministers of the community (*quae ministrae dicebantur*). He executed professed Christians who were not Roman citizens. Professed Christians who were citizens he remanded to Rome for trial.

Pliny reported to the emperor that, as a result of these and other measures, progress had been made toward eradicating this "degenerate cult" (*superstitionem praevam*). Pliny does not claim that any active Christians recanted their faith and reviled Jesus. However, he does advise Trajan that the temples were being repopulated and the flesh of sacrificial animals was again being sold "everywhere" (*passimque*).

In their response to the Philippian Christians, the magistrates of Philippi might have utilized Pliny's concept of *hetaeria*. The category of *hetaeria* would have given these magistrates a rationale for their efforts to undermine and destroy the burgeoning Christian community. In such a scenario, the Christians of Philippi became subject to condemnation for the offense of membership in an illicit society.

As at Bithynia, the threat posed by the Christians' proliferation at Philippi was economic, religious, and political. Virtually all of the temples and shrines identified in section 7 of the Introduction (above) utilized animal sacrifices. Nonparticipation in these rites thus meant a diminution of the sales of these animals as well as an implicit critique of the deities to whom these sacrifices were directed.

In his study of the rituals at temples and sanctuaries of Asia Minor, Price (1984a, 208–9) indicates that the most important feature of the ritual involved the pouring and/or sprinkling of the sacrificed animal's blood. Some part of the slaughtered animal might then be placed upon the cult table proximate to the statue of the emperor. The remainder would customarily then be apportioned among the hierophants and others who were present (ibid., 208).

Under Paul's tutelage such practices would have become antithetical to the Christians of Philippi. From Paul, Philippi's Christians would have come to appreciate that no animal's blood had any power at all. Rather, it was *the blood of Christ* that was supremely powerful!

That Paul already held strongly to such a perspective is evident from such passages as 1 Corinthians 10:16a and 11:25, 27. In Romans 3:25 he expresses his view in the following terms: "(Christ Jesus) whom God put forward *as an expiation by his blood*." Romans 5:9 expresses a comparable view: "therefore we are now *justified by his blood*." Conversion to Christ thus profoundly undermined the rationale for participation in rituals based on the blood of animals.

From the perspective of Philippi's magistrates, Paul presented a fundamental challenge to the colony's "system" of cults. The refusal of Christians to participate in the officially sanctioned cults of the colony could not be tolerated.

While the magistrates of Philippi did not have the extensive powers that Pliny did, significant options were still at their disposal. These measures included (1) harsh interrogations, possibly involving an image of the emperor; (2) public shaming, including denunciation by the colony's heralds (*praecones*); (3) confiscation of property; (4) loss of civic office; (5) ejection from the approved guilds (*collegia*); (6) prohibition from the market (*agora*); (7) prohibition from attending games and spectacles at the theater; (8) expulsion from the colony; (9) torture and imprisonment for Christian slaves.

This last measure, the torturing of Christian slaves, might have represented an important initiative for the magistrates at Philippi just as it was an important tool for Pliny. As Harrill has observed (2006, 158), the Romans viewed the body of the slave as "a privileged site for the production of truth through torture."

13. Philippians Authored from Rome

Several factors internal to Philippians support the conclusion that Rome was the location from which Paul authored this letter: (1) Paul is in a situation of *sustained* imprisonment; (2) he is at a location where a verdict of death can be pronounced against him; (3) numerous members of the praetorian guard are present at Paul's location; (4) a Christian community of significant size exists where Paul is located; (5) he is at a location where members of "Caesar's household" are present.

Two factors within the letter indicate that Paul's situation is one of sustained imprisonment. Philippians references a number of trips between Philippi and Rome, and a significant amount of time would have elapsed while this travel was taking place (see commentary on 4:15 and 2:25-30). Paul remained in chains while this travel was taking place. Second, Paul reports that a serious division has occurred with the Christian community where he is now located, and two factions now proclaim Christ in different ways (see commentary on 1:14-18). A significant interval of time would be required for this division to occur and for the competing proclamations to emerge.

Parenthetically it is useful to mention that "sustained imprisonment" may involve a period of five or more years. Josephus testifies that, at the approximate time of Paul's imprisonment, the Roman authorities kept a number of Jerusalem priests in chained custody in Rome for over five years (*Vita* 3). The governor Felix sent these priests to Rome in AD 59. Josephus himself traveled to Rome in AD 64 to secure their release.

Rome is also favored as a venue for the composition of Philippians because Paul is at a location at which he may receive a verdict of death (see commentary on 1:20; 2:17; 3:10). Paul's sense is that, once his verdict is pronounced, it will be final. There is no higher authority at any other location to whom he will be able to appeal. From Caesarea or from Ephesus, a death verdict might be appealed to the emperor in Rome. For capital verdicts rendered in Rome, there is no appeal.

The third factor favoring Rome is that Paul is at a location where praetorian guards are numerous. At 1:13 Paul's words *en holō tō praetoriō* should be translated "throughout the whole praetorian guard." Lightfoot (1888, 99-104; cf. Bockmuel 1998, 75) provides an extended argument that these words do not merely reference a location where Roman officials stay but rather denote the location of the emperor's security detail, his praetorian guards.

Paul's claim is that his witness is reaching throughout "*the whole*" guard, implying that the praetorians are around him in significant numbers. The fact that Paul's next phrase, "and to all the rest" (*kai tois loi-*

pois pasin), clearly references a group is a further argument that *persons* are meant in the preceding clause (O'Brien 1991, 92; similarly, Reicke 1970, 283; full discussion in Cassidy 2001b, 126–27).

Since the praetorian guards constituted the emperor's bodyguard, they were principally found in Rome in close proximity to the emperor. Inscriptions have been cited to argue that one member of the praetorian guard served in the vicinity of Ephesus. However Bruce (1983, 12) has shown that the soldier mentioned in these inscriptions was actually a *former* member of the praetorians who subsequently worked as a "station officer" (*stationarius*) on a Roman road in the province of Asia.

The fourth internal factor favoring a Roman venue is that Philippians implies Paul's proximity to a numerically substantial Christian community. Paul's own letter to the Roman Christians, especially his greetings in Romans 16:3-15, argues for a relatively large Christian community in the capital. As mentioned above, this community has split into two factions. In Philippians 1:14-18 both the minority and the majority factions are portrayed as undertaking a significant preaching of the gospel. Certainly for Caesarea, it is difficult to imagine a community large enough to sustain two evangelizing factions.

The fifth indication that Philippians was written from Rome is Paul's reference to Caesar's household at the end of the letter. In 4:22 Paul conveys greetings to the Philippian Christians from "those of Caesar's household" (*ek tēs kaisaros oikias*). In his excursus on this phrase, Lightfoot (1896/1961, 171–78) shows that this term applies to the large number of *libertini* and slaves who were employed in the imperial service as well as to the emperor's blood relatives. In Weaver's analysis of 660 inscriptions pertaining to Caesar's household (1972, passim), Rome, Italy, and North Africa were the locations for 96 percent of those who served in this capacity.

Regarding external attestation for Rome as the location for Philippians, brief mention should be made of the Latin preface to Philippians that is attributed to Marcion. The preface first explains that the Philippians were Macedonians who accepted and persevered in the faith. The author then states that Paul "praises them, writing to them from Rome, out of prison, by Epaphroditus" (full discussion in Cassidy 2001b, 125–26, 267).

As a complement to this consideration of the factors that favor Rome, it is useful to note a key weakness in the cases that have traditionally been made for Caesarea and Ephesus. Both of these sites lack the feature of an extended imprisonment that will potentially end in execution.

According to Acts 24:27, Paul was in chained custody in Caesarea for more than two years. This length of time fulfills the criterion of sustained imprisonment. Nevertheless, there is no possibility of a death sentence at Caesarea, and Philippians definitely envisions such a possibility.

In terms of sustained imprisonment and the possibility of a death sentence, the case for Ephesus is negligible. Two texts from Paul's Corinthinian letters speak of Paul's grave sufferings at Ephesus, and these reports of his abject suffering must be respected in any proposed "reconstruction" of Paul's journey. Nevertheless, neither of these texts speaks of imprisonment, let alone *sustained imprisonment with chains*. At 1 Corinthians 15:32 Paul states, "I fought with wild beasts at Ephesus." In 2 Corinthians 1:8 he writes of " the affliction (*thlipseōs*) we experienced in Asia . . . we were so utterly unbearably crushed that we despaired of life itself."

In 2 Corinthians 11:23, in Paul's catalogue of the sufferings he has endured as a servant of Christ, he claims that he has "far more imprisonments" (*en phylakais perissoterōs*) than his opponents. Again the suffering that Paul endured in these imprisonments is not to be minimized. Yet shorter term imprisonments (recall Acts' description of Paul's overnight imprisonment at Philippi) are not to be confused with the *extended* imprisonment involving praetorian guards and chains that Philippians speaks of.

14. The Date of Philippians

The date at which Paul finalized Philippians cannot be precisely determined. This indeterminacy is due in part to uncertainty regarding the time of Paul's arrival in Rome and the length of his extended imprisonment there.

Lüdemann (1984, 108ff.) has proposed that Paul's ministry ended after he reached Jerusalem in AD 52 or AD 55. Such a proposal cavalierly minimizes the value of the final seven chapters of the Acts of the

Apostles as well as the reports concerning Paul's status as a prisoner in Rome that are given in 2 Timothy. Regarding Lüdemann's thesis, Rainer Riesner observes (1998, 226), "a chronology of Acts that finds Paul in Rome in AD 62 presents fewer riddles than does his disappearance from the history of Christianity after a stay in Jerusalem in the year AD 51 or at latest, AD 55, as suggested by the reconstruction of G. Lüdemann." In his own chronology, Riesner proposes that Paul departed Caesarea in the custody of a centurion sometime in AD 59 and that he was a prisoner in Rome during the years 60 to 62 (ibid., 332).

Others would place Paul's arrival in Rome and his martyrdom in that city later in the 60s. Brown (1996, 428), for example, locates Paul as a prisoner in Rome from AD 61 to 63 with death after the summer of 64. Guthrie (1990, 1004) indicates that various scholars hold the view that Paul's death did not occur until AD 67 or 68 near the very end of Nero's regime. Ramsay (1893, 245) refers to "the widely entertained opinion that St. Paul was executed in AD 67 or 68."

Acts 28:30 indicates that Paul was in Rome as a chained prisoner for two years. However, as Fitzmyer has observed (1987, 20), Luke's final sentence does not mean that Paul's imprisonment ceased when the two years had passed: "The mention of 'two whole years' (28:30) does not imply that he died immediately thereafter no matter what interpretation is given to the enigmatic ending of Acts." Again, in conjecturing about the length of Paul's stay in Rome, the phenomenon of priests from Jerusalem being chained prisoners in Rome for *five years* until Josephus secured their release must be kept in view.

Under the scenario of a relatively late date of composition, Philippians might not have been completed when the news of Nero's projected tour of Greece reached Paul. Nero's trip was remarkable because it was not for any military or diplomatic purpose. Rather Nero's objective was to gain personal *glory* by means of victories in athletic and artistic competitions.

Nero was to depart for Greece in October of AD 66 and would spend more than a year on this grand "tour" (Griffin 1985, 230). For all that Paul knew, Philippi (a location revered by the Julio-Claudian emperors) might well be on Nero's itinerary, and such a visit could pose particular challenges for the Philippian Christians.

15. The Unity of Philippians

Numerous commentators on Philippians have questioned whether the extant text is a single unified letter. Not infrequently, the canonical letter is said to be a composite of three or more letters that Paul composed and sent to Philippi over a period of time.

Markus Bockmuel provides an overview of this discussion and identifies two principal factors that lead scholars to doubt the literary unity of the letter. The first factor (1996, 20): "There seems . . . to be little obvious logic in the overall organization of the argument." The second factor: in its present form, Philippians "has a number of rough transitions, which have suggested to scholars the possibility of seams between two, or more commonly, three different letter fragments" (ibid., 21).

For many scholars, the startling change to a new topic (and tone!) that occurs at 3:2 supports the theory that the section 3:2–4:3 constitutes a separate letter or letter fragment. Paul's comments about the Philippians' gift in 4:10-20 are also often considered to constitute a separate letter.

This commentary argues that Paul actually has a coherent overall strategy in writing Philippians. It will be shown below that the perspectives Paul expresses in sections 1:1–3:1, 3:2–4:9, and 4:10-20 all contribute effectively to an integrated letter. The theory of multiple letters thus cannot be supported on the grounds that canonical Philippians lacks an integrated message. With reference to the abrupt change that occurs at 3:2, Martin's argument that a major interruption occurred in the apostle's dictation at this point (1987, 40–41) may be decisive.

16. Philippians as a Prison Letter

Philippians is a unified letter, but what "type" of letter is it? In *Typoi epistoliki*, written during the first century AD, an author commonly referred to as Pseudo-Demetrius, identified twenty-one types of ancient letters and provided a brief example of each type (Murphy-O'Connor 1995, 96–97). Stanley Stowers lists fifteen types of letters (1986, passim). These letters range from letters of friendship and family letters, to letters of praise and blame, to letters of exhortation and advice, a broad heading that encompasses eleven letter types.

Remarkably, Philippians contains trace elements of practically all 21 of Pseudo-Demetrius's categories and all of Stowers's categories. Murphy-O'Connor rightly concludes (1996, 98): "No one category can do justice to the complexity of a Pauline epistle. Virtually all of Pseudo-Demetrius's types are to be found in every letter."

Philippians certainly embodies elements of the friendship letter, the letter of thanksgiving, and the other types just listed. However, Philippians also reflects two letter types not identified either by Pseudo-Demetrius in the first century or by most modern commentators. Philippians is a "prison letter." It communicates the perspectives of a chained prisoner to a beloved community (Tamez 2017, 23–35). Philippians is also a "counter-imperial" letter. In it the writer challenges the cult of Roman emperors and also the slave system over which these emperors preside.

Before Paul authored Philemon and Philippians, is there evidence for the existence of letters of some complexity being written from prison? Rapske (1994, 226–327) considers a number of petitions formulated by prisoners seeking release. He notes that a prisoner might engage a professional scribe to draft such a petition and then deliver it to the appropriate official once the prisoner had signed it. Yet clearly there is a major distinction between a prisoner's relatively concise petition for release and an extended letter such as Philippians that treats a number of topics in a nuanced way.

In general, Paul's critique of Roman patterns is indirect. In Philippians, there is no castigation of any emperor by name, no direct criticism of the emperor cult, and no express call for an end to the Roman-maintained slave system. Nevertheless, Philippians sets forth powerful indirect criticisms regarding all of these aspects of imperial life through Paul's affirmations of Jesus's dominion in such passages as Philippians 2:9-11 and 3:20-21.

Indirectness regarding political matters can be observed in such Roman authors as Cicero. Doty (1973, 2) has noted that Cicero was concerned *not* to write anything that might be intercepted and used against him. In effect, Cicero did not want his writings to bring him and his allies into chains.

Two cases involving charges of *maiestas* are relevant here as illustrations of the danger that Paul faced in composing Philippians. While in prison, Sextius Paconianus, a former praetor, composed "verses" (*carmina*) considered to be disrespectful of the majesty of Tiberius. Accordingly Tiberius ordered that Paconianus be strangled to death (Tacitus, *Annals* 6.39).

Under Nero another case involving *carmina* very nearly cost the composer his life. At a dinner gathering the praetor Antistius delivered *carmina* critical of the emperor (Tacitus, *Annals* 14.48). He was thereupon accused of treason (*maiestatis delatus est*) and would have been summarily executed if it had not been for the intervention, to Nero's displeasure, of Thrasea Paetus.

Parenthetically, Nero later contrived to condemn Thraesa himself. Among Nero's charges, Thrasea evaded the annual oath of loyalty to Nero and had not offered a sacrifice "for the welfare of the emperor and his celestial voice" (Tacitus, *Annals* 16.22). As a consequence, Thrasea committed suicide in AD 66.

How might the contents of Philippians have come to the attention of the Roman authorities? This question focuses attention on other aspects of Paul's circumstances beyond the very fact that he is in chains.

Is Paul in some form of gated prison? Is he in the camp of the praetorians? Is he in the type of rented dwelling presumably referenced in Acts 28:16, 30? Whatever his location, he is under close surveillance. He may be directly chained to his guard (Seneca, *Epistle* 5, 7). Possibly Paul may be draped with body chains with praetorian guards stationed outside of his quarters.

Presumably Paul's praetorian guards kept him under close surveillance. In addition, trained spies and paid informers might have played a role in Paul's custody. From Augustus onward, *speculatores* (military spies in civilian garb) served at the emperor's personal discretion as a subunit within the praetorian guards (Hirschfeld 1913, 586).

Epictetus, formerly a slave of Epaphroditus, Nero's powerful secretary for petitions (*a libellis*), later gained renown for his philosophic discourses. (Epictetus will be cited again at 4:17 below.) In one of his *Essays* (4.13.5) Epictetus describes the following scenario of entrapment: "A soldier, dressed like a civilian, sits down by your side, and begins to speak ill of Caesar, and then you too, just as though you have received from him some guarantee of good faith by the fact that he began the abuse, tell likewise everything you think, and the next thing is—you are led off to prison in chains."

Writing decades after Epictetus, Philostratus portrays a similar scenario for the attempted entrapment of the philosopher Apollonius. In the episode that Philostratus describes, the spy, operating under the orders of Domitian, surreptitiously entered the prison where Apollonius was confined. This informant then attempted to gain comments from Apollonius for the purpose of discrediting him (*Life of Apollonius* 7.27).

Paul's standard closing verses at 4:21-23 indicate that his letter was successfully completed. Nevertheless, there were still obstacles to the successful transmission and reception of the letter. Two scenarios should be considered.

In the first scenario, Paul entrusted the letter to Timothy and/or Epaphroditus, who carried the letter to Philippi. On arriving there, the letter carrier(s) took responsibility for formally presenting the letter, perhaps drawing on the talents of Christian actors. Certainly, its contents posed a danger for those to whom it was addressed (Standhartinger 2013, 159). The letter thus was probably authoritatively read and/or performed in a clandestine setting.

In the second scenario, Paul's letter to the Philippians never left Rome but was actually confiscated by the imperial authorities. Such a scenario initially seems startling. It must be emphasized, however, that Paul is in *dangerous* circumstances and engaged in a *perilous* project. He is under surveillance in Nero's Rome, and in his letter he is proclaiming that Jesus, not Nero, is *Lord*!

If Paul's letter was confiscated by the imperial authorities (conceivably to be introduced as evidence at Paul's imperial trial), how then did Philippians survive to be included in the collection of Paul's letters? Hypothetically, a *copy* of the letter was made at the time of composition, and this copy was somehow safeguarded by the Christians of Rome who were favorable to Paul (see on 1:14-15b below).

Another possibility is that Timothy and/or Epaphroditus prepared for their mission to carry the letter to Philippi by memorizing it. As explained below in the commentary on 2:19-24 and 2:25–3:1, David Rhoads (2006, 176) hypothesizes that Paul would enact this requirement to ensure that his letter was read with proper nuance, proper emphasis, proper drama. If Paul's physical letter was confiscated, it would have been possible for Paul's delegate to present his letter absent the text!

17. Paul's Purposes in Philippians

It is possible to analyze Paul's specific purposes in Philippians under the following six headings. A more detailed analysis will follow in the commentary proper.

1. *To convey information about his situation.* To update the Philippians regarding his own situation is one of Paul's principal purposes. Paul's situation is complex, encompassing personal and judicial factors. At the outset he stresses that his chains have not prevented him from advancing the gospel (1:2). In fact it has become widely known among the praetorian guards that his chains are for Christ (1:13).

Encouraged by Paul's own witness, a majority of the Roman Christians have been emboldened to proclaim Christ (1:14, 15b-16). A minority, however, while proclaiming Christ, seek to marginalize Paul as they do so (1:15a, 17).

With respect to his judicial circumstances, Paul envisions both the possibility of his release and the possibility of his condemnation (1:19-26; 2:17; 3:10). Paul does not explain how he came to be in chains or the precise charges against him. Also he does not refer to his precise location in Rome. Presumably the Philippians are already informed about these aspects.

Finally, Epaphroditus has recovered from his illness, and Paul anticipates sending Epaphroditus back to Philippi (2:27-28). Pending the outcome of his case, Paul also envisions sending Timothy to Philippi (2:22-23).

2. *To provide insights regarding Christ.* Philippians is fundamentally a letter about Christ. References to Christ permeate the letter from beginning to end. Paul is intensely engaged in formulating and expressing the new insights about Christ that he had gained in his circumstances as a prisoner in Nero's Rome.

Philippians 2:6-11 is the crowning passage regarding Christ in this letter and probably the crowning passage regarding Christ in all of Paul's writings. The profundity of the insights expressed in these verses suggests that Paul reflected on them and meditated on them for weeks, months, and even longer.

Traditionally, scholars have proposed either a "kerygmatic" or an "ethical" interpretation of these verses. Aspects of both of these interpretations will be affirmed in the commentary below. Nevertheless, Paul's insights in these six verses have not been adequately assessed by scholars working within these two traditional categories.

It has been widely recognized that Paul traces Jesus's trajectory from equality with God downward to the lowest form of death and then upward to the place of highest exaltation. It has also been widely recognized that Jesus's death on a Roman cross in 2:8 represents the pivot at which the downward journey ends and the upward journey commences. Nevertheless, these valid insights barely touch the richness and the complexity of the *Roman* factors that Paul had in view when he composed these verses.

To plumb the depths of Paul's meaning, it is useful to approach Philippians 2:6-11 as a prayerfully conceived drama that comprises eight separate, but related, scenes. The *action* delineated in each scene must be carefully considered. Similar attention must be give to the *characters* present in each scene. What visual images does Paul convey to his readers as he depicts each scene?

In 2:7-8, when Paul images Jesus "taking the form of a slave" (*morphēn doulou labōn*) and then embracing "the slave's form of death" (*thanatou de staurou*), he presents two arresting counter-imperial visualizations. Recall that the Roman Empire was a slave-based enterprise. Paul's two dramatic scenes postulate Jesus's solidarity with slaves in an unprecedented and challenging way.

Similarly, once it is comprehended that Paul envisions the same Roman authorities who perpetrated Jesus's unjust crucifixion (scene 3) subsequently prostrating themselves before the exalted Jesus (scene 5), it becomes clear that a radical critique of these authorities is being presented. The same authorities are also implicitly critiqued when Paul portrays the oppressed slaves of their empire now participating with full dignity in confessing that Jesus is Lord to the glory of God the Father (scene 8).

In summary, Phil 2:6-11 delineates Jesus's status path as a profound challenge to the Roman system. Paul's meditative drama profoundly challenges the cult of Rome's emperors. It also implicitly challenges the system of slavery on which the empire is based.

Later, in 3:10, Paul demonstrates that he has reflected still more deeply on the Roman character of Jesus's death and on the power of his resurrection. Paul intimates his desire to share Christ's suffering, "becoming like him in his death" (*symmorphisomenos tō thanatō autou*) in order that he may attain the resurrection.

Because he himself is now in the midst of a Roman legal process, Paul is now able to reflect more carefully on the judicial "process" that Jesus suffered under Pilate. Just as Jesus received an official trial, Paul will have such a trial. Just as a Roman governor delivered the verdict of *maiestas* against Jesus, so will a Roman emperor pronounce a verdict of *maiestas* against Paul.

Further, just as Roman personnel oversaw the execution of Jesus, so will Roman personnel have responsibility for Paul's execution. Just as Jesus's execution was effected by Roman power, so will Paul's own approaching death be effected by Roman power.

Paul's third important insight regarding Christ is expressed in 3:20-21 where he delineates Christ's power. Earlier, in 2:9-11, Paul portrayed the cosmic scope of the Father's power. In 3:20-21 he profiles the universal cosmic power of "the Lord Jesus Christ."

In contrast with the power of Nero and his confederates to reify and degrade the body, Jesus has the surpassing power to transform the human body into "a body of glory like his own" (*tō sōmati tēs doxēs autou*). The risen Jesus has the power to subject "all things" (*ta panta*) to himself.

Philippians contains other significant insights regarding Christ (for example, Christ as the foundation for joy is treated in section six above). Paul illuminates Christ in virtually every part of his letter. In Gordon Fee's words (1995, 64), "Everything is in, by, of, and for Christ Jesus."

3. *To strengthen the Philippians against adversaries.* The third purpose of Paul's letter is to afford strength to the Philippians against their opponents. In three passages (1:27-30; 2:14-18; 3:18-21) Paul encourages the Philippian Christians in the face of persecution by the Roman authorities of Philippi. In a fourth passage (3:2) he strives to prevent any undermining of the Philippians' community life by "the circumcisers."

4. *To promote unity in the community.* To promote unity among the Philippian Christians is another of the letter's principal concerns. It is widely recognized that Paul encourages unity at 1:27; 2:2-4; 4:2-4; cf. 2:14. Unity is desirable in and of itself. In the face of persecution by the Roman authorities, the importance of unity is inestimable.

When Paul delineates Jesus's self-emptying in 2:6-8, he provides the Philippians with a model for the conduct that he has encouraged at 1:27b and 2:2-4. Christians who are citizens are called to the unity-oriented virtues of humility and self-giving. These virtues are to be expressed in their dealings with those who are citizens like themselves. These virtues are also to be manifested when they are dealing with Christians of the community who are slaves.

In 4:2-3, when Paul publicly urges Euodia and Synteche to reconcile their differences, he does not mention the grounds for their dispute. Possibly a division has arisen because these two women disagree regarding the best approach for the community to follow in responding to the Roman magistrates. Another possibility is that the division concerns the appropriate way for treating Christian slaves.

Whatever their dispute, Paul urges these two women to reconcile their differences. When the life of a community is being threatened from outside, unity is such a priority that all personal rivalries must be set aside and all disputes over issues settled.

5. *To respond carefully to the Philippians' gift.* To recognize the Philippians' donation to him and to express his reflections regarding this gift are certainly among Paul's purposes for this letter. Significantly, Paul uses eleven verses (in a letter of 104 verses) to acknowledge and comment on the gift that Epaphroditus has brought.

In commentaries on Philippians, it has been widely noted that Paul does not *directly* express gratitude for this gift. Equally significant is that Paul never indicates the use to which he will put it. Nevertheless, he is concerned to acknowledge the benevolent intentions that led the Philippians to gather a gift and send it in Epaphroditus's care.

The key to Paul's "reserve" regarding the gift probably lies in the character of the coins that comprised it. Paul's terminology suggests that this gift was *monetary,* and he might well have had reservations about using the imperial coins that comprised it. These coins were presumably minted at Philippi and embossed with the countenances and pretentious titles of Nero and his Julio-Claudian predecessors. Located now at the center of Nero's Rome, Paul appreciates to a greater extent the role of these coins in promoting the cult of this charlatan "lord."

6. *To express and encourage joy.* Paul's sixth purpose in writing Philippians is to express and encourage joy. "Joy" (*charis*) is a pervasive con-

cept in Philippians. In its noun and verb forms, the term appears sixteen times within a letter of four chapters.

For Paul, joy is "no evanescent emotional quality" (Martin 1987, 45). Rather joy is an abiding gladness that derives from the contemplation of Christ and from close communion with him. Joy is, in effect, *Christ-centered*. It is a gladness regarding Christ that the Philippians share with one another and with Paul (2:17-18; 2:28).

His reflections in such passages as 2:6-11 and 3:20-21 indicate that Paul has pondered the stages of Jesus's status path. As a consequence, Paul has become permeated with joy over who Christ is and what Christ has accomplished and will accomplish. Joy is for Paul both a present and an eschatological reality (Standhartinger 2013, 163). Paul's desire to encourage Christ-oriented joy is overflowing. He exuberantly uses *chairete* twice in a single verse (4:4): "*Rejoice* in the Lord always; again, I will say *rejoice*."

As is the case with the topic of "peace" (see commentary on 4:7, 9) Paul's emphasis that Jesus is the true foundation for joy represents a challenge to the claims advanced for the Julio-Claudian emperors relative to "joy." Within Paul's lifetime, Philo wrote that the entire world has unsurpassed "joy" (*charan*) as a consequence of Gaius's accession (*Embassy* 19, cf. 15). Seneca (*De clementia* 1:2) subsequently made a comparable claim on behalf of Nero: (Because of this emperor's utterances) "peoples and cities gather reasons for rejoicing" (*laetitiae causas populi urbesque concipiunt*).

18. The "Narrative" Embedded in Philippians

The content of Philippians is centered on Paul's affirmations concerning Christ and his exhortations to the Philippians regarding their life in Christ. When the letter is read carefully, it emerges that Paul's affirmations regarding Christ and his exhortations to the Philippians are conveyed within a coherent historical narrative.

Paul's letter features historical characters, plots and subplots, settings, and unfolding time—all of which are key elements for narratives (Cassidy 2007, 2–3). Rome and Philippi are the principal earthly settings within Philippians. Developments occur at these two sites in a way that is reminiscent of Charles Dickens's interweaving of events at Paris and

London in *A Tale of Two Cities*. As is evident in 2:6-11, Paul's letter also portrays characters, plots, and sites pertaining to the cosmic level.

Paul is the leading protagonist in this narrative. Philippians details his uncompromised faithfulness to Jesus despite significant opposition. The interactions among Paul, the Philippian Christians, and the Roman authorities are *intelligible*. They constitute the historical "plot" of the letter.

In this plot, Paul has embarked on a mission on behalf of Jesus Christ. He has proclaimed Christ at Philippi and founded a Christian community there. While doing so he faced persecution from the Roman authorities of the colony, and his friends at Philippi are now experiencing this same persecution. Paul himself is now persecuted in Rome, the capital of the empire.

Various subplots can also be identified within Philippians. One such subplot concerns the efforts of Epaphroditus to render assistance to the chained Paul. The Philippian Christians have selected Epaphroditus as their delegate to bring a monetary gift to Paul in Rome. Epaphroditus risks his life to carry out this dangerous mission. A surprising twist ensues, however, when Paul opts not to make use of the gift that Epaphroditus has brought to him.

A second subplot concerns the division that Paul's arrival in Rome has engendered among the Christians already resident in the capital. A majority of the Roman Christians are encouraged by Paul and proclaim Christ with greater boldness. However, a minority of the Roman Christians oppose Paul and seek to marginalize him. This anti-Paul minority nevertheless continues to proclaim Christ, and Paul rejoices in this aspect of the situation.

19. Philippians' Subversiveness When Performed

As discussed above, in 2:6-11 Paul fashioned a "Christ drama" comprised of two acts, each encompassing four scenes (see the exegesis of these verses below). Some of the concepts that Paul embedded in this drama constituted a direct challenge to the emperor cult, for example, the concept that Jesus's name is above every other name. Other concepts such as the eternal shaming of Roman officials and the coequality of slaves in proclaiming the name of Jesus were embedded beneath the surface and would not have been easily apprehended until the letter was performed.

Hans Dieter Betz (2013, 16) has employed the term "covered speech" (*verdeckte Sprache*) in reference to Philippians, and James Scott (1990, 4–16) has classically used the term "hidden transcript" to characterize this type of writing. In addition to 2:6-11, this phenomenon of covered meaning is present in other passages in the letter such as 3:19-21. Regarding the acceptance of hidden nuances, David Rhoads (2006, 128) has emphasized that the audience must have an abiding trust in the reader/performer commissioned to present the letter.

Both Epaphroditus and Timothy have the credentials necessary to give an authoritative interpretation of Paul's meaning in his Christ drama. Under their guidance, Christian members from Philippi's resident acting troupe may have performed the memorable scenes of Philippians 2:6-11 in such a way as to disclose their counter-emperor dimensions of meaning. Christian slaves themselves might have participated actively in the performance of these scenes.

Also, Timothy and/or Epaphroditus might have brought the counter-emperor dimensions of meaning present in 3:19-21 to light by eliciting chanting from Christian actors and other community members. If these verses were staged in such a manner, the chanted "dis-praises" by the Philippian Christians would have represented a powerful antidote to the chanted praises of Nero that were characteristically organized by Nero's sycophants at Philippi and elsewhere.

Commentary

Outline of Philippians

I. Opening of the Letter (1:1-11)
   A. Address and Salutation (1:1-2)
   B. Thanksgiving (1:3-11)
II. Overview of Paul's Situation (1:12-26)
   A. Paul's Chains Advance the Gospel (1:12-13)
   B. Paul's Chains Engender Division (1:14-18)
   C. Paul's Potential for Death or Life (1:19-26)
III. The Same Conflict at Philippi and Rome (1:27-30)
IV. Harmony and Unselfishness (2:1-5)
V. Drama Depicting Christ's Descent to a Roman Cross Followed by Cosmic Exaltation (2:6-11)
VI. Further Encouragement for the Philippians (2:12-16)
VII. Paul Again Envisions His Death (2:17-18)
VIII. The Mission of Timothy (2:19-24)
IX. The Mission of Epaphroditus (2:25–3:1)
X. Paul's Response to a Threat from the "Circumcisers" (3:2-7)
XI. Paul's Communion with Christ in Life or Death (3:8-16)
XII. Paul's Response to a Threat from "the Enemies of the Cross of Christ" (3:17–4:1)
XIII. Entreaty to Euodia and Synteche (4:2-3)
XIV. Encouragement to Rejoice and Be Grounded in Christ (4:4-9)
XV. Response to the Philippians' Gift (4:10-20)
XVI. Concluding Greeting and Benediction (4:21-23)

Philippians 1:1-11
I. Opening of the Letter

Introductory Comments

THE FIRST ELEVEN VERSES of Philippians consist of the address and salutation (1:1-2) and the thanksgiving (1:3-11). These components are characteristically present in Paul's other letters whose authorship is not in dispute. (The absence of the thanksgiving component in Galatians is a significant exception.) Within each component, Paul includes material that is pertinent to the situation of the Philippians or to his own situation.

In the salutation section (1:1-2) Paul refers to himself and Timothy as "slaves of Christ Jesus" (*douloi Christou Iēsou*). It will become clear that Paul's opening use of the word "slave" is related to his astonishing characterization of Jesus as a "slave" (*doulos*) in 2:7.

The thanksgiving section (1:3-11) includes prayer (1:4, 9-11). It also introduces ideas that are essential to the letter (Bockmuel 1998, 57). "Communion in the gospel" (1:5) and "the day of Jesus Christ" (1:6, 10) are two of these ideas. Two other major concepts introduced are "my chains" (*tois desmois mou*) and "the defense and confirmation of the gospel" (*tē apologia kai bebainōsei tou euangeliou*), both referenced in 1:7.

Paul's mention of his chains distinguishes Philippians from all of his other uncontested letters save for Philemon. As discussed in the Introduction, Philippians is a "prison letter" and thereby in a different category from 1 Thessalonians, 1 and 2 Corinthians, Galatians, and Romans.

Additional elements regarding the character of Paul's situation as a prisoner will emerge as the letter continues. Paul's initial references indicate that he is an official Roman prisoner, as opposed to being the captive of bandits. He is chained and situated in a juridical process. Precisely in this setting, Paul is engaged with presenting a "defense" of the gospel.

Tracing the Train of Thought

The opening of Philippians consists of two units: the salutation (1:1-2) and the thanksgiving/prayers (1:3-11).

A. Address and Salutation (1:1-2)

1:1. Paul's first words identify him as the sender of the letter and depict him and Timothy as Christ's slaves: **"Paul and Timothy, slaves of Christ Jesus."** Paul's name, his self-designation as a slave, and the reference to Christ Jesus are each topics that require attention.

It is usual for Paul to name himself at the beginning of his letters. Yet owing to the profoundly *Roman* character of Philippi and controversies involving the Philippian magistrates, Paul's name may have particular meaning in this letter.

Paulos, his name in Greek, directly corresponds to the Latin *Paulus* (alternatively spelled *Paullus*). In Latin, the feminine *Paulla* also appears (Hemer 1985, 183).

Acts 16:37-38 and 22:25-29 make clear that Paul was a Roman citizen, and, as such, he would have possessed the citizen's usual three names: *praenomen*, *nomen*, and *cognomen*. Paulus would have been his cognomen. In the first century AD, this would have been the principal name by which he was known in the Latin- and Greek-speaking regions of the empire (Solin, 1996, 1024–25; Hemer 1985, 179).

At the time of his birth, in addition to receiving the customary three names, Paul probably received a fourth name, "Saul," as a *supernomen*. This Hebrew name would have reflected the desire of Paul's parents to associate their son with Saul, the first Jewish king who was also of the tribe of Benjamin (see below on 3:4-6).

With respect to the interactions between Paul and the Roman authorities who are mentioned in Philippians, it may be significant that the *cognomen*, Paulus, was utilized by three prominent Roman families in the first Christian century: the Aemilii Pauli, the Vetteni Pauli, and the Sergii Pauli (Sherwin-White 1978, 153–54). Paul's *praenomen* and *nomen* are not known; however, Harrer has conjectured that Paul's lineage might have connected him to the Aemilian *gens* (1940, 22).

If this was the case, Paul's full Roman name, including his Hebrew supernomen might have been *Lucius Aemilius Paullus Saul* (ibid., 33). If Paul did have Aemilian lineage, then his mission at highly Romanized Philippi had an ironic dimension: Lucius Aemilius Paullus was the Roman general who first brought Macedonia under Roman rule.

Paul names Timothy as a cosender of the letter. However, since the lines that follow are written in the first person singular (and by someone bound with chains), it is evident that Paul himself has composed this highly personal letter. Paul may nevertheless envision a key role for Timothy in the transmission and performance of the letter.

As noted, Paul identifies himself and Timothy as "**slaves of Christ Jesus.**" The RSV translates *douloi* as "servants," but the word "slaves" more exactly renders Paul's meaning. Because *doulos* was, in effect, a term of dishonor in the Graeco-Roman world (although not necessarily in the Septuagint), Paul's use of this word to characterize himself probably was a shock to the Philippian Christians (Fee 1999, 63). Nevertheless, Paul's self-designation is not "accidental." In 2:22 he uses a verbal form of *doulos*, in *edouleusen eis to euangelion* ("worked as a slave for the gospel").

There are three dimensions of meaning present in Paul's self-designation as a slave at 1:1. These aspects have to do, in one way or another, with Christ. Boundaries between them are not demarcated rigidly.

Paul's first dimension of meaning is that he (and Timothy) belong to Christ in the way in which slaves belong to their masters. Paul has earlier used *doulos* with this meaning at Gal 1:10 and Rom 1:1. They are Christ's slaves because they are *owned* by him. In a way analogous to Roman slaves, their role is to follow the will of the one who owns them. As Paul will indicate later in 3:12, it is Christ Jesus who has made Paul his own.

Paul's second dimension of meaning pertains to the chains that he wears. In Roman society chains confirmed the slave status of an individual. As noted in the Introduction, slaves are not identified by any particular insignia or type of clothing. Chains, however, conventionally indicated that the one so chained was a slave.

As the letter proceeds, Paul will thrice indicate that he is in chains (1:7, 13, 14). These chains confirm his identity as Christ's slave. Roman slaves *unwillingly* accept the chains that their masters confer. Slave Paul *willingly* accepts the chains assigned to him by his master. Indeed at 1:13 he explains that "my chains are because of Christ." Paul is in chains because Christ, his Lord, wills it for him. He is also in chains because he has been relentless in his testimony regarding Christ his Lord.

Paul's third dimension of meaning pertains to Christ's status as a slave. In this dimension Paul affirms his communion with Christ who took the form of a slave and embraced the slave's form of death. Paul will not explicate Christ's downward trajectory until 2:6-8. Nevertheless, Christ's self-emptying to the point of a slave's death is already in Paul's view, and at 1:1 this chained prisoner indicates that he is a slave in communion with "slave" Jesus—who is paradoxically Paul's Lord.

Important social consequences for the Christian community at Philippi can be seen to flow from Paul's designation of himself as a slave. For Paul did not express this term, *doulos*, in a vacuum but rather in the opening of a letter to a Christian community in which slaves were present. Further, Paul himself almost certainly had personal contacts with slaves during his initial visit to Philippi.

On the assumption that the Christian community at Philippi had grown rapidly (see Introduction above), it is useful to consider Paul's perspective on a variety of topics pertaining to participation by slaves in worship and in other aspects of community life. The following mundane questions can open windows that have not been opened for centuries.

How were slaves "positioned" during worship in Paul's Philippi? Were slaves always proximate to their owners? Was there a separate slaves' section? Also what, if any, liturgical ministries were open to slaves? Could slaves assist if music was utilized in the community's liturgies? Could literate slaves proclaim biblical texts? And did slaves require the permission of their owners to serve in these capacities?

Christian owners' treatment of their slaves is a topic that Paul presumably also had in his view. Slaves ordinarily might be punished through such harsh measures as whipping, collaring, chaining, branding. Paul now understands that such practices by Christian masters are proscribed (see on 2:9). What is Paul's perspective regarding other important practices? Under what circumstances could/should Christian slaves be manumitted? Under what circumstances could/should Christian owners sell their slaves? Such questions would not receive a fully consistent response for three centuries, until Gregory of Nyssa (Ramelli 2016, 172–89).

Paul's experiences with the harshness of slavery at three sites—Amphipolis, Ephesus, and Corinth—might have paved the way for him to affirm the worth of slaves when he wrote to the Philippians. According to Acts 17:1, Paul passed through Amphipolis when he departed from Philippi. According to Acts 19, Paul conducted a ministry of more than three months' time at Ephesus. Finally, Acts 18:11 depicts Paul initially ministering at Corinth for a period of eighteen months. Amphipolis, Ephesus, and Corinth were all noteworthy sites for slave trading.

Because of its proximity to Thrace, Amphipolis served as a point of departure for slaves being brought from Thrace for transportation to other slave centers in Greece and Italy. Thracian slaves could be found throughout the empire, including the capital (Harris 1980, 126; Harris 1999, 74; Finley 1968, 171; Thompson 2003, 260). At Amphipolis, a seven-foot funeral marker was erected, probably within the first century AD, to commemorate the success of Aulus Caprilius Timotheus as a "slave trader" (*sōmatemperos*).

This marker depicts a slave trader leading a cohort of twelve slaves, eight of them male and chained at the neck (Duchene 1986, 517–21). Paul might never had met Capreilius or viewed his funeral stele. Nevertheless, he could have encountered actual processions of chained slaves at Amphipolis.

Extensive slave trading also took place at Ephesus. From the end of the Republic and continuing into imperial times, Ephesus was a "hub" for the slave trade, and its "slave market" (*statarion*) was widely known (Harris 1999, 74–75; Scheidel 2011, 301). Sometime after AD 40, the slave traders of Ephesus funded a public inscription to honor the Roman aristocrat C. Sallustius Crispus Passienus as their patron (Scheidel 2011, 300).

During his time at Corinth Paul would have found himself proclaiming Christ in yet another center for slave trading. Particularly after the fall of Delos (Magie 1950, 282) Corinth's traffic in slaves increased (Gordon 1964, 172, 177). Recent excavations point to the existence of a slave market (*statarion*) adjacent to the principal market (*agora*) of the city (Harrill 1995, 73).

In addition to Amphipolis, Ephesus, and Corinth, Paul presumably encountered slave traders at other locations. Biweekly "slave fairs" were commonly held in various provincial cities. Conceivably Paul might have become knowledgeable regarding *ergastulae*, prisons in rural locations where agricultural slaves were chained and housed for the night (Bradley 1994, 101).

Later in his journey, after he himself had been placed in chains, Paul might have encountered chained slaves at Puteoli. After Rome, Puteoli was probably the second largest market in Italy for the trading of slaves (Harris 1980, 126). It was known as "the new Delos," a reference to the former center of Greek slave-trading (Gordon 1964, 172; Thompson

2003, 33). According to Acts 28:14, Paul stayed seven days at Puteoli, meeting with members of the Christian community there. During this interval, still guarded in chains, it is possible that he viewed the slave market at which chained slaves were being auctioned.

In addition to the foregoing reflections regarding Paul's visual contacts with oppressed slaves, one arresting literary reference encapsulates the perspectives that Paul might have gained from literature or from personal contacts that he might have had with despairing slaves. These visceral words regarding slavery were expressed by the freed slave Publius Syrus: "It is beautiful to die instead of being degraded as a slave" (*occidi est pulchrum, ignominiose ubi servias*; *Sententiae* 489, cited by Harrill 1995, 1, 9, 193).

The letter to Philemon should be kept in view when considering how Paul might have "processed" the topic of slavery. Philemon precedes Philippians (Cassidy 2001b, 81–84, 135–38). In Philemon, Paul himself is in chains, presumably under military supervision. The circumstances under which slaves are chained are different from Paul's circumstances. Nevertheless, the experience of his own chains might have promoted Paul's reflections about slaves and chains.

In Philemon, Paul is thinking through the issue of slavery. The focus of his reflections is on Onesimus, a slave who has reached Paul's side seemingly without his Christian master's knowledge. Onesimus himself has become a Christian under Paul's guidance. In writing to Philemon to urge Philemon's manumission of Onesimus, Paul is offering guidance as to the mind of Christ regarding *one* Christian slave (ibid., 79, 251) What is the mind of Christ regarding *all* slaves? That is the topic that Paul is now taking up in Philippians.

As noted, the third element requiring attention in 1:1a is Paul's use of the name "Christ Jesus" (*Christou Iēsou*). This is the first of twenty occurrences of these two names in the letter. In some instances the order of the names is reversed to read "Jesus Christ." Bockmuel (1998, 51) and others have observed that the two names, "Christ" and "Jesus," appear to be reversible without any change of meaning. In addition, Philippians has seventeen references to "Christ" alone and one reference to "Jesus" alone.

Two features of Paul's address in 1:1b set it apart from the types of address that he typically uses in his other letters. Instead of explicitly referencing "the church" (*ekklēsia*) at Philippi (something that he will do at 4:15), he addresses **"all who are consecrated in Christ Jesus at Philippi"** (*pasin tois hagiois en Christō Iēsou en Philippois*).

In formulating this address Paul expresses several nuances of meaning. First, the Philippians are dedicated/consecrated to God (Reumann 2008, 58). Second, they have this status not because of their own virtue but because Christ has effected their consecration (Fee 1995, 65). Third, *all* of the Philippian Christians have this standing. Paul will again reference "*all* who are consecrated" in 4:21 at the end of the letter. These inclusive references underscore the priority that he places on the community's unity.

The second feature of 1:1b that represents a departure from Paul's form in his other letters is the wording **"with the bishops and deacons"** (*syn episkopois kai diakonois*). Paul evidently appreciates the presence of these ministers at Philippi. Although it is difficult to determine the precise forms of service in which they are engaged, it is significant that Paul expressly references two types of ministers.

Episkopos does not appear elsewhere in Paul's uncontested letters. It appears in 1 Tim 3:2 and Titus 3:1 (cf. Acts 20:28) where it may identify a person serving as overseer or supervisor with a special interest in guarding the apostolic tradition (BDAG 2000, 379).

In secular Greek use, *episkopos* commonly has the meaning of "overseer," "guardian," "supervisor," "inspector" (LSJ 1968, 657). Well before Paul, Athens sent inspectors (*episkopoi*) to its subject states (ibid.). Closer to Paul's time, five municipal officers at Rhodes were recognized as a council of *episkopoi* (Deissmann 1901, 230). Also at Rhodes the office of *episkopos* is listed among the religious offices of the Temple of Apollos (ibid., 231).

Within his undisputed letters Paul uses *diakonos* in reference to a Christian minister only at Rom 16:2 when he uses it to identify Phoebe. (Paul describes himself and Apollos as *diakonoi* in 1 Cor 3:5.) In the pastorals *diakonos* appears in 1 Tim 3:8, 12, and *diakoneō* appears at 1 Tim 3:10, 13).

In secular Greek, *diakonos* exhibits a range of both secular and religious meanings. It may initially have meant "servant" or "messenger." It also identifies attendants or officials in temples and religious cults (LSJ 1968, 398).

Given the prominence of the cult of Isis and Sarapis at Philippi (see Introduction), a citation from Magnesia (Moulton-Milligan 163, 149) indicating that the cult of these two deities in that city was served by a priest (*hiereus*) who presided over a college of *diakonoi* may be significant.

The Isis cult at Philippi involved a *hierys* but seemingly did not involve *diakonoi* (see Collart 1937, 453 for a listing of the cultic offices). Nevertheless Paul and/or the Philippian Christians, especially former devotees of Isis, might have known of the role of *diakonoi* in other Isis settings and appropriated *diakonoi* as a term for identifying Christian ministers at Philippi.

Hawthorne (1983, 7–9) is representative of commentators who urge that *episkopoi kai diakonoi* be translated as "bishops who are deacons." While such a translation is grammatically possible, *episkopoi* of this type are not identified in the existing Greek sources.

Precisely how those designated bishops and deacons functioned in the church of Philippi cannot be determined. It has been suggested (Silva 1988, 41, referencing Chrysostom) that these ministers collected the gift that was delivered to Paul by Epaphroditus (2:25; 4:17). It also is possible that Epaphroditus himself was a deacon.

Once again, from the standpoint of the Roman officials at Philippi, any ministry by *episkopoi* and *diakonoi* would be considered suspect. The decurions and magistrates *officially* supervised the religious cults of Philippi. Paul has now generated an *unauthorized* religious assembly. This assembly is well enough established to warrant ministries by bishops and deacons.

The next element of Paul's greeting (1:2) is familiar because he uses almost identical versions of it in all of his undisputed letters: **"Grace (*charis*) to you and peace (*eirēnē*) from God our Father and the Lord Jesus Christ."**

"Peace" (*eirēnē*) may be understood as the condition of wholeness and harmony that results from God's freely extended grace (Bockmuel 1998, 56). Here and at 4:7 and 4:9 also, peace is ultimately derived from God and/or Christ. It is not derived from Augustus or any other emperor.

"Grace" (*charis*) appears also at 1:7 and 4:23 and is one of Paul's most frequently used terms. It occurs sixty-six times within his undisputed letters. *Charis* is regularly translated as "grace" or "favor." As Harrison (2003, 88) and Reumann (2008, 65) have observed, however, the root concept may be that of "power." The closeness between "grace" and "power" is noted by BDAG (2000, 1080): "In some cases it (*charis*) is hardly to be differentiated from *dynamis*...."

In 1:2, 1:7, and 4:23, *charis* can be taken to mean "benevolent power." Benevolent power results in "favor." It ultimately results in "salvation." Here in 1:2 Paul is affirming that benevolent power is held and exercised by the Father and the Lord Jesus Christ. This conferral of benevolent power is totally unmerited. O'Brien has correctly stated (1991, 51): "Grace is not achieved by human work. It is totally free and unearned."

This clause imports two other facets of meaning that are important for the interpretation of Philippians. First, Jesus is depicted as being *with the Father*. Second, he is referenced with the title "Lord" (*kyrios*).

Paul indicates to the Philippians that "God our Father" *and* "the Lord Jesus Christ" exercise benevolent power whose effect is peace. Paul's meaning is that the Lord Jesus Christ is as much the source of "grace and peace" as God the Father (Hawthorne 1983, 12).

When Paul says that Jesus is *with the Father*, he indicates that this is Jesus's *present* status. *How* Jesus came to be with the Father in glory is a central feature of Paul's narrative in this letter. In effect, Paul's use of this customary salutation takes on an important new dimension of meaning because he will subsequently describe Christ's downward path and his upward path in returning to the Father with the Father's assistance.

In 1:2b Paul affirms to the Philippians that Jesus *is* Lord. As the letter unfolds, Paul will indicate the attributes that Jesus possesses because he is "Lord."

B. Thanksgiving (1:3-11)

The verb *eucharistō* ("I give thanks") signals the beginning of the thanksgiving section of the letter (1:3-11). This section (and the letter as a whole) is highly christocentric. There are four explicit references to "Jesus Christ" and to "Christ" (1:6, 8, 9, 11) here. In addition, Paul uses the term "gospel" in 1:5 and 1:7 in reference to Christ. (See comment on 1:7.)

Because Paul's vocabulary and grammar in the thanksgiving section are somewhat challenging, it is useful to approach these verses with two fundamental questions in mind: to whom does Paul express thanks and precisely for what is he thankful?

The first question is plainly answered at the outset: Paul is thankful to God. The answer to the second question is more complex. Paul is thankful for the "communion" (*koinōnia*) that he shares with the Philippians. He is grateful for the communion that they share with Christ. He is grateful also for the communion that they share with respect to his chains and with respect to his defense and confirmation of the gospel.

Paul immediately and directly expresses thanks to God (1:3): "**I thank my God in all my remembrance of you.**" Paul has in view his previous positive history with the Philippians. As he remembers this history he thanks God *for the Philippians*.

Paul then indicates in 1:4 that he makes this thanksgiving "**with joy**" (*meta charas*). Joy is a leitmotif of this letter, and this is its first appearance. *Charis* and its cognates appear no fewer than sixteen times in Philippians.

In approaching the meaning of *koinōnia* in 1:5 and 1:7, it is useful to note that these are two of the six instances in which Paul uses forms of this word in Philippians (also at 2:1; 3:10; 4:14; 4:15). Paul uses *koinōnia* in several of his other undisputed letters, and the range of meanings that this terms takes on has been extensively analyzed (for example, Campbell 1932; McDermott 1975; Koperski 1996, 81–87).

In 1:5 Paul expresses his gratitude for the Philippians' "**communion in the gospel**" (*tē koinōnia eis to euangelion*). The term "gospel" is also a term the Paul uses extensively in Philippians (nine times). It is a term whose fundamental meaning is "Christ." Gordon Fee's important insight on this usage deserves to be cited in full (1995, 82): "By the 'gospel' especially in Philippians, Paul refers primarily neither to a body of teaching nor to proclamation. Above all, the gospel has to do with Christ, both his person and his work."

In 1:6 Paul expresses his confidence that God will bring the good work already begun among the Philippians to completion "**at the day of Jesus Christ.**" He has now shifted his thoughts to the future. Jesus Christ, the person who is central to the entire letter, will return with full sovereignty on a certain "day." On this day, Jesus will bring to completion the good work that is even now in evidence among the Philippians.

The concept of Christ's sovereign advent is present elsewhere in the letter. In 1:10 Paul omits Jesus's name and refers to "the day of Christ." He also uses "day of Christ" in 2:16. Further, Paul's affirmation in 4:5b, "the Lord is near," is conceptually related to his previous "day of Christ" references.

In formulating the concept of Christ's "day," Paul may have been influenced by the eschatological "day of Yahweh" heralded in Joel 2:2 and Amos 5:20. Previously Paul has made reference to "the day of our Lord Jesus Christ" in 1 Cor 1:8 and 5:5 and also in 2 Cor 1:14. He has also vividly imaged "the day of the Lord" coming "like a thief in the night" in 1 Thess 5:2. His four references to "the day of Christ" in Philippians serve to emphasize that Christ's "day" far surpasses "Augustus's day" or any days dedicated to a Roman emperor.

In Egypt and Asia Minor a certain day of each month was termed *sebaste* and dedicated to the worship of the emperor (Deissmann 1978, 359). In Asia Minor an "emperor's day" was observed on the twenty-fourth of every month in order to commemorate Augustus's birthday on that date in September (Price 1984a, 106). Because of its strong Augustan heritage, one or more "Augustus days" on the calendar of Philippi's imperial observances is virtually certain.

Several important juridical and penal concepts are present in Paul's next verse (1:7): **"It is right that I should think about you all since I have you all in my heart sharing in grace both in my chains and in the exoneraton and vindication of the gospel."**

The middle clause in 1:7 is translated here with the meaning that Paul is holding the Philippians in his heart. The Greek is ambiguous, and Paul possibly means that the Philippians are holding *him* in their hearts (Sumney 2007, 12). Whatever his precise meaning, Paul is generally underscoring that he and the Philippians share in close communion (*synkoinōnous*) with Christ and one another. They have been sharing in Christ's grace (=benevolent power) since Paul's initial ministry at Philippi. This communion will be fully manifest on the day of Christ's sovereign return (3:20-21).

In the next clause in 1:7, Paul makes his first reference to his chains (*tois desmois*). He will refer to these chains three more times in the next ten verses (1:13, 14, 17). These metal chains are extremely important for an understanding of Paul's circumstances.

The RSV as well as other translations use "imprisonment" as a translation for *desmos*. However, the fundamental meaning of words with the *desm-* root is that of "binding" (Staudinger 1990, 1:289). When *desm-* is translated as "imprisonment," a situation in which the prisoner is bound with chains should be understood.

In addition to Philippians, five other New Testament texts depict Paul in chains (Philemon, Colossians, Ephesians, 2 Timothy, and the Acts of the Apostles). In Philemon, *desmios*, "prisoner" (literally, "the one bound"), appears in vv. 1 and 9, and *desmois* appears in vv. 10 and 13.

In Colossians *desmōn* appears strikingly in 4:18, the final verse of the letter. In Ephesians *desmios* occurs in 3:1 and 4:1. In 6:20, *halysis* is used, and the image is that of "an ambassador in chains" (*presbeuō en halysei*). *Halysis* also occurs in 2 Tim 1:16 where it is said of Onesiphorus that "he was not ashamed of my chains" (*kai tēn halysin mou ouk epaischynthē*).

The similar use of *halysis* and *desmos* in Acts to identify Paul's condition suggests that Luke understands both terms as designating metal chains. In Acts 21:33 the Roman tribune orders Paul "to be bound with two chains" (*dethēnai halysesi dysi*). In Acts 26:29 Paul uses *desmos* in decrying the chains that bind him: "except for these chains" (*parektos tōn desmōn toutōn*). In Acts 28:20 Paul uses *halysis* in proclaiming "I am bound with this chain" (*tēn halysin tautēn perikeimai*)

Josephus uses verb forms with the *desm-* root to describe how Tiberius relegated Agrippa into chained custody. Agrippa was literally chained to a centurion (*Jewish Antiquities* 18.6). Six months later, when Gaius ordered Agrippa's release, he stipulated that a gold chain be given to Agrippa. The weight of this chain was equal to the weight of the iron chain (*tē sidēra halysei*) with which Agrippa had been bound (*Jewish Antiquities* 18.10).

Agrippa's situation sheds light on Paul's situation in other ways as well. For a short period, Agrippa was transferred, still in chains, "from the camp" (*stratepedou*) back to the "house" (*oikian*) where he had formerly lived. According to references at Acts 28:16, 23, 30, the location of Paul's military custody was "an individual dwelling" (Rapske 1994, 384).

Paul may have been chained to one or more of his praetorian guards just as Herod Agrippa was chained to a centurion. Chains may have bound Paul's wrists together (Longenecker 1995, 364, commenting on Acts 28:20). A third possibility is that Paul may have been subjected to a heavy body chain similar to those used to secure the conspirators who faced Nero in AD 65 (Suetonius, *Nero* 36.2).

Many of those to whom Paul was writing would have had little difficulty envisioning the particular features of Paul's chains and other features of his custody. In effect, these Christians participated in "the narrative world of the letter" (Koperski 1996, 74). Some members of the Philippian community, especially slaves, may already have experienced the magistrates' chains. Also some of the Roman veterans now living at Philippi might themselves have guarded prisoners and been physically chained to them.

The Philippian Christians can also be presumed knowledgeable about the administrative aspects of Paul's situation. They would envision the written documents to be assembled by various officials and clerks in Rome. They could also anticipate the various types of proceedings that Paul might be facing, including the possibility of a preliminary hearing.

The Philippians' initiative in sending Epaphroditus to assist Paul indicates their awareness that Paul's form of custody allowed him to have visitors. In Agrippa's somewhat comparable situation, his *libertini* were able to visit him and bring him bedding and provisions (Josephus, *Jewish Antiquities* 18.7). The gift the Philippians sent via Epaphroditus indicates their awareness that funds could be used to assist Paul's personal expenses (4:12-18). According to Acts 28:30, Paul's custody as he awaited the adjudication of his case was "at his own expense" (*en idiō misthōmati*).

Were the Philippians apprised that administrative fees could sometimes be charged for cases appealed to the emperor? It is significant that from the time of Claudius, civil appeals to the emperor's court from the province of Asia required a deposit of 2,500 denarii (Oliver 1979, 552). If Paul faced comparable fees, then his response to Epaphroditus's gift is all the more remarkable (see commentary on 4:14-19).

Paul's meaning in the final clause of 1:7 is rich and complex. In this clause (as at 1:5 and elsewhere in the letter), "gospel" refers to Christ. Paul is thus using two legal terms, "exonerate" (*apologia*) and "vindicate" (*bebaiōsei*) with reference to Christ. Both *apologia* and *bebaiōsei* were common terms in first-century judicial proceedings (Deissmann 1901, 108), but Paul combines them in a remarkable way.

Paul also uses *apologia* in Phil 1:16. He has used this word and its cognates in his earlier letters, for example, in 1 Cor 9:3; 2 Cor 7:11; 2 Cor 12:19. *Apologia* and its verbal forms are also used in judicial scenes in the Acts of the Apostles (22:1; 24:10; 25:8, 16; 26:1, 2, 24). *Apologia* is used with reference to Paul's juridical proceedings in 2 Tim 4:16.

The function of the prefix *apo* in *apo-logia* is to urge dismissal of the charge (LSJ 1968, 208). On the assumption that Paul has Jesus's trial in view as he engages in his own juridical process, Paul can be regarded as calling boldly for the withdrawal of the Roman verdict against . . . *Jesus*.

Previously Paul has focused on Jesus's crucifixion as scandalous (1 Cor 1:23; Gal 5:11; cf. 1 Cor 1:13; 2:2, 8; 2 Cor 13:4; Gal 3:1; 6:14). Now, because of the verdict looming in his own case, he focuses on the Roman proceedings that resulted in Jesus's crucifixion. It now becomes a part of Paul's trial strategy to petition that his judge (the emperor or the emperor's delegate) repudiate the *logion* pronounced against Jesus by the Roman governor of Judea.

Paul is now reflecting at a most profound level regarding the testimony that he himself will present before the emperor. *Jesus* is the basic, all-encompassing reason why Paul is in chains. Paul knows unalterably that any courtroom dialogue that he might have will revolve around Jesus. Certainly Paul will not defer to any imperial comment discrediting Jesus as a justly condemned zealot (*lēstēs*). Should Nero or his delegate advert to Pilate's decree (*titulus*) against Jesus, Paul's immediate response would be to demand that Pilate's verdict be expunged.

As noted, Paul uses "vindicate" (*bebaiōsei*) as a complement to *apo-logia*. These two nouns are joined by the conjunction "and" (*kai*), governed by the same article, *tē*, and modified by the same phrase, "of the gospel" (*tou euangeliou*).

Paul has used verbal forms of *bebaiō* in 1 Cor 1:6 (often translated "confirm") and in 2 Cor 1:21 (often translated "establish"). Philippians 1:7 contains the only use of *bebaiōsis* as a noun in the New Testament. From the work of Deissmann (1901, 108), it emerges that *bebaiōsis* may refer to surety for "recovering" something invalidly sold.

Paul's focus here is entirely on Christ. If "recovery" is the root meaning of *bebaiōsis*, that which is being recovered pertains to Christ. What, regarding Christ, needs to be "recovered"?

Because of an invalid, blasphemous verdict, the name of Christ has been degraded and besmirched. It is thus the "reputation," the "good name" of Christ that must now be "recovered." The reputation of Christ must be "vindicated" from the "scandal" that Roman crucifixion has conferred on it. Recall that Paul uses *skandalon* in reference to the crucifixion in 1 Cor 1:23.

Certainly Paul's proposals are audacious! He first calls for the setting aside of the unjust verdict pronounced by the Roman authorities against Jesus (*apologia*)! He then calls for the vindication (*bebaiōsis*) of the "high" name, the reputation, of Jesus.

Paul's great boldness on behalf of Christ presumably will be pondered at some length by the Philippians. The objectives that Paul is projecting for his testimony are lofty. Yet let it not be thought that these considerations regarding the vindication of Jesus's "name" are far-fetched. For, in 2:9-11, Paul will indicate the Father's decisive intervention for the sake *of the name* of Jesus.

Paul recognizes that he will not be able to carry out such testimony unaided, and he relies on Christ's "benevolent power" (*charis*) to assist him. As discussed at 1:2, "power" is a fundamental meaning of *charis*. Paul is facing the overwhelming power of the Roman state. He is relying on the beneficent power of Jesus to safeguard and strengthen him.

To repeat, Paul is engaged in a bold endeavor to exonerate and vindicate Christ. The concepts of honor and dishonor are central to what Paul describes. The Roman authorities seek to *dishonor* Paul by chaining him. Paul brushes aside this attempt at *dishonor* and strives to bring *honor* to the name of Jesus. Paul relies on the surpassing beneficent power of Jesus for assistance in achieving this objective.

In 1:8 Paul begins with an oath: "**For God is my witness.**" (He uses identical or similar wording in 1 Thess 2:5, 10; Rom 1:9; 2 Cor 1:23.) This oath adds depth to the claim of his next words: "**I yearn for you all with the affection of Christ Jesus.**"

There are three elements in Paul's claim. First, the verb translated "yearn for" (*epipothō*) is an indication of the emotional closeness between Paul and the Philippians. This verb occurs also at 2:26 and 4:1; see also 1 Thess 3:6; Rom 1:11; and 2 Cor 5:2; 9:14. Second, "all" (*pantas*) expresses that Paul has a unified community in his view. As noted above, this unified community includes both free and slave Christians.

Third, Paul's yearning is "with the *affection* of Christ Jesus." (The RSV translators render *splanchnois* as "affection" here and at 2:1 and as "heart" at Phlm 7, 12, 20.) In writing this phrase Paul expresses that his longing to be with the Philippians has its origin in the risen Christ's surpassing love.

Christ's deep love embraces Paul and embraces *all* of the Philippians.

In 1:5 Paul recalled that he and the Philippians share the high calling of "communion" (*koinōnia*) in Christ. Here he affirms that he is caught up with them in the surpassing love that originates from Jesus Christ.

At 1:9 Paul reiterates what he has already affirmed in 1:4, namely, that he is in a posture of prayer toward the Philippians. The objective of his prayer is that the Philippians' own love may abound more and more. Additionally, he petitions that their love grow by means of **"knowledge"** (*epignōsei*) and **"all discernment"** (*pasē aisthēsei*).

In the next two verses (1:10-11) Paul identifies three consequences that will follow from such an abounding love.

First, the Philippians will be able to **"discern what is excellent."** Second, they will be **"kept pure and blameless for the day of Christ."** Paul's reference here to "the day of Christ" is close to his expression in 1:6.

The concepts "pure and blameless" are similar to those in his admonition in 2:13 where he exhorts the Philippians to be *"blameless and innocent, children of God without blemish in the midst of a crooked and perverse generation."* Since Paul seems to have Roman moral degradation in view in 2:13 (see comments below), "pure" (*eilikrineis*) and "blameless" (*aproskopoi*), the terms he uses here, may also relate to Roman moral degradation.

The third consequence is that the Philippians will be filled **"with the fruit of righteousness."** Paul indicates that this righteousness comes **"through Jesus Christ"** and concludes that all of this is oriented **"to the glory and praise of God."**

This intimation that events concerning Christ pertain to the "glory" (*doxan*) and praise of God is crucial for the meaning of Philippians as a whole. In 2:11, in the final scene of Paul's Christ drama, a universal confession is made affirming that Jesus is Lord "to the *glory* of God the Father."

Philippians 1:12-26
II. Overview of Paul's Situation

Introductory Comments

Three major topics constitute 1:12-26, the first section of the body of the letter.

1. 1:12-13: Paul's chains advance the gospel
2. 1:14-18: Paul's chains engender division
3. 1:19-26: Paul's potential for death or life

Below, in "Tracing the Train of Thought," these thought units will be analyzed without separate introductions.

Earlier in the letter (1:5) Paul has indicated to the Philippians his continuing communion with them for the sake of the gospel. He now reports to them in 1:12-13 that the cause of the gospel, that is, the cause of Christ, is advancing as a result of his chained custody in Rome.

Paul does not dwell on the aspects of his circumstances that concern his location, the nature of his accommodations, and his daily regimen. The presumption is that the Philippians already know something about these aspects.

Paul's chains are central to the advance of the gospel. With apparent satisfaction Paul relates that his chains have brought Christ to the attention of the "whole" praetorian guard and to "all the rest." Further, most of the members of the Christian community at Rome have been encouraged by Paul's witness. These now testify to Christ "without fear."

Nevertheless, Paul's chains have had a negative effect. A minority of Christians have started to proclaim Christ in such a way as to afflict Paul in his chains (1:17). These Christians are preaching Christ, but they do so (1:15) "from envy and rivalry." This is a distressing development. Paul makes the best of this situation by focusing on the fact that Christ is still being proclaimed.

Paul then reflects about the possibility of his release and the benefits that such an outcome would bring to the Philippians (1:19-26). It is significant that, while his release is a distinct possibility, so too is his death. Paul is actually hard-pressed to determine his own preference.

Having shared his inner conflicts in 1:21-25, Paul then informs the Philippians that his renewed ministry with them is his ultimate preference, and he even anticipates the reunion they will have (1:26). In writing these words, Paul is projecting that his trial will end with an acquittal. As time elapses and the letter continues, however, the possibility of a verdict of condemnation reemerges.

Tracing the Train of Thought

Overview of Paul's Situation (1:12-26)

A. Paul's Chains Advance the Gospel (1:12-13)

Paul's words in 1:12a, "**I want you to know**" (*ginōskein de hymas boulomai*) open the body of the letter. Here Paul adopts another feature of ancient letter writing, the disclosure form (O'Brien 1991, 86). Prescinding from any description of the material conditions of his custody, Paul affirms the impact that his chains are having on those around him. Paul's central affirmation is that "**the things that have happened to me have served to advance the gospel**" (*ta kat' eme eis propokēn tou euangeliou*).

Paul explains that there are two principal ways in which the gospel is now advancing. First, it is advancing through Paul's "testimony" to members of the praetorian guard. Second, it is advancing by means of emboldened proclamation by some members of the Christian community at Rome.

In 1:13 Paul relates that "**it has become known throughout the whole praetorian guard and to all the rest that my chains are for Christ.**" For purposes of exposition, the phrase "and to all the rest" will be taken up after clarifications are made regarding the character of Paul's testimony to the praetorian guards.

As noted in the Introduction, Augustus provided parcels of land at Philippi to the discharged members of his personal guard. These praetorian veterans subsequently played a significant role in shaping the Roman ethos of the colony. Augustus's praetorians played a far more significant role *at Rome* as he proceeded to fashion the empire. The praetorian guard later functioned prominently during the regimes of Augustus's successors, especially at the points of transition between emperors.

Paul's claim here is that virtually all of the praetorian guards have become aware that his chains are for Christ. He does not indicate precisely how this information has become known so widely. Presumably, the reports that Christ was connected with Paul's chains circulated both directly and indirectly.

If Paul were chained to his guards in the manner that Josephus reports Herod Agrippa being chained to his guards (*Jewish Antiquities* 18.6.5ff.), Paul may have spoken directly to them regarding Christ. Alternatively, Paul's guards may have learned of Paul's commitment to Christ as a result of overhearing Paul's conversations with Timothy (2:19-22), with Epaphroditus (2:25-30), and/or "with the brethren who are with me" (4:21b).

While Paul's guards have become aware that Paul's chains are for Christ, Paul does not state that he has brought any of his guards to faith in Christ. Nevertheless, his claim is still sweeping in its scope: throughout *the whole praetorian guard*, it is now known that Paul's chains are for Christ.

The possibility that Paul's communications with his guards brought information *to him* regarding conditions in imperial Rome should be considered. The involvement of the praetorian guards in imperial matters was especially pronounced during the era of Nero. The praetorians took the initiative to install Nero as emperor!

In response, Nero paid these guards a large donative and also provided land to them at the new colony of Antium. He paid a similar donative to ensure the praetorians' loyalty after he murdered his mother (Watson 1981, 110), and yet another donative for their critical assistance at the time of the Pisonian conspiracy in AD 65 (Tacitus, *Annals* 15.67). At the time of Galba's uprising, one of the coprefects of the praetorians influenced the guards as a whole to withdraw their allegiance from Nero and bestow it on Galba (Plutarch, *Galba* 2.1-2).

When Paul decries abuses by "the enemies of the cross of Christ" in 3:18-19, he probably has Nero and his confederates in view. From the praetorians Paul could have learned of multiple instances of the emperor's deviant and idolatrous behavior. The praetorians knew everything regarding Nero's malicious and bizarre practices. The phrase "known throughout the whole praetorian guard" thus suggests that various items of information about Nero were reaching Paul via the praetorians.

As noted in the Introduction, Paul's words in 1:13a, "and to all the rest" (*kai tois loipois pasin*), indicate that a second group of persons was being impacted by Paul's witness. Paul is probably referring now to the members of the emperor's staff (see 4:22 regarding *tēs kaisaros oikias*, "Caesar's household") who are responsible for his case (Bruce 1980, 261; Fee 1995, 114).

Within the imperial bureaucracy, the department *a cognitionibus* had the responsibility to collect information and prepare opinions for the emperor in cases involving imperial prisoners (Abbott 1911, 362). The secretary of this bureau administered the emperor's court of law (Millar 1984, 94). Unlike the Christians of Rome, the staff of *a cognitionibus* did not previously know that Christ was the explanation for Paul's chains (Marshall 1992, 21).

Paul indicates in 1:13b that it has become clear both to the praetorians and to these others **"that my chains are for Christ"** (*hōste tous desmous mou en christō*). Here *en christō* is best taken as a dative of cause (Zerwick/Grosvenor 1988, 593; cf. Sumney 2007, 19). Paul is experiencing chains *because of* Christ. Paul is in chains because of the testimony that he has been giving concerning Christ.

Nevertheless, Paul may also use *en Christō* with a second meaning. In his chains, Paul remains *in Christ*. In other words, Paul remains in communion with Christ (and with Christ's suffering) even while he is in chained custody.

B. Paul's Chains Engender Division (1:14-18)

Paul's description of his situation continues in 1:14-18, a passage often regarded as a "cross" for the interpreter (*crux interpretum*) because of the difficulty in explaining the motivation of the group that is causing Paul distress. This group is clearly composed of Christians, but what is their motivation? Along with the majority, this minority is committed to the preaching of the gospel. Nevertheless, the members of the minority are preaching Christ in such a way as to harm Paul.

An explanation for the approach of the minority may be detected in Paul's earlier letter to the Romans. In particular Rom 15:18-19 and 13:1-7 may shed light on the situation that Paul is now experiencing as he writes to the Philippians.

At the end of Romans, Paul indicates his travel plans to his readers. After noting the immense scope of the apostolic mission that he had already completed, Paul projects his next missionary undertaking (Rom 15:18-19): "since I no longer have any room for work in these regions, and since I have longed for many years to come to you, I hope to see you in passing as I go to Spain, and to be sped on my journey there by you, once I have enjoyed your company for a little. At present, however, I am going to Jerusalem with aid for the saints. For Macedonia and Achaia have been pleased to make some contribution for the poor among the saints in Jerusalem."

In the chronology of Paul's writings, Romans predates Philemon and Philippians. Both Philemon and Philippians reflect Paul's circumstances as a Roman prisoner who has been in chains over an extended interval of time. Since there is no mention of his being bound with chains in Romans, it is safe to conclude that the letters in which Paul is manifestly in chains were written *after* Romans (Cassidy 2001b, 81–84, 135–38). In writing his letter to the Romans, Paul did not envision that chained custody would be the condition under which he would arrive in Rome.

In the scenario now being proposed, Paul's arrival in Rome *in chains* was profoundly disconcerting for a minority of the capital's Christians. In effect, this minority judged that Paul's chains disqualified him from preaching the gospel.

For this minority, Paul himself failed to observe the teaching regarding subjection to the imperial authorities that he had set forth in Rom 13:1-7. Paul's failure to observe his own teachings caused him to incur the wrath of the Roman authorities. He has presumably engaged in some form of nefarious conduct. For this reason he cannot continue to serve as an authoritative expositor of the gospel.

This minority may also have concluded that Paul's status as a chained prisoner might constitute a danger for the entire Christian community at Rome. In tumultuous Rome, the vigorous proclamation of Christ by a prominent chained prisoner could conceivably result in the chaining of many Christians!

Chains have the potential to generate shame. In 1:20 Paul will advert to the fact that chains might normally confer shame on the prisoner. Nevertheless Paul avows that this will not be so for him.

In the secular literature of the time, there are references to chains engendering shame for the chained prisoner and among the prisoner's associates and close friends. The shame of chains might continue even after the prisoner gained release. Josephus indicates that Titus and Domitian took an unusual step to obviate Josephus's shame when they ordered his release from chains. They ordered that Josephus's chains be severed by an axe (as opposed to unlocking them), thereby conveying that Josephus never should have been in chains (*Wars* 4.10.7).

Seneca, Nero's tutor for the emperor's first five years, wrote of fair-weather friends who flee "at the first rattle of the chain" (*Epistle* 9.9). The contrasting image of a friend *not* deterred by chains is provided by 2 Timothy's description of Onesiphorus: "he was not ashamed of my chains, but when he arrived in Rome, he searched for me eagerly and found me" (2 Tim 1:16b-17).

In 2 Timothy Paul is also portrayed admonishing Timothy not to be shamed by Paul's chains (2 Tim 1:8 author's translation): "Do not be ashamed (*mē oun epaischynthēs*) of testifying to our Lord, nor of me his chained one (*eme ton desmion autou*)." Second Timothy also depicts Paul himself resolutely refusing to be shamed even though he is suffering (1:12): "and therefore I suffer as I do. But I am not ashamed" (*all' ouk epaischynomai*).

Once again, in 1:14-18, Paul describes two responses to his chains, the positive response of the majority of Roman Christians and the negative response of the minority. In these verses Paul shifts back and forth in his description of responses by the majority and minority. Hawthorne (1983, 36) and other interpreters have discerned a chiastic pattern in these verses. In any analysis of Paul's style of presentation, the gravity of the insight he expresses in 1:16b must not be ignored.

In 1:14 Paul begins by characterizing the positive response of the majority. He then portrays the negative response of the minority in 1:15a only to resume speaking of the positive attitude of the majority in 1:15b-16. In 1:17 he turns again to the minority, elaborating their negative motives. In 1:18, as he presents his overview of the situation, he includes one additional phrase critiquing the minority and one additional phrase commending the majority. Paul's positive commendations for the majority can be examined together.

In 1:14 he identifies three ways in which the majority's proclamation of Christ has been strengthened because of his chains (*tois desmois mou*). The majority has become **"more confident in the Lord"** (*en kyriō pepoithotas*) **"much more bold"** (*perissoterōs tolman*) and **"without fear"** (*aphobōs*).

In 1:15b Paul characterizes the majority as proclaiming Christ from **"good will"** (*di' eudokian*) toward Paul, but also toward God (Reumann 2008, 180). The complement to the majority's motivation "from good will" comes in 1:18, where Paul characterizes their proclamation as being **in truth** (*alētheia*).

In 1:16a Paul expands his favorable comments regarding the majority. He states that they operate **"out of love"** (*ex agapēs*) for him (Fee 1995, 120). He then adds, in 1:16b, a note that is of extreme consequence. He states that the majority has embraced his own view: **"recognizing that I am put here for the exoneration of Christ"** (*eidotes hoti eis apologian tou euangeliou keimai*).

This last clause discloses Paul's insight that his mission as a chained prisoner in Rome has been divinely entrusted to him. This mission involves the "exoneration of Christ." What is now indicated by the words **"I am put here"** (*keimai*) is that Paul's bold commitment to exonerate Christ is divinely appointed for this space and time (Reumann 2008, 191, extensive note; BDAG 2000, 537; Zerwick/Grosvenor 1988, 593).

Earlier in the letter, in 1:7, Paul referenced his commitment to "the exoneration of Christ" (*apologian tou euangeliou*). He mentions this commitment now, adding that he has been divinely appointed for this mission. He will auspiciously reference this mission again in 2:11 when speaking of the definitive magnification of Jesus's name.

Paul now recognizes that Tiberius (through Pilate) unjustly condemned Jesus as a violator of *maiestas*. As a consequence of this verdict, the sacred name of Jesus was degraded throughout the empire of the Julio-Claudians. Now, in the providence of God, Paul has been appointed for the exoneration of Jesus's name.

Paul has been brought to Rome in chains under Nero to accomplish his mission at the heart of the empire. He has been divinely appointed for this undertaking. He has been "put *here*" (*keimai*) for it. This divine appointment to exonerate Christ at the heart of the empire does not necessarily mean that Paul considers Rome his final destination. For, in 1:24-25 he evidently contemplates a return to Philippi.

As indicated, Paul characterizes the response of the minority of Roman Christians negatively in 1:15a, in 1:17, and by one phrase in 1:18. He uses "envy," a complex term to indict this group (Böttrich 2004, 96–98). In 1:15a he describes the approach of the minority in the following way: **"Some indeed preach Christ from envy and rivalry"** (*tines men kai dia phthonon kai erin*). Because "envy" (*pthonos*) and "rivalry" (*eris*) appear in the lists of vices in Gal 5:20-21 and Rom 1:29, it is startling that Paul here attributes these qualities to Christians who are engaged in the proclamation of Christ.

In 1:17 he continues his severe criticism of the minority: (they) **"proclaim Christ out of selfish ambition, not sincerely, but seeking to afflict me in my chains"** (*hoi de ex eritheias ton Christon katangellousin ouch hagnōs oiomenoi thlipsin egeirein tois desmois mou*). In criticizing them for acting "out of selfish ambition" (*ex eritheias* is so translated by BDAG 2000, 309), Paul indicts the minority for marginalizing him while burnishing their own credentials as evangelists for Christ. In 2:3 Paul uses the same term (*eritheian*) when he warns the Philippians themselves against acting from "selfish ambition."

Finally, in 1:18 Paul characterizes the proclamation of the minority as being **"with pretext"** (*prophasei*). In other words, what appears to be true on the surface is actually not true. In contrast, as noted above, the proclamation of the majority is "with truth" (*alētheia*).

There are two additional points to consider regarding 1:14-18. First, Paul adopts a "high road" toward the minority. These Christians are, in effect, contributing to his sufferings. Yet Paul rejoices in the fact that they are authentically proclaiming Christ (1:18b): **"Christ is proclaimed and in that I rejoice."** Paul's capacity for benevolence toward the minority in Rome thus lays a foundation for the appeals that he will make for self-sacrificing conduct on the part of the Philippian Christians (2:1-4; 4:2-4).

Second, the complex developments that Paul alludes to in these verses indicate that he is well informed regarding events within the Christian community in Rome. Certainly Paul has access to Timothy (1:1-2; 2:19-22) and to Epaphroditus (2:25-30). These two collaborators would be reliable sources of information. It has presumably taken time for the approaches by the majority and the minority to develop and coalesce. Paul might have met personally with members of the majority during this interval.

As noted, Paul ends 1:18 with "I rejoice" (*chairō*), marking the end of a thought unit. In 1:19a, perhaps after an elapse of time, he resumes: **"Yes I shall rejoice"** (*alla kai charēsomai*). Joy is a leitmotif in this letter. Whatever his own circumstances, Paul cannot be separated from his contemplation of the propitiousness of Christ's entire endeavor. The magnificence of what Christ and the Father have wrought engenders an abiding joy in Paul. Paul also derives joy from being "in the Lord."

C. Paul's Potential for Death or Life (1:19-26)

Paul now turns to reflections concerning his future. In 1:19b he writes, **"For I know"** (*oida gar*), and then proceeds to indicate two things about which he is certain. The first aspect known to Paul is **"that through your prayers and the provision of the Spirit of Jesus Christ, this will turn out for my salvation."**

As indicated in the Introduction, a threefold communion is operative throughout Philippians. This communion is among Christ, Paul, and the Philippian Christians. This communion is referred to in the present verse. The prayers of the Philippians and the intercession of the Spirit sent by Christ (Bockmuel 1998, 84) will bring Paul through the present dangers.

Many translators and commentators render *sōtēria* here as "deliverance" (for example, the RSV, NIV; Hawthorne 1983, 40). However, Paul seems not merely to affirm his release—which may not happen—but rather his ultimate *salvation*, something that will certainly occur.

Paul also speaks of Christ as "savior" (*sōtēr*) in 3:20. In this latter verse Paul adverts to Christ's arrival as the savior who will transform the fragile human body into a body of glory. Paul's meaning is the same here. He is concerned with Christ's ultimate intervention. Paul may or may not gain "deliverance" at his Roman trial (see below). Yet he will ultimately receive the "salvation" that Christ will confer on him. Here he is thus expressing confidence in his "eschatological salvation" (Fee 1995, 128). He will also urge the Philippians to focus on such "salvation" in 1:28 and 2:12.

In 1:20 Paul considers two outcomes that he expects to experience as aspects of salvation. On the one hand (1:20a), **"it is my eager expectation and hope that I shall not be at all ashamed"** (*tēn apokaradokian kai elpida mou hoti en oudeni aischynthēsomai*). On the other hand (1:20b), **"but that with all boldness now as always Christ will be glorified in my body, whether by life or by death"** (*en pasē parrēsia hōs pantote kai nyn megalynthēsetai Christos en tō sōmati mou, eite dia zōēs eite dia thanatou*).

Paul knows that no human tribunal has the capacity to confer indelible shame on him. Jesus suffered earthly "shame" at the time of his arrest, trial, and execution. Yet no such shaming occurred before the heavenly tribunal. So too with Paul. Because he relies on his right standing with Jesus Christ (whom 2 Tim 4:8 refers to as "the righteous judge"), Caesar's chains and any negative verdict at Caesar's tribunal will be unable to visit indelible shame on Paul.

In 1:20b the Greek word *megalynthēsetai* (rendered by the RSV as "honor") has the fundamental meaning of "make great, glorify" (Zerwick/Grosvenor 1988, 594). A verse in which Paul expresses his hope to glorify Christ is hardly surprising in christocentric Philippians. Yet Paul now specifies that his hope is to glorify Christ either through his own death or else by continued life. No single verse in Philippians encapsulates the meaning of the letter. Yet this clause, along with 2:11, can be taken as fundamental to Paul's meaning in the letter: the glorification of Christ above every other entity.

Paul does not use *megalynthēsetai* here to mean that his own life or death will succeed in making Christ greater (Hawthorne 1983, 43). Rather, it is his hope and expectation that his life or death will serve to make Christ, *who is already great*, known to a larger audience. Paul's endeavor is to glorify Christ, to praise Christ, by his own faithfulness to Christ in life or in death.

Paul uses the phrase "with all boldness" (*en pasē parrēsia*) as a modifier for *megalynthēsetai*. *Parrēsia*, the key word in this phrase, means "resolute testimony" in circumstances of intimidation, particularly intimidation by the regnant political authorities (Schlier 1964, 5:871-86; Marrow 1982, 65–67; Cassidy 1987, 45–56). Conceptually, it is related to *tolman*, "confident," the word that Paul uses in 1:14 to indicate that the majority has caught something of Paul's "fire" in their own testimony for Christ.

In 1 Thess 2:2 Paul uses *parrēsia* within a sentence in which persecution by the political authorities is in view. He reminds the Thessalonians of how he had previously been shamefully treated *at Philippi* and then had declared the gospel with boldness at Thessalonica while experiencing great conflict there also. Within the undisputed letters, the only other occurrence of *parrēsia* occurs in 2 Cor 7:4, where pressure from the political authorities is not involved.

In Ephesians and Acts Paul is depicted as a chained prisoner who testifies "with boldness" (*en parrēsia*). Ephesians 6:19-20 presents prisoner Paul requesting prayers that utterance be given him to testify to the gospel "with boldness" (Cassidy 2001b, 99–104). In Acts 26:26, 29 Paul highlights his chains in testifying "boldly" (*parrēsiazomenos*) before the governor, Porcius Festus, and Herod Agrippa. In the final verse of Acts (28:31), Paul continues to testify to the Lord Jesus Christ "with all boldness" (*meta pasēs parrēsias*) as a chained prisoner in Rome (Cassidy 2014, 133–35).

Paul avows that the sphere in which Christ is to be magnified is "in my body" (*en tō sōmati mou*). Many commentators correctly urge that *sōma* refers to Paul's whole being here, as opposed to "a narrowly corporeal meaning" (Collange 1979, 60). Yet in view of Paul's two uses of this word in 3:21, the dimension of physical corporality must not be minimized. Paul is very conscious that his *corporal* body may be brutally treated in a Roman execution. Nevertheless he is confident that, should this happen, he will receive from Christ "a body of glory."

When he reflects "whether by life or by death," Paul imparts to the Philippians that his death at the hands of the imperial authorities is a distinct possibility. The Christians at Philippi have presumably already foreseen that Paul's condemnation and execution may occur. A death verdict for cases appealed to the emperor is always possible and perhaps even likely.

Nevertheless, Paul does not speak of his death as certain at any point in Philippians. He also adverts to the *possibility* of his death in 2:17, 3:10, and 3:21. What the Philippians might regard as "new information" in this verse is Paul's *equanimity* regarding death.

In the next four verses (1:21-24), Paul discloses how his internal thought processes give rise to a preference for continued life. In 1:21-22a Paul indicates that both life and death are positive outcomes and indicates a benefit from continuing to live: "**For me to live is Christ and to die is gain. If I live in the flesh that means fruitful ministry for me.**" As with so many other passages in the letter, these verses are permeated with Christ. In 1:21a Paul affirms that his earthly life *is* Christ (*to zēn christos*); in 1:21b he regards death as a gain (*kerdos*). Paul's meaning is thus that both outcomes result in Christ. The result of death is "gain" (=Christ) just as the result of continued life is *Christ*.

In 1:22b-23a Paul indicates his perplexity in trying to assess these two alternatives: **"which I shall choose I do not know"** (*kai ti hairēsomai ou gnōrizō*). **"I am hard pressed between the two"** (*synechomai de ek tōn duo*). This latter verse has given rise to a great variety of interpretations. Among the more astonishing proposals is that Paul is actually considering suicide. This proposal is forcefully rebutted by Fee (1995, 141), among others.

Because Paul is not deluded over the role that the Roman authorities will play in deciding his future, it is best to take these words as a soliloquy in which he reflects on the attractiveness of continued life in Christ and the full gain of Christ in death. The following paraphrase may capture Paul's sense here: "If I had to choose martyrdom or life, both choices are so attractive to me that I hardly know which I would choose."

In 1:23b Paul discloses the alternative he prefers: **"I have the desire to depart and be with Christ for that is far better"** (*tēn epithymian echōn eis to analysai kai syn Christō einai pollō gar mallon kreisson*). Here the verb "depart" (*analysai*) is used metaphorically for death (Sumney 2007, 30).

Nevertheless, Paul indicates in 1:24 that he is influenced by what is more beneficial *for the Philippians*: **"But to remain in the flesh is more necessary for you."** Accordingly he announces (1:25), **"I know that I shall remain and continue with you all for the sake of your progress and joy in the faith."** Philippians 1:24 and 1:25, when taken with 2:24, indicate that Paul attaches the highest priority to the Philippian community.

Additional light is shed on Paul's words in 1:24-25 by what he writes at 2:24 and also at 1:30. In 2:24 Paul indicates that he will travel to Philippi upon his release. Travel eastward to Philippi represents a clear shift from his previously projected plans to travel to Spain (Rom 15:28). The explanation for Paul's decision to change his itinerary may reside in the fact that the Philippian church is undergoing persecution (1:30). Upon his own release from chains, Paul's first priority will be to reunite with the Philippian Christians in order to strengthen them by means of his personal presence.

In 1:26 Paul urges that the Philippians take his coming (literally his "arrival") to them again as a cause for their boasting and exulting in Christ: **"so that your jubilation in Christ Jesus may abound because of my arrival again among you."** In this instance "in Christ Jesus" denotes both the ground and the mode of the Philippians' jubilation. Christ Jesus alone is the reason for Paul's return to Philippi. And it will be the occasion for jubilation *in* Christ Jesus (Bockmuel 1998, 95).

Paul's use of "arrival" (*parousia*) may also function to counter an aspect of the emperor cult, namely, the arrival (*parousia*) of the emperor with immense pomp and circumstance. Paul's "arrival" will not have the trappings of the Roman emperor with his retinue.

The underlying premise for Paul's reflections in these verses is that he does not fear Roman execution. He will not be cowed by any threats or saber rattling from the imperial authorities. They can *only* execute him! Such an execution will enable him to gain Christ fully!

Philippians 1:27-30
III. The Same Conflict at Philippi and Rome

Introductory Comments

Having communicated at some length regarding his own circumstances, Paul turns his attention to the situation of the Philippians.

What 1:27-30 indicates about the phenomenon of persecution at Philippi is important for the interpretation of the letter as a whole. In this section Paul links his own persecution by the imperial authorities in Rome with the persecution that the Philippian Christians are experiencing from the imperial authorities at Philippi. The persecution that Paul himself earlier experienced at Philippi underlies what he writes in this passage.

In these verses Paul encourages the Philippian Christians not to be frightened by their opponents, that is, not to be intimidated by any measures that the Roman magistrates might employ. The Philippian Christians are to stand firm "in one spirit with one mind" (1:27b).

These last words represent Paul's first expression of concern for unity within the letter. He expresses this concern in the context of reflections regarding persecution. When there is an attack launched against a community, it is important to maintain internal and external unity. No Philippian Christian should consider breaking ranks to seek advancement through collusion with the Philippian magistrates (see below on 2:3).

The magistrates who are engaged in this intimidation and persecution are themselves headed for *annihilation* (1:28b). In contrast, the outcome for the Philippian Christians who stand firm is *salvation* (1:28c)

Tracing the Train of Thought

Paul is now focusing his attention on the situation of the Christians at Philippi. His words to them presume that they are experiencing persecution from the Roman magistrates who administer the city. Public beatings, the confiscation of property, etc., are among the types of persecution employed by the Roman duumviri at Philippi. (See Introduction, section 12, above.)

In 1:27a, Paul uses the adverbial form *monon*, translated as **"just one thing,"** to indicate the importance of what he now presents regarding worthy conduct and unity. He uses *monon* in a similar way in Gal 1:23, 2:19, and 3:2.

In secular usage, *politeuesthe* pertains to the conduct of those who are the citizens of a city ("live as free citizens"; LSJ 1968, 1434). Noting that Paul has citizenship in view when he uses the cognate *politeuma* in 3:30, O'Brien (1991, 147) considers that public conduct is the focus in the present passage. In effect Paul is counseling the Philippians: **"let your public living be worthy of the gospel of Christ"** (*axiōs tou euangeliou tou christou politeuesthe*).

The Philippian Christians who are Roman citizens are in Paul's view when he gives this counsel. Nevertheless, Paul encourages the Christian slaves of Philippi to conduct themselves worthily in public to the degree that it is within their capacity. For both free and slave, the standard is "the gospel of Christ," that is to say, the gospel which is Christ (Fee 1995, 162). It is a standard for the Philippians to embrace (1:27b) **"whether I come to see you or am absent."**

Continuing in 1:27c Paul emphasizes the importance of unity: **"that you stand firm in one spirit striving together with one mind for the faith of the gospel"** (*stēkete en heni pneumati mia psychē synathlountes tē pistei tou euangeliou*). Paul counsels unity at other points in the letter (2:3; 4:2). The persecution that he mentions in 1:30 is a particular impetus for the unity he advocates here at 1:27.

Paul has used forms of "stand firm" (*stekō*) in previous letters (1 Thess 3:8; 1 Cor 16:13; and Rom 14:4), and he will use *stēkete* again in 4:1. His use of this term in Philippians may have a military frame of reference (Reumann 2008, 265). If it does have a military valence, there would be an irony: in effect, Paul would be asking the Philippian Christians who are the descendants of *Roman* veterans to exercise military-like discipline as they face the intimidations of the *Roman* magistrates.

Paul's emphasis on discipline and unity is especially apposite if the magistrates of Philippi are actively trying to recruit members of the Christian community into acting as informers. As discussed in the Introduction, Pliny was able to penetrate the inner life of the Christian community at Bithynia-Pontus by means of an informant (*ab indice*). The magistrates at Philippi might be employing comparable tactics.

Paul now urges (1:28a) that the Philippians **"not be at all frightened by anything that comes from opponents"** (*kai mē ptyromenoi en mēdeni hypo tōn antikeimenōn*). As noted, the Roman authorities at Philippi are the opponents in view here.

In 1:28b and then in 1:29 Paul gives two compelling reasons why the Philippians should not be "frightened" (*ptyromenoi*) by the colony's magistrates. These officials are headed toward annihilation whereas the Philippian Christians are headed toward salvation (1:28b): **"This is a sign of annihilation for them and of your salvation and this from God"** (*hētis estin autois endeixis apōleias hymōn de sōtērias kai touto apo theou*).

In many translations *apōleia*, the word Paul employs here, is rendered "destruction." A more careful analysis supports the stronger meaning of "annihilation." When *apōleias* is used with transitive meaning it refers to the destruction one causes. Yet it may also be used intransitively for the destruction one experiences (BDAG 2000, 127).

Within his undisputed letters, Paul uses *apōleias* twice in Philippians (also at 3:19) and once in Romans (9:22). In each instance he also employs a polar opposite term. Here the contrasting term is "salvation" (*sōtērias*). In 3:19, the contrast word is "savior" (*sōtēr*). In Rom 3:23, the contrasting term is "glory" (*doxan*). Within the divine framework, the steadfast faithfulness of the Philippians is evidence for their salvation and for their persecutors' condemnation (Sumney 2007, 37).

Further, just as the *salvation* of the Philippian Christians is future and eternal, so is the *annihilation* of their opponents future and eternal

(Vincent 1902, 35). This depiction of the annihilation of the Roman persecutors will be echoed in 3:20. An alternative depiction of their eternal abasement is given in 2:9-11.

The second reason that Paul puts forward (1:29) for encouraging unity is the nobility of suffering for the sake of Christ. Paul begins with a divine passive (1:29): **"It has been granted to you"** (*hoti hymin echaristhē*). He then indicates what has been granted: that **"for the sake of Christ you believe in him."** It has also been granted that the Philippians **"suffer for his sake"** (*kai to hyper autou paschein*).

Paul's grammatical construction in these verses is difficult (Sumney 2007, 37–38). Nevertheless, it is clear that the Philippians' sufferings pertain to Christ. He is the one in whom they have believed, and he is the one for whom they now suffer (cf. 2 Cor 12:10). That they are now called to suffer on behalf of Christ is actually a privilege that has been granted to the Philippians.

In 1:30, Paul uses the term "conflict" and notes three related conflicts: **"having the same conflict that you saw with me and now hear to be mine"** (*ton auton agōna echontes hoion eidete en emoi kai nyn akouete en emoi*).

The noun *agōn* and its verbal form *agōnizomai* admit of a range of meanings, including "warfare," "battle," "conflict," "struggle," "contest." *Agōnizomia* initially referred to "warfare" (Moulton-Milligan 1930, 8). Because Paul has had the experience of physical force used against him at Philippi (Acts 16:22b-24) and the experience of physical force used against him now at Rome (his chains and guards), he probably uses *agōna* here in the sense of "battle" or "conflict."

Paul uses "the same" (*ton auton*) to indicate that the three instances of conflict have the same origin. The first conflict is Paul's experience at the time of his initial visit to Philippi fifteen to twenty years earlier. The second conflict is Paul's present experience in Rome. The third conflict is the one the Philippian Christians are now enduring at Philippi. As Vincent has observed (1902, 36; cited in the Introduction), the common feature in each conflict is that the Roman authorities are the perpetrators.

Paul's use of the verb "saw" (*eidete*) in 1:30 suggests that some of the Christians at Philippi were present during the momentous events that occurred during Paul's initial visit to the colony when he and Silas were treated brutally and shamefully. The vividness of the scene in which the magistrates tore the clothes off the two missionaries and had them publicly beaten embedded the incident in the memories of those who witnessed it (Williams 1995, 288).

Paul's use of the present participle, "having" (*echontes*), indicates that the Philippians themselves are now experiencing the conflict that Paul previously experienced. The Philippian magistrates thus continue the measures that their predecessors enacted against Paul and Silas. The range of measures available to the magistrates in their persecution has been described in section 12 of the Introduction.

In the final clause of this verse, "and now hear to be mine," Paul references the third conflict. Paul now suffers mistreatment from the Roman authorities in the capital. The Philippians have already heard of Paul's sufferings in Rome, presumably from oral reports. (They will learn more about his situation when this letter is read/performed publicly.) In response, the Philippian Christians have sent Epaphroditus to him with a monetary gift (see on 4:10-20).

Philippian 2:1-5
IV. Harmony and Unselfishness

Introductory Comments

Philippians 2:1-4 contains counsel regarding unity that reinforces the counsel Paul has already given in 1:27. These verses also contain encouragement regarding self-giving that looks forward to Christ's paradigmatic self-emptying in 2:6-8.

In the Greek, verses 2:1-4 form a single complex sentence. This sentence introduces the Christ drama Paul portrays in the following verses. Philippians 2:5 is a bridge verse, effecting the connection between Paul's counsel for self-giving and his delineation of self-giving, par excellence, in 2:6-8.

Tracing the Train of Thought

As just noted, Paul's first sentence in this new section is complex. In four opening conditional clauses Paul asks rhetorically (2:1), **"if there is** encouragement in Christ, if any consolation of love, if any communion in the spirit, if any loving compassion." Paul's basic meaning is that all of these conditions have been fulfilled (Sumney 2007, 40; Bockmuel 1998, 104; cf. 2 Cor 5:7).

In the main clause of the sentence, Paul urges (2:2a): "**complete my joy**" (*plērōsate mou tēn charan*). He then indicates the ways in which the Philippians should complete his joy. They should do so (2:2b) "**by being of the same mind; having the same love; being harmonious in their outlook.**"

Having experienced severe disunity within the Christian community of Rome, Paul is the more concerned to encourage unity at Philippi. He ardently desires that the Philippians be "of the same mind" (*to auto phronēte*) and "harmonious in their outlook" (*sympsychoi*). These attributes are related to the "humility" that Paul recommends in the following verse.

Antithetical to the unity that Paul is promoting are "selfish ambition" (*eritheian*) and "empty glory" (*kenodoxian*). Paul decries both of those motivations at 2:3a: "**not acting from selfish ambition or empty glory.**"

Paul has used "selfish ambition" (*eritheia*) earlier, in 1:17, when he described the motivation with which the minority of Roman Christians were proclaiming Christ. *Eritheia* also appears in 2 Cor 12:20, Gal 5:20, and Rom 2:8.

It is difficult to determine Paul's exact nuance here, but in the secular Greek of his time, *eritheia* often meant "canvassing for public office," "intriguing," or "a self-seeking pursuit of political office by unfair means" (LSJ 1968, 688). If Paul were using *eritheia* in 2:3a with this last nuance, he would actually be warning the Philippian Christians against seeking advancement through collusion with the political authorities.

Paul's use of *kenodoxia* in this verse also deserves attention. His only other use of this compound term is in Gal 5:26, which uses an adjectival form of the word. In translating this word, the RSV and other translators adopt "vainglory." More accurately, the meaning is "empty glory."

Paul's use of *kenodoxia* in 2:3a foreshadows the forms of *kenos* and *doxa* that appear in the Christ drama of 2:6-11. The verb form, *ekenōsen* ("emptied"), holds a decisive meaning when it occurs in 2:6. *Doxa* itself appears in the final scene of the drama, in 2:11, when it refers to the glory of God. *Doxa* also means "God's glory" in 1:11, 4:19, and 4:20. When it occurs at 3:19 and 3:21 it serves to contrast self-idolaters who "glory" in their shame with the disciples of Jesus who await from him a body "of glory."

Paul's next words (2:3b-4), **"but with humility, regarding others above yourselves, not looking out only for your own interests but also for the interests of others,"** may well have constituted "social dynamite" at Philippi.

Paul first counsels "humility" (*tapeinophrosynē*) and then reflects that humility will enable the Philippians to regard others as "better" or "above" (*hyperechontas*) themselves. Because of what he will write in 2:7 regarding Jesus "taking the form of a slave," it is evident that those who are slaves at Philippi are not outside of Paul's view when he asks the Philippians to treat others as their betters.

Although he does not draw any inference regarding slaves, Howard Marshall still perceives that there is a powerful social radicalism expressed in Paul's words in this verse (1992, 45): "This is revolutionary stuff."

In effect, Paul is counseling a mode of conduct that has the potential for undermining the premises and practices that constitute the Roman system of slavery. Paul's words urge the free Christians of Philippi to treat one another with deference. His words also encourage all slaves to treat one another with deference. Finally, and most radically, his words exhort the free Christians of Philippi to treat those who are slaves with deference.

Assuming the public exposition of these verses at Philippi, it is not difficult to imagine the free Christians of Philippi rising to their feet with the words: "This upends everything!" To what degree did Paul advocate such a perspective during his own visits to Philippi? Galatians 3:28 indicates that Paul embraces such an upheaval with regard to Jew/Gentile, male/female, free/slave. It is possible that Paul did not apprehend the radical love of Jesus Christ for slaves until some years after his initial visit(s) to Philippi. In effect, Paul's letter may have brought to the Philippians perspectives regarding slaves that they had not heard previously from him.

At this critical juncture, Paul moves to ground his appeal on the example of Jesus Christ! His next words are (2:5): **"Have this way of thinking in you which was also in Christ Jesus"** (translation of Sumney

2007, 44). In effect, the approach that Paul has just recommended to the Philippian Christians has its origin in the self-emptying of Jesus Christ. The Philippian Christians, including Christian slaves, are now to ponder the model of Jesus, who took the form of a slave and accepted the slave's form of death.

Philippians 2:6-11
VI. Drama Depicting Christ's Descent to a Roman Cross Followed by Cosmic Exaltation

Introductory Comments

Owing to the central importance of these verses and to the focused attention that they have received in Pauline studies, it is important to provide a framework for the exegesis of this passage. This commentary argues that Paul composed 2:6-11 as a "Christ drama" while in Roman chains. Such a view challenges the prevailing interpretation that these verses are based on a preexisting "hymn," one taken over by Paul or else previously composed by him. (See O'Brien 1991, 188–93 for a full discussion of theories regarding the origins of this hymn.)

Another preliminary consideration is that 2:6-11, especially 2:6-8, exhibit features such as repetition, parallelism, and cadence. These elements contribute to the transitions between scenes and enhance the drama's overall impact with reference to descent and ascent.

In the interpretation now proposed, Paul's drama consists of two *acts*: 2:6-8 and 2:9-11, each comprising four *scenes*. Act 1 opens with a meditative scene in which Christ exists with the Father and is equal to the Father. In the second scene, Christ takes the form of a slave. In the third scene Christ accepts a sentence of death. The fourth scene depicts Christ's death by Roman crucifixion. Throughout the first act, Christ is the leading actor, although the Father is continuously present.

In the first scene of Act 2, the Father exalts Jesus to the highest place. In the second scene, the Father bestows the highest name on Jesus. In scene 3, every being in the universe bows before Jesus. In scene 4, every tongue proclaims that Jesus is Lord to the glory of the Father. Throughout the second act, the Father is the leading actor. The Father takes Jesus from the cross to the highest place and the Father renders the entire universe subject to Jesus.

By dividing his drama into two acts, Paul has developed a compelling exposition in which content is well served by form. In the scenes of Act 1, Paul's ideas tend to overflow the confines of normal sentence structure. Nevertheless, the sequence that Paul unfolds has the capacity to engage his audience powerfully.

What were Paul's purposes in composing 2:6-11? Traditionally, commentators have argued that Paul's purpose was "ethical" or "kerygmatic." (See O'Brien 1991, 203–5, 256–62, for an extended discussion of these two interpretations.)

Those emphasizing a kerygmatic purpose have argued that Paul wanted to provide the Philippians with doctrinal teaching about Christ, for example, Christ's preexistence, incarnation, death, and exaltation. Because these doctrinal-kerygmatic features are particular to Christ, they are not aspects for the Philippians to imitate (Bockmuel 1998, 122). Advocates of a kerygmatic purpose also argue that Paul is affirming to the Philippians that they now already participate in Christ's life.

Interpreters emphasizing an ethical purpose have argued that Paul desired to present Christ's self-emptying as an example for the Philippians to imitate in their dealings with one another. As indicated in the preceding exegesis of 2:3b-5, Paul is manifestly concerned to encourage the Philippians in their humble service to one another.

While Paul certainly has kerygmatic and ethical concerns in his view as he fashions his Christ drama, his rich meaning abundantly overflows these traditional categories. For example, Paul does provide key doctrinal insights regarding Christ. Yet these insights simultaneously serve to counter the propaganda of the Julio-Claudian emperors.

Paul's love for Christ and for the Father permeate both acts and all of the scenes of his drama. Paul loves Jesus Christ in all of Christ's dimensions and stages. He loves Christ Jesus who did not grasp his preexistent glory with God but rather emptied himself. Paul marvels at the radical self-emptying that Christ undertook. He is in holy awe that Jesus Christ entered willingly into "the realm of evil" in which he accepted a wrongful and degrading death.

Paul similarly loves God the Father. He loves the Father who preexisted with Jesus. Because he knows of the Father's decisive intervention on behalf of the unjustly crucified Jesus, Paul intuits the Father's benevolent oversight as each stage of Christ's downward trajectory occurs. Paul loves the Father for exalting Christ. He loves the Father for vanquishing all who participated in the crucifixion of Christ, the Roman authorities and the suprahuman agents of evil.

The preceding paragraphs introduce the profundity and the richness of Paul's perspective in 2:6-11. The position adopted in this commentary is that Paul formulated these insights as a chained Roman prisoner. These insights were the culmination of months and possibly years of reflections concerning Jesus's trajectory and the love of Jesus for slaves. Philippians 2:6-11 is not a work composed by some other author or by Paul himself in another setting. Only as a prisoner in chains, at the end of his long journey with Christ, is Paul able to formulate these profound insights.

In addition to viewing 2:6-11 as an instruction and encouragement for the Philippians, these verses can be viewed as a foundation for Paul's possible testimony before Nero. Because of their counteremperor and counterslavery thrust, these verses would not function to win Paul's acquittal. Rather, they would help Paul to give a full and faith-filled response to the question: "Who is Jesus Christ and what is owed to him?"

Tracing the Train of Thought.

In 2:5 Paul wrote, "Have this way of thinking in you which was also in Christ Jesus." Christ Jesus remains the subject of Paul's next clause in 2:6: **"who being in the form of God from all eternity, did not count equality with God a thing to be grasped"** (*hos en morphē theou hyparchōn ouch harpagmon hēgēsato to einai isa theō*).

In 2:6, the two phrases "in the form of God" and "equal to God" serve to interpret each other. Part of the difficulty in determining the meaning of "form of God" (*morphē theou*) is that the noun *morphē* appears only three times in the New Testament: in the present verse, in the following verse, 2:7, and in the longer ending of Mark's Gospel, Mark 16:12.

"Form of God" is the translation adopted here for *morphē theou,* but Paul's meaning pertains to "the essential nature and character of God" (Vincent 1902, 57–58). Christ is equal to the Father as regards the Father's "form."

When this affirmation of Christ being "equal to God (*isa theō*) is considered against the claims that various emperors were "god" or "equal to God," the dimension of Paul's meaning in opposition to the emperor cult emerges. As Heen has noted (2004, 144) the claim that Julius Caesar was "like a god" (*isa kai theon*) had been made by Nicolaus of Damascus at the time of Augustus.

Numerous inscriptions acclaiming Nero, the last Julio-Claudian, as a "god" are also extant. An inscription from the island of Cos (Deissmann 1978, 345) establishes that in AD 53, Nero was acclaimed there as "the good god" (*agathō theō*). Other inscriptions simply add "god" as a prefix to Nero's name (Price 1984b, 82) resulting in "god Nero" (*theos Nero*).

In his *Roman History* (62.5.2), Dio Cassius describes a public event that occurred in Rome in AD 66. After acclaiming Nero as "lord" (*despota*) in Naples, the Armenian king Tiridates traveled to Rome. There he prostrated himself before Nero, acclaiming him as "my god" (*ton emon theon*), and adding that he worshiped Nero just as he worshiped Mithras.

Calpurnius Siculus also speaks of Nero as a god. This Latin poet wrote during the years of Nero's ascendancy (Watson 1996, 281). Five lines from his fourth *Eclogue* hold special importance for the interpretation that aspects of Phil 2:6 constitute a challenge to the emperor cult: "Thou too, Caesar, whether thou art Jupiter himself on earth in altered guise, or one other of the powers above concealed under an assumed moral semblance (for thou are very God)—rule, I pray thee, this world, rule its peoples for ever! Let love of heaven count as nought with thee: abandon not, O Sire, the peace thou hast begun!" (Duff translation 1968, 257).

The reference to "Caesar" in Calpurnius's first line is a reference to Nero (ibid., note b). Calpurnius ponders whether Nero is actually Jupiter (or a comparable god) descended to earth and now concealed under "an assumed moral semblance." In line three, Calpurnius proclaims that Nero "is truly god" (*es enim deus*). The poet would thus persuade Nero not yet to abandon his work of bringing peace on earth. Rather, he must rule earth's people for ever (*aeternus populus rege*).

Not only Phil 2:6 but the entirety of 2:6-11 subverts the idolatry of Calpurnius's obsequious verses! Paul's affirmations concerning Jesus's initial equality with the Father and then Jesus's downward trajectory into human form provide an almost direct rebuttal to the factitious

Jupiter–Nero descent concocted by Calpurnius. Similarly Phil 2:9-11 represents Paul's decisive counter to Calpurnius's rhapsodic pleading with "god" Nero lest Nero prematurely take leave of the world to return to heaven.

In portraying Christ Jesus as coequal to God, Paul is implicitly portraying him as coequal to God *the Father* (see on 1:2). The close bond between the Father and Jesus is implied throughout 2:6-11.

Paul uses the participle *hyparchōn* to affirm that Christ is in the form of God "from all eternity" (Zerwick/Grosvenor 1988, 595). An alternate translation is that Christ "always existed" in the form of God (Hawthorne 1983, 87). "Eternity" functions as a key temporal reference for the drama that Paul is presenting. The first scene of Act I is set against the backdrop of eternity. Several scenes then occur within history. The final scenes of the drama are again positioned against the backdrop of eternity.

In the initial scene of Paul's drama, only Jesus and the Father are present. No one else is present. Because God (*theos*) cannot be imaged, Paul's visualization may be focused on Christ, Christ enfolded by "majesty."

In scene 2 of Paul's drama, Christ acts magnanimously and momentously. In scene 1, Christ did not consider "equality with God a thing to be grasped at." In scene 2 he begins a descent.

Paul's description in 2:7 is as follows: **"But he emptied himself taking the form of a slave, being born in the human likeness, being recognized as human"** (*all' heauton ekenōsen morphēn doulou labōn, en homoiōmati anthrōpōn genomenos kai schēmati heuretheis hōs anthrōpos*)

The conjunction "but" (*alla*) reverberates. Paul uses this conjunction to indicate that Christ's entry on such a downward trajectory was *fully contrary* to Paul's expectations and to the expectations of everyone else.

Philippians' emphasis is on *Christ's* self-emptying to embrace the form of a slave. This contrasts with Gal 4:4, where the emphasis falls on *the Father's* sending forth the Son: "But when the time had fully come, God sent forth his Son born (*genomenon*) of woman, born (*genomenon*) under the law."

What fundamental meaning does Paul intend with the words "form of a slave" (*morphēn doulou*)? Paul has just clarified the meaning of "form of God" (*morphē theou*) by employing the phrase "equal to God" (*isa theō*). For Christ to be in the form of God is to be equal to God. In a similar fashion, for Christ to take the form of a slave means for him to become equal to a slave. In effect, Christ "adopted the nature, the characteristic attributes, of a slave" (Hawthorne 1983, 86).

Paul affirms Jesus's character as a slave even before affirming Jesus's human identity. Only with his next clause does Paul indicate, by way of amplification, that Jesus is born in human likeness. Conceivably Paul might have reversed the order of these two participial phrases to make his presentation more "logical." Philippians 2:7 would then read: "But he emptied himself, being born in the human likeness, taking the form of a slave. . . ." This was *not* Paul's approach. Paul accentuates Jesus's identity as a slave even before he references Jesus's incarnation.

Another feature of Paul's presentation in 2:7 is that it does not mention other aspects of Jesus's historical identity. Paul does not mention that Jesus was free born, a *peregrinus* from the Roman perspective. Paul also refrains from mentioning Jesus's royal Jewish lineage: "a descendant of David" (Rom 1:3).

The profound implications of Paul's depiction of Jesus as a slave have scarcely been adverted to in Pauline studies. A few commentators have observed that, just as slaves were fully lacking in human rights, Jesus emptied himself of his human rights (Moule 1970, 268; Feinberg 1980, 42; Bruce 1991, 53; O'Brien 1991, 222). However, this is only a marginal dimension of Paul's meaning in portraying Jesus as a slave.

Paul's presentation of Jesus as a slave in 2:7 has obvious consequences for the life of the Christian community of Philippi. Paul's conceptualization not only dignifies slaves; it simultaneously challenges free persons and slave owners. Subsequent scenes in the drama of 2:6-11 have the same effect.

Joseph Hellerman (2005, 129–42) affirms that, in delineating Christ's downward status path, Paul juxtaposes Christ's "course of shame" (*cursus pudorum*) with the imperial "course of honors" (*cursus honorum*). Paul's delineation of Christ embracing the form of a slave establishes that Christ is following a *cursus pudorum*.

In 1:1 Paul identified himself as Christ's "slave" (*doulos*). In now using "slave" (*doulos*) as a designation for Christ (Paul's own Lord), Paul is profoundly enlightening the Philippian Christians who are citizens and simultaneously stirring the hearts of those who are slaves. Roman citizens who accept Paul's teaching are to regard their own slaves and the slaves around them as persons of worth who are embraced by Christ. The slaves at Philippi are to realize their fundamental dignity as beloved by Christ who became a slave in solidarity with them.

What was responsible for Paul's insight that Jesus embraced the identity of a slave? Paul may have been led to understand Jesus as a slave once he came to appreciate that crucifixion was quintessentially the slave's form of death. At some point in his journey, Paul reached the critical insight that crucifixion was the characteristic Roman form of death for slaves. Paul may have gained this decisive insight from literary sources with which he was familiar prior to his arrival at Rome. References to crucifixion as the slave's form of death occur in the writings of such authors as Cicero, Tacitus, and Valerius Maximus.

Cicero, for example (*Second Oration against Verres* 5.169), refers to crucifixion as "the supreme and ultimate punishment for a slave" (*servitutis extremum summumque supplicium*). Similarly in a work dedicated to Tiberius, Valerius Maximus (*Factorum ac dictorum memorabilium libri IX* 2.7.12) speaks of "the slave's punishment" (*servile supplicium*). In *Histories* 2.72, Tacitus refers to "the punishment usually inflicted upon slaves" (*supplicium in servilem modum*). In *Histories* 4.11, Tacitus considers it noteworthy that a *libertus* actually died by means of a slave's punishment (*servili supplicio expiavit*).

If literary sources did not afford Paul the insight that crucifixion was the slave's quintessential form of death, he might have gained this perspective from visits to slave markets in the cities to which he traveled. Certainly he could have gained this insight once he reached Rome and was proximate to the Esquiline Hill, the capital's infamous site for the crucixion of slaves.

Tacitus indicates the existence of a place in Rome that was officially designated as the site for the execution of slaves (*in locum servilibus poenis sepositum*; *Annals* 15.60). Tacitus elsewhere indicates that the Esquiline Hill was this site (*Annals* 2.32; cf. Suetonius, *Claudius* 34). Horace (*Epode* V) also identifies the Esquiline Hill as this gruesome location. Horace notes that "Esquiline vultures" (translation of *esquilinae alites* given in Smart 1895, 88) eagerly sought the flesh of those crucifed and exposed there. Paul's guards may have taken him past this site, or its horror might have been recounted to him by the Christians of Rome.

In Paul's view, what was Jesus's *motivation* for taking the form of a slave and embracing the slave's form of death. Philippians 2:9-11, John 13:4-5, and John 15:15 provide grounds for asserting that Paul understood Jesus as being fundamentally motivated by a love for slaves.

In Phil 2:9-11 slaves are accorded a standing comparable to that of everyone else. Slaves, like all others, participate in bending their knees in homage to Jesus. Like all others, slaves participate in the magnification of the name of Jesus. Although the Father is the principal agent in these scenes, he does not act independently of Jesus. A beneficent attitude toward slaves is thus the stance of Jesus as well as the stance of the Father.

If Paul was familiar with the Johannine traditions concerning Jesus's farewell supper, he could have derived insight regarding Jesus's beneficence toward slaves from that source. According to John 13:4-5, Jesus performed the work of a slave in washing his disciples' feet (Cassidy 2015b, 119–23). In John 15:15 Jesus indicates that, up until this point, these disciples have been his "slaves" (*douloi*). He now sets aside their standing as slaves (*douloi*) and confers on them the status of "friends" (*philoi*).

Clearly these Johannine sayings are focused on Jesus's initiatives regarding his disciples and do not explicitly encompass the slave population in Judea. Neverthleless, in this Johannine paradigm, slaves (*douloi*) become friends (*philoi*), and Paul might have reflected that this transformation represented the mind of Christ for slaves in other circumstances. Precisely, Paul might have concluded that this slave-to-friend transformation represented the mind of Christ (cf. 1 Cor 2:16) for the Christian slaves of Philippi.

In Gal 3:28 (cf. 1 Cor 12:13) Paul wrote: "There is neither Jew nor Greek, there is neither slave nor free (*ouk heni doulos oude eleutheros*), there is neither male nor female; for you are all one in Christ Jesus." Now in Philippians he is able to advance his insight regarding the fundamental love of Jesus Christ for slaves.

Paul may have had a second related insight concerning Jesus's embrace of the form of a slave. Jesus adopted the identity of a slave in order to respond to the evil of slavery and to the perpetrators of this evil.

Within a slave-based empire, Paul's detailing of Jesus's radical affirmation of slaves is profoundly counterimperial. Within an empire where slavery is pervasive and considered to be a part of the natural fabric of society, Paul's proclamation is that Jesus enobles slaves. Philippians 2:6-7 is thus arguably the most powerful passage of the New Testament in terms of the radicality of Christ's love. Jesus's love reaches toward those suffering under a state-authorized *system of slavery*.

Paul next writes (2:8a): **"he humbled himself becoming obedient unto death"** (*etapeinōsen heauton genomenos hypēkoos mechri thanatou*). In this third scene of Paul's Christ drama, Jesus is imaged receiving and accepting a sentence of death that is unjust. In this scene, Jesus's trial before Pilate is in Paul's view.

In Paul's contemplation of this scene, various agents of evil play roles. Jesus suffers from the machinations of the chief priests of Jerusalem, the Roman governor Pilate, and various members of Pilate's military detachment. Jesus, the innocent one, is condemned to death on grounds of "treason" (*maiestas*). The emperor Tiberius is implicitly in the background of this scene, lending his authority to Pilate's verdict against Jesus.

Paul began his drama with the Father and Jesus existing prior to history. Jesus now is immersed in human history. As regards political geography, he is within the confines of the Roman Empire. He is within the confines of a Roman governor's praetorium.

While Jesus is the principal figure in scene 3, the Father is not absent from the scene. The Father assesses the unjust verdict delivered against Jesus. The Father recognizes the perpetrators of this verdict. Jesus submits to this wrongful verdict, virtually offering no resistance.

Paul's meditations about Jesus in this scene may have deepened as a result of Paul's own juridical situation. For Paul himself is now on the verge of receiving an unjust verdict. As was the case with Jesus, Paul will receive an *official* verdict, one duly authorized by the Roman government.

Why did Jesus submit to a manifestly unjust verdict? As Paul contemplates this scene, what purpose does he ascribe to Jesus? In Paul's vision Jesus's acceptance of this unjust verdict was a part of his response to the presence of evil. Jesus's overarching purpose was to respond to virulent evil and to overcome it. In part, this is the meaning of "redemption" (*apolytrōsis*), Paul's concept in 1 Cor 1:30.

The fourth and concluding scene of Act 1 is delineated in 2:8b by the phrase "**even death on a cross**" (*thanatou de staurou*). The conjunction "even" (*de*) serves to convey Paul's sense of wonderment that Christ's self-emptying has taken him to crucifixion—the slave's form of death. Slaves *involuntarily* undergo the repugnant death of crucifixion. Jesus, this scene's principal character, *voluntarily* undergoes the slave's form of death.

Pontius Pilate is present in this scene by reason of the *titulus* that Paul gazes at above the cross. Pilate has ordered Jesus's death on the grounds that Jesus (who *is* "majesty") violated the emperor's "majesty." Paul also views the centurions and soldiers who are implementing Pilate's orders. Paul is cognizant of the hatred of the Jerusalem chief priests (Paul's former allies) as they pressure Pilate for Jesus's crucifixion (Cassidy 2015a, 203–24).

Tiberius is implicitly present again in this scene. Pilate and the crucifying soldiers are not in the employ of Parthian satraps or other potentates. Rather, they are ultimately selected by, trained by, and paid by the Roman emperor and his delegates. The procurator and his soldiers are carrying out Tiberius's protocols for crucifixion, including Jesus's being scourged and stripped naked.

In addition to perceiving the human malefactors who are the perpetrators of Jesus's death, Paul probably recognizes the involvement of suprahuman agents of evil, whom he elsewhere refers to as "principalities and powers" (1 Cor 15:24; cf. Rom 8:38). In Phil 2:8 Paul does not explicitly advert to the role of these malefic agents in Jesus's crucifixion; however in Phil 2:10, he implies that they too are subjected to the exalted Jesus by the Father. Colossians portrays God overcoming these evil entities precisely at Jesus's cross (2:15): "(God) disarmed the principalities and the powers and made a public example of them, triumphing over them in it (the cross)."

The implicit presence of the Father in scene 4 must be emphasized. The Father is present in addition to the human and suprahuman characters just identified. The Father has been implicitly present in scenes 2 and 3. This implicit presence is disclosed by the *explicit* and decisive intervention that the Father makes in the first scene of Act 2.

The death of Jesus was not only an instance of a harsh and cruel death. It was also a *wrongful death*. Paul now sees this more clearly because he himself is proximate to a wrongful death at the hands of the successors of the Romans who tried and executed Jesus. Further, the Father has acted to nullify the Roman-sanctioned death of Jesus because the Father has recognized the egregious injustice of the verdict under which Jesus was crucified.

A final point regarding Phil 2:8 concerns the "obedience" that Paul mentions. To whom was Jesus obedient when "he *became* obedient unto death"? (The participle *genomenos* literally means "becoming" and is translated "became" by convention.) Given what Paul has previously stated in Gal 1:4, he presumably understands that Christ's obedience is to the Father. In Gal 1:4 Paul wrote that Christ "gave himself for our sins *according to the will of our God and Father.*" Christ's obedience to the Father can also be taken as grounds for the Father's intervention on behalf of Christ in Phil 2:9-11.

Before proceeding to describe the Father's role in 2:9-11, Paul may have taken extended time to reflect anew regarding Christ's conduct in the four scenes of the Christ drama that he is contemplating. In doing so, Paul may have experienced overwhelming *gratitude* to Christ for Christ's profound self-emptying and for his profound humility. In Gal 3:20 he previously wrote, "I live by faith in the Son of God, who loved me and gave himself for me." Paul may have had a similar experience of gratitude as he pondered the profundity of Christ's self-emptying.

Paul may also have experienced a deepening of his own love for Jesus Christ. Apart from 1 Cor 16:22, Paul's love for Christ is not proclaimed explicitly in his undisputed letters, but rather is implicit. Ephesians proclaims the author's explicit love for Christ powerfully in the final verse of the letter (6:24): "Grace be with all who love our Lord Jesus Christ with love undying."

In 2:9a, Paul limns the first scene of Act 2: "**Therefore, God has exalted him to the highest place**" (*dio kai ho theos auton hyperypsōsen*). The two conjunctions *dio kai* (rendered here as "therefore") indicate that what has occurred *elicits* the Father's response. Other translations that identify the Father's response as *evoked* are: "That is why" (Zerwick/Grosvenor 1988, 596) or "As a consequence, therefore" (Hawthorne 1983, 90, following BDAG).

Commentators have traditionally proposed that Paul understands the Father's intervention as elicited in response to Christ's self-emptying (for example, Bockmuel 1998, 140–41) or in response to Christ's "obedience" (Sumney 2007, 48). Such interpretations neglect *the Roman crucifixion* of Jesus that Paul has in his view.

For Paul, it is not only that Jesus radically empties himself into humiliating suffering. Paul also views Jesus as *unjustly* brutalized and killed by official representatives of the Roman emperor.

For this reason, the Father now intervenes to set aside the Roman verdict against the good name of Jesus and to enact judgment on the Roman leaders who blasphemed Jesus's name. Because of their transgression against Jesus, all representatives of the Roman regime will be abjectly subjected to the very one whom they have degraded and killed (see comments on 2:10 below).

In Paul's schematization, four scenes comprise the second act of this Christ drama. In Act 2, scene 1, Paul depicts the Father exalting Christ to the highest place. In scene 2 the Father bestows the highest name on him. In scene 3, every knee bows at the name given Jesus. In scene 4 every tongue confesses that Jesus is "Lord" to the glory of God the Father.

In all four scenes of Act 2 Paul presents God the Father as the initiating actor. Jesus is the principal recipient of the Father's initiatives. The other characters implicitly present in scenes 3 and 4 include the Roman officials previously identified in Act 1. They are within the universe-wide gathering depicted in these scenes. Slaves are present within this gathering. There is no longer any criterion for segregating and subordinating them.

Syntactically, 2:9-11 is a single sentence with two main verbs: "exalted to the highest place" (*hyperypsōsen*) and "bestowed" (*echarisato*). *Echarisato* governs a two-part subordinate clause that begins in 2:10a (O'Brien 1991, 232).

The Acts of the Apostles twice employs "exalted" in ways that illuminate Paul's meaning in 2:9. In Acts 2:23, Peter proclaims that Jesus has been raised up and is *exalted* at the right hand of God. In 5:31 Peter and the apostles testify: "God *exalted* him (Jesus) at his right hand as leader and savior."

In 2:9 God exalts Christ to the highest possible degree (Fee 1995, 221). There is no place higher than the place to which the Father has brought Jesus. The Father has taken Jesus "to the loftiest height" (BDAG 2000, 1042).

The subject of this intervention is "God" (*theos*). Paul's usage throughout the letter establishes that he is identifying God *the Father*. The outcome in the final scene of this Christ drama will be "the glory of God *the Father*" (2:11b). In 1:2 Paul has previously extended grace "from God *our Father*" (*apo theou patros hymōn*). In 4:20 at the end of the letter, he will express glory "to our God and *Father*" (*tō de theō kai patri hymōn*).

The place *from which* the Father exalts Jesus is the cross of Jesus's crucifixion. How can the Father be depicted approaching the cross? Perhaps Paul views the Father as resplendent light. In Paul's meditation, God, who is light that can scarcely be imaged, draws near to the cross, with love, to disengage Jesus from the cross. God the Father brings Jesus upward, upward to the loftiest place.

There is only a single upward movement. In describing this movement Paul does not explicitly mention Jesus's resurrection or ascension (Fee 1995, 220). In this scene, Jesus's exaltation "encompasses" his resurrection just as in Act 1 taking the form of a slave "encompassed" Jesus's nativity.

This portrayal of *exaltation* serves as the framework for what Paul will present in the two following scenes of this second act, scenes 3 and 4. In wondrously accomplishing the resurrection of Jesus, the Father overcame the power of death. However, a "narrow" emphasis on the resurrection would not provide the framework for the judgment concerning Jesus's wrongful death that will be presented in the following scenes. Jesus is exalted to the highest place because it is from that place that a response to the malefactors who were responsible for his death will emerge.

Commentators frequently observe that the Father has brought Jesus from "the depths" to "the heights." This is not a careful-enough rendering of Paul's meaning regarding the point of origin. The Father has lifted Jesus precisely *from the cross*. In effect, the Father now commences to "extricate" Jesus from the wrongful death that evildoers effected. Besides bringing Jesus *spatially* to the highest place, the Father also brings Jesus *temporally* into the realm of eternity. Jesus is with the Father at the highest place for time that is *without end*.

The Father's next initiative regards Jesus's name (2:9b): **"and bestowed on him the highest name"** (*kai echarisato autō to onoma to hyper pan onoma*). What is this exalted name?

The prominence of the title "Lord" (*kyrios*) in 2:11 weighs heavily in support of the view that "Lord" is the name that Paul has in view in 2:9 (Hawthorne 1983, 91; O'Brien 1991, 238). Further, "Lord" (*kyrios*) is the translation that the Septuagint uses to represent the proper name of the God of the Old Testament. O'Brien notes that the bestowal of this name by God is the rarest of all honors (1991, 238; cf. Isa 42:8).

Paul's thus understands God's bestowal of the name *Lord* on Jesus as the conferring of an honor that cannot be surpassed. It is an honor that fully dissolves the shame that Pontius Pilate and Tiberius enacted against Jesus's name at Golgotha. The imparting of *kyrios* is more than the bestowal of a title. The Father's conferral of the name "Lord" is also the bestowal of an *identity*. Hawthorne rightly observes (1983, 91), "not only does Christ *possess* the title, 'Lord,' he *is* Lord."

The consequences of this bestowal of *kyrios* are now set forth (2:10a): **"so that at the name belonging to Jesus, every knee must bow"** (*hina en tō onomati Iēsou pan gony kampsē*). This clause expresses what Paul beholds as he contemplates this new scene in the drama of Christ's exaltation.

Jesus now holds full sovereign power. His grandeur and his majesty are manifest. The possessive form *Iēsou* ("of Jesus") indicates that the title "Lord" now belongs to him (O'Brien 1991, 240). The name now given to Jesus is so powerful that its very pronouncement engenders consequences in every sphere of the universe. The positive consequences are worship and salvation. The negative consequences are judgment and shame.

Paul potentially derived the image of knees bending at the name of Jesus from Isa 45:23 (ibid., 241). He may visualize something resembling a sustained genuflection, or perhaps an even more profound bowing of the upper body to the ground when he writes these words. In the secular Greek familiar to the Philippian Christians, one of the meanings of *kamptō* is "submission" (LSJ 1968, 873), and this seems to be Paul's principal meaning here.

Paul then specifies (2:10b), **"in heaven, on earth, and under the earth"** (*epouraniōn kai epigeiōn kai katachthoniōn*). The three terms he employs are masculine genitive plural adjectives used substantively (Sumney 2007, 50). By using these all-encompassing terms, Paul envisions beings in every realm as those who are called to render homage to the exalted Jesus. Paul has initially indicated that there were no exceptions by writing *"every* knee" (*pan gony*). Now he elaborates that all beings in *every* realm of the universe must render homage to Jesus.

Paul's claim that inhabitants of these three spheres are subservient to Jesus contravenes the claim that the Latin poet Ovid (circa 43 BC–AD 17) made on behalf of Jupiter and Augustus. In his adulation of Augustus, Ovid wrote (*Metamorphoses* 15.858-66): "Jupiter controls the heights of heaven and the kingdom of the triformed universe but the earth is under Augustus's sway."

Paul identifies three realms of the universe in 2:10b. He may identify *four* distinct groups within the three realms: angelic beings located in heaven, living human beings on earth, demonic beings, and deceased human beings located under the earth (Bruce 1991, 74).

Paul seemingly envisions that the prostration of demonic beings is "an act of submission to one whose power they cannot resist" (O'Brien 1991, 243). In 2:8 Paul did not indicate expressly the involvement of any powers from the cosmos in Jesus's death. Yet his reference to beings "under the earth" here in 2:10 may mean that he has them in view.

For the humans involved in Jesus's crucifixion, compelled prostration may be a matter of judgment as well as "a matter of shame" (Bockmuel 1998, 147). Such shame is mentioned in Isa 45:24b: "All who have raged against him will come to him and be put to shame" (translation by O'Brien 1991, 241).

Tiberius, Pilate, and the others who authorized and carried out Jesus's crucifixion are presumably among the "all" who now fall prostrate before Lord Jesus. Tiberius has not a shred of *maiestas* remaining. Nor does Augustus, nor Gaius, nor Claudius, nor Nero. These five Julio-Claudians now experience varying degrees of shame as they now formally acknowledge Jesus's majesty. Their acknowledgment of Jesus is made before the entire universe. It is made for all eternity.

An additional aspect to be noted regarding scene 3 is the absence of any such entity as "the Roman Empire." By implication, the Roman Empire itself no longer exists. Paul's perspective in this regard is breathtaking. The most powerful political entity hitherto known has simply vanished from the universe!

The book of Revelation proffers a comprehensive indictment of the Roman Empire for its abuses and vividly describes its demise (Cassidy 2001a, 109–14). Paul's words regarding the empire's demise in Phil 2:10-11 are more subtle. Nevertheless, Paul's perspective in these verses is light years away from the perspective that he earlier expressed in Rom 13:1-7.

Philippians 2:10 does not indicate how the Roman Empire ended. However, all of its rulers, all of the Julio-Claudian emperors and their confederates, are now prostrate before Lord Jesus. Jesus was crucified according to the "system" of this empire. The empire, so to speak, acted against Jesus "officially." The perpetrators of this unspeakable evil now have their deed fully disclosed. Their prostration before Jesus endures forever.

Jesus voluntarily entered into a "zone of sin," in which slavery's evil was rampant. Now the Father has lifted Jesus up from the slave's form of death. In scene 3 there are no more slaves. Those who were formerly slaves on earth now join voluntarily with the others who are citizens of heaven in an act of profound homage to Jesus. These former slaves are enobled by their participation in this worship. They now render profound praise as persons free from every form of bondage.

Paul evolves an almost seamless transition into scene 4 (2:11a): **"and every tongue shall accclaim that Jesus Christ is Lord"** (*kai pasa glōssa exomologēsetai hoti kyrios Iēsous Christos*). The cast of characters for scene 4 is the same as it was for scene 3. The Father is present. Jesus is present. All intelligent beings from the three regions of the universe are present. These beings proclaim without exception ("every tongue," *pan glōssa*) that Jesus is Lord.

As in scene 3, so in scene 4, those who have wounded the *maiestas* of Jesus are brought to acknowledge that he is Lord. "Shall acclaim" (*exomologēsetai*), the verb that Paul employs here, may convey the meaning of "begrudging acknowledgment" as well as "confess with thanksgiving" (Bockmuel 1998, 146–47; cf. Zerwick/Grosvenor 1988, 596).

Strikingly, Paul now envisions Nero and his Julio-Claudian predecessors acknowledging Jesus with the title that they arrogated to themselves so aggressively. This title is "Lord" (*kyrios*). The Julio-Claudians, to varying degrees, prized this title and expropriated it for their exclusive use. As regards Gaius, Aurelius Victor reports the protocol (*Epitome de Caesaribus* 3.8) that Gaius always be addressed as "lord" (*dominum*). Similarly, Claudius is referred as "the lord" in an Egyptian papyrus from the year 49 and in an Egyptian ostracon from the year 54 (Deissmann 1978, 353).

During Nero's reign there was a remarkable upsurge in the use of *kyrios*. Adolf Deissmann describes an ostracon from his personal collection in which the two words "Nero lord" (*Nerōn kyrios*) appear without any modifier (ibid., 354). Deissmann has also identified various papyri and ostraca in which the genitive form, *Nerōnos tou kyriou* ("of Nero the lord"), appears along with a number such as 6 or 9 to indicate the specific year of Nero's reign in which the document was published (ibid., 105, 173). Peter Arzt-Grabner (2011, 4) has recently determined that, within the Duke Database for Documentary Papyri, there are documents that utilize this dating formula for every year of Nero's fifteen-year reign.

Harrison (2003, 88) also draws attention to a papyrus from Egypt in which the Roman prefect refers to "the grace of the lord" in referring to Nero. (This phrase, "the grace of the lord," also sheds light on Paul's closing at 4:23; see below.) Arzt-Grabner (2011, 5) cites this same papyrus and notes that in Acts 25:26 the governor Festus uses *kyrios* without Nero's name when he indicates that he has nothing to write "to the lord" (*tō kyriō*).

In addition to the above relatively concise references to Nero as "lord," the Boeotian town of Acraphiae acclaimed Nero in more embellished terms in a decree published in AD 67, during Nero's Greek tour (Deissmann 1978, 354). According to the Boeotian decree, Nero was *ho tou pantos kosmou kyrios Nerōn* ("the lord *of the whole world* Nero"; emphasis added).

Deissmann (ibid., 358) also documents adjectival reference to Nero's "lordship." The possessive adjective *kyriakos* appears twice in a decree published by another prefect of Egypt in AD 68. This decree refers to "the lord's finances" (*tais kyriakais psephois*) and to "the lord's treasury" (*ton kyriakon logon*).

Given Nero's predeliction for the title "lord," Paul's boldness in affirming Nero's compelled proclamation that Jesus is "Lord" is breathtaking. Nero, the all-powerful "lord" is now brought to confess in humility that Jesus alone is "Lord." In contrast with Nero and those allied with him, the tongues of the other assembled beings acclaim Jesus's identity as Lord with sentiments of "praise and thanksgiving" (Lightfoot 1888, 115) even as in a liturgy (Collange 1979, 107).

Once again, former slaves participate fully in the confession and praise of Jesus. During their lives on earth these slaves were constrained to use the term "lord" (kyrios) to address those who owned them. These former slaves now have a place among the human and angelic beings whose joy in the proclamation of the *Lord* Jesus is unbounded.

Paul knows the degradation, the abuse, and even the deaths that slaves suffered from their owners. These owners now stand exposed before the assembled multitude for presuming to have functioned as ersatz "lords," for presuming to exercise a kind of lordship that belongs only to Jesus.

Paul's concluding phrase (2:11b), **"to the glory of God the Father"** (*eis doxan theou patros*) indicates that the glory of God the Father" is the the ultimate outcome for the final scene of Act 2 and the final scene of the entire drama. Nevertheless, the reality of the Father's glory has been implicit in all of the earlier scenes of the drama.

Christ was initially with the Father in glory. Christ's taking upon himself the form of a slave was to the glory of the Father. When Jesus accepted an unjust sentence and suffered the slave's form of death, the Father was not absent (Bruce 1991, 80; Bockmuel 1998, 148). The Father's decisive intervention to bring Jesus from the cross to the highest place manifests the Father's glory just as it vindicates Jesus.

Paul affirms the Father's glory not only in 2:11. Paul expresses this also at the beginning and end of the letter. In 1:11 he references "the glory and praise of God" (the Father), and in 4:20 he affirms that "glory" (*doxan*) is appropriately accorded to the Father.

Before proceeding to the next section of Paul's letter, an effort should be made to view Paul's Christ drama as a counter to a putative "Nero drama" at Philippi's impressive theater. Heen (2004, 130) has observed that the spectacles at many ancient theaters often possessed a cultic dimension. A drama promoting the cult of Nero might have utilized the trajectory that Calpurnius Siculus delineated for Nero in his fourth *Eclogue*.

The following "Calpurnian" drama might have been performed at Philippi's theater. In scene 1 the god Jupiter enters earth in disguised form. In scene 2 Jupiter commences to rule the peoples of the earth forever. In scene 3 he brings peace to all whom he rules. In a fourth scene it is disclosed that Jupiter and Nero are one and the same. In the fifth scene Jupiter-Nero is torn between his home in heaven and his rule on earth. In the final scene, the cries of the audience prevail on Nero, and he consents not to abandon his earthly mission for a return to heaven.

If such a "Nero-drama" or any dramas comparable to it were performed in the theater of Philippi, Paul presumably would have knowledge of them. The various scenes in Paul's "Christ drama" might have had the secondary purpose of countering the *form* of an emperor-cult spectacle. Certainly, the contents of Paul's drama effectively countered the *contents* of any emperor-cult dramas created by propagandists such as Calpurnius.

Because it is grounded in Paul's *contemplation* of Jesus Christ and his praise of Christ's name, Paul's Christ drama is far more than an exposure of the ultimate demise of Roman power. Nevertheless, Paul's scenes do express a prophetic judgment against an imperium purporting to be eternal.

Certainly, given conditions at Philippi, any "full production" of Paul's drama would have to have been clandestine. A rhetorically powerful reading of these verses could be coordinated by Timothy and/or Epaphroditus. These two "commissioned agents" (see on 2:19-24 below) might have involved the *archimimus*, *choragiarius*, and *locator scaenicorum* from Philippi's resident theater group. Suitable clandestine settings would have been required for such "underground theater" productions.

Philippians 2:12-16
VI. Further Encouragement for the Philippians

Introductory Comments

The time that Paul required for the formulation of his Christ drama cannot be known. These scenes may have required intense reflection and prayer by Paul for weeks, months, or even longer. Possibly, after formulating this "peak" section of the letter, Paul did not resume writing until an additional period of time had elapsed.

When he continues his letter with 2:12-16, Paul moves to the topic of the Philippians' discipleship at Philippi. In effect, these verses constitute a second bookend for the auspicious Christ drama. Paul's words in 2:1-4 encouraging the Philippians to consider others better than themselves constituted the first bookend.

Tracing the Train of Thought

In 2:12a Paul uses the conjunction "**therefore**" (*hōste*) to signal the beginning of a new section. Paul's next words, "**my beloved**" (*agapētoi mou*), express the cordial warmth with which he regards the Philippians. As noted in the Introduction, Paul shares a profound communion with the Philippians, and "my beloved" reflects that communion. He will employ this term twice more at the conclusion of the letter (4:1).

Paul's principal counsel within this section is expressed in 2:12c: "**work out your salvation with fear and trembling**" (*meta phobou kai tromou tēn heautōn sōtērian katergazesthe*).

It is important to approach the meaning of "salvation" (*sōtērian*) in this passage by considering the other instances in which this term occurs in the letter. In Philippians, salvation encompasses the community's protection from persecution and ultimately from "annihilation." This was Paul's meaning when he stated in 1:28 that the Philippians corporately were headed toward salvation while their persecutors were headed toward "annihilation" (*apōleias*). He expresses a similar view in 3:20 in stating that Christ, the Savior (*sōtēr*), will intervene for the Philippians while their opponents suffer "annihilation" (*apōleia*).

Certainly, the Philippians do not earn salvation. Here, as in 1:27, Paul urges his hearers to live in a manner worthy of the salvation *that Christ bestows on them*. Paul's words "with fear and trembling" are words that he has used previously in 1 Cor 2:3 and 2 Cor 7:15. Paul may be emphasizing that the Philippians are wise to fear those who seek to derail them from salvation. In other words, the Philippians should treat the perils of their situation seriously.

Paul has preceded this counsel by two clauses (2:12b and 2:12c): "**as you have always obeyed**" (*kathōs pantote hypēkousate*) and "**not only in my presence but much more in my absence**" (*en tē parousia mou monon alla nyn pollō mallon en tē apousia mou*). Paul's recollection is that the Philippians up to this point have consistently complied with his counsels. They sought to follow Paul's instructions when he was ministering among them. How much more is compliance called for when Paul is away from them because of his chains.

In writing about the Philippians' obedience to him, Paul may also have in view the Philippians' uncompromised obedience to God. Indeed,

Paul attests to God's decisive role at Philippi when he writes (2:13), "**For God is at work in you to will and act according to good purpose.**"

In 2:14-16 Paul additionally counsels, "**Do all things without grumbling or disputing that you may be blameless and flawless children of God without blemish in the midst of a crooked and perverse generation among whom you shine as lights in the world, holding fast to the word of life in order that I may have reason for boasting on the day of Christ that I did not run in vain or labor in vain.**"

As Fee (1995, 242) and others have observed, Paul's phrasing in 2:14 seems to reflect concepts from Exodus and Deuteronomy regarding Israel's murmuring against Moses (Exod 16:2) and Moses's rebuke of Israel (Deut 32:5). Because of Paul's use of such concepts here, various commentators (for example, Collange 1979, 112) have concluded that he is actually referring to the proponents of circumcision, whom he castigates in 3:2ff.

This proposed Moses-related interpretation is rendered inadequate when attention is properly focused on Paul's use of "in the midst of" (*meson*) in 2:15. The Philippians are to be blameless and flawless *in the midst* of "a crooked and perverse generation" that surrounds them precisely at Philippi. In other words, although Paul's language is influenced by his knowledge of the Septuagint texts regarding Israel, his basic intent is to speak about conditions at Philippi. As Fee notes (1995, 245) Paul's words are "a fair reflection of his view of pagan society."

Paul is thus warning his readers that the milieu of Roman Philippi is "crooked and perverse." The idolatrous cult of the Roman emperor is at the center of the "crookedness." Sexual misconduct in the setting of Philippi may also be in Paul's view.

In 2:14, Paul gives his counsel regarding the Philippians' conduct in such circumstances. They are to do all things "without grumbling or disputing" (*chōris gongysmōn kai dialogismōn*). This counsel looks to the internal patterns of the Christian community, one of Paul's consistent concerns throughout the letter, for example, 2:2-4 and 4:2-3.

By adhering to Paul's wisdom, the Philippians will be "blameless" (*amemptoi*), "flawless" (*akeraioi*), and "without blemish" (*amōma*). They will thus shine as lights in the world and be "holding fast" (*epechontes*) to the word of life (2:16).

In 2:16, for the third time in the letter, Paul refers to Christ's future arrival. Here his specific reference is to "the day of Christ" (*eis hēmeran Christou*). As analyzed in 1:6 and 1:10, Paul employs this term in reference to the solemn arrival of Christ with full majesty. This affirmation regarding "the day of Christ" represents a challenge to all observances of "the emperor's day" at Philippi proper.

One aspect of Christ's majestic arrival will be his assessment of all human endeavors. In 2:16 Paul desires to have grounds for "boasting" (*kauchēma*) concerning his ministry to the Philippians. Using words similar to those in Gal 2:2c, Paul expresses the hope that he did not "run in vain" (*eis kenon edramon*). He wants also to boast that he has not "labored in vain" (*eis kenon ekopiasa*).

Philippians 2:17-18
VII. Paul Again Envisions His Death

Introductory Comments

For several reasons 2:17-18 should be taken as a distinct thought unit. The majority of scholars would place it with 2:12-16. A small minority (noted in Hawthorne 1983, 104) would place it with 2:19-30. Nevertheless, these two verses represent a break with what has preceded because Paul is shifting his attention from Philippi to his own perilous situation. The visceral intensity that characterizes these verses separates them from the following less intense verses concerning travel to Philippi by Timothy and Epaphroditus.

This section of Paul's letter should not be approached as though it were penned from a scholar's study. Paul is writing from chained custody, and he is writing about the possibility of his own martyrdom.

Tracing the Train of Thought

Paul is being held in chained custody on capital charges. Previously in the letter he has drawn attention to the real possibility of his execution and has recounted that such a "departure" will bring him to Christ. He now reflects anew about his prospects for death, using the vocabulary of martyrdom. Martin (1988, 122–23) holds that these verses express "the most solemn personal reference of the whole letter."

The opening words of 2:17, **"But even if"** (*all' ei kai*), seem to indicate that a new development has occurred in Paul's judicial situation. This development may presage his condemnation, for in the remainder of 2:17-18 Paul speaks of his death as a sacrifice and remarkably affirms this outcome as an occasion for joy: **"I am poured out as a sacrifice and service for your faith, I rejoice and I rejoice with you all. Likewise you also should rejoice and rejoice with me."**

Three aspects of Paul's meaning in these verses are noteworthy. First, Paul is utilizing concepts that pertain to the sacrificial death of a martyr: "I am poured out" (*spendomai*), "sacrifice" (*thysia*), and "service" (*leitourgia*). In this reference to the pouring out of his blood, Paul may be influenced by such sacrifice-oriented Old Testament passages as Num 15:8-10. The martyr's death embraced by Jesus himself is unalterably a more fundamental point of reference for Paul.

Second, Paul will retain his solidarity with the Philippians, should Christ be calling him to die a martyr's death. His words "for your faith" (*tēs pisteōs hymōn*) probably indicate that Paul's proximate martyrdom is related to the Philippians' own steadfast faith. He will be poured out for the cause of *their* faith—which is his own faith (Sumney 2007, 57; cf. Zerwick/Grosvenor 1988, 597).

"Joy," the third important feature in these two verses, is a leitmotif within Philippians. Paul uses "rejoice" (*chairō*) four times in 2:17b-18. He first affirms, "I rejoice" (*chairō*), and then, "I rejoice with you all" (*synchairō pasin hymin*). Then he urges the Philippians, "You rejoice" (*hymeis chairete*) "and rejoice with me" (*synchairete moi*). It is remarkable that Paul encourages these rejoicings within the context of the possible martyrdom that he is facing.

Imperial propaganda heralds the emperor as the ground for joy (see Introduction). In contrast, *Jesus* is the ground for Paul's joy and for the rejoicing of the Philippians with him. The ruling emperor may cause Paul's blood to be poured out. Nevertheless, the ominous scenario that Paul is facing will not diminish his joy in Jesus and his rejoicing over what Jesus has accomplished.

Philippians 2:19-24
VIII. The Mission of Timothy

Introductory Comments

Philippians 2:19-24 represents a shift in Paul's perspective regarding his future. The martyrdom he pondered in 2:17 now seems less imminent. Paul does not know from day to day how his judicial process will play itself out, but the travel plans he projects in 2:19-30 suggest that he has now detected signs that he may soon be released. While Paul is now able to project travel for Timothy (and Epaphroditus, 2:25-30), he still needs to wait to see "how it will go with me" (2:23b) before he sends Timothy.

Paul is envisioning a mission of considerable difficulty for Timothy. The difficulty is twofold. First, Timothy will have to complete an arduous physical journey; and second, on his arrival at Philippi, Timothy will have to achieve a successful reading or performance of Paul's letter.

These verses reference Paul's interactions with Timothy and, less directly, Paul's interactions with others who are less supportive of him. His circumstances as a chained prisoner allow for such interactions. Paul seems able to visit and consult members of his support group. Nevertheless, his visitors are presumably under surveillance

The initial segment for travel between Philippi and Rome was on the Via Egnatia from the colony to the Greek port of Dyrrhachium on the Adriatic coast. The second segment was by ship to Brundisium on the southeast Italian coast, a crossing of less than a day with good winds. The third segment was from Brundisium to Rome via the Appian Way (Ramsay 1906, 384).

Bockmuel (1998, 31–32) puts the total distance at approximately 1,300 kilometers and projects daily travel by foot at 30 kilometers. By this reckoning, the travel time required would be approximately 43 days each way. Citing Cicero's travel from Rome to Thessalonica and reports by other ancient authors, Lightfoot (1988, 33) conjectures that the journey to Philippi could have been made in one month.

In the analysis of David Rhoads, Timothy and/or Epaphroditus would have received an auspicious mandate from Paul over and beyond the assignment of carrying the letter safely to its destination. This second mandate concerned the successful reading and/or performance of the letter. Rhoads (2006, 176) uses the term "commissioned agent" to identify their responsibility. Rhoads conjectures that emissaries such as Timothy and Epaphroditus could have been asked by Paul to memorize the letter before departing to bring it to its destination.

Tracing the Train of Thought

In 2:19-24 Paul indicates that he has positive and negative reasons for sending Timothy to Philippi. Positively, he considers Timothy well suited for such an undertaking. Negatively he draws a contrast with those who are unsuitable for such a mission.

In 2:22 Paul remarks that the Philippians "**know his** [Timothy's] **tested character**" (*dokimēn*), which implies that Timothy has been at Philippi previously. In focusing on Paul's initial ministry at Philippi (Acts 16:12-40), Luke does not say that Timothy was jailed with Paul and Silas and does not explicitly remark on Timothy's presence in any of the other episodes that transpired at Philippi.

However, Luke does portray Timothy present with Paul prior to and subsequent to Paul's visit to the colony. In Acts 16:3 Paul wanted Timothy to accompany him on mission and took the extraordinary step of circumcising him. Timothy then presumably journeyed with Paul northward toward Philippi. Since Luke notes Timothy's subsequent presence with Paul and Silas at Beroea (Acts 17:14), it is reasonable to conclude that Luke understands Timothy to have been present at Philippi as well. Timothy's familiarity with Philippi is also suggested by Luke's report in Acts 19:22 that Paul sent Timothy and Erastus on a mission back to Macedonia from Ephesus.

In utilizing Timothy as his emissary here, Paul is not breaking new ground. According to 1 Thess 3:2, Paul sent "Timothy our brother and God's co-worker in the gospel of Christ to establish you in your faith and exhort you." Also in 1 Cor 4:17, Paul writes, "Therefore I am sending you Timothy, my beloved and faithful child in the Lord, to remind you of my ways in Christ." As Margaret Mitchell has argued (1992, 62), there are benefits to be realized from Timothy's role as envoy that are different from the benefits Paul achieves by personally visiting a community.

In 2:20a, Paul reveals his high estimation of Timothy by stating that he and Timothy are "**of equal spirit**" (*isopsychon*). In 2:22b Paul characterizes the relationship that Timothy has with him "**as a son with his father.**" Paul then adds that Timothy "**has worked with me as a slave for the gospel**" (*syn emoi edouleusen eis to euangelion*).

As noted previously, when Paul writes "the gospel" in this letter his reference is to Christ. Paul is thus carrying forward the image that he presented at 1:1, namely, the image that he and Timothy are "slaves of Christ." The insight that Christ himself embraced the form of a slave (2:7) is also undoubtedly in Paul's view here.

On another level of meaning, Paul's words in 2:22 reference *the work* that is done by slaves, a datum with which Paul is well familiar as a result of his travels. Paul certainly knows that many slaves are consigned to unrelenting arduous labor for their masters. The words "work as a slave" thus proclaim that Paul and Timothy have labored arduously and unrelentingly for Christ.

Paul's words in 1 Cor 15:10 provide a context for what he now expresses in Phil 2:22. In 1 Cor 15:10a Paul emphasizes the grace that has made his ministry for Christ possible. He then writes in 1 Cor 15:10b: "I worked harder than any of them" (*perissoteron autōn pantōn ekopiasa*).

In Phil 2:22 Paul again remarks that he has worked for Christ in a most obdurate way. He has worked harder than "all the rest" because he has worked for Christ just as slaves are constrained to work for their earthly masters. Philippians 2:22 may thus be taken as an amplification of 1 Cor 15:10b.

In 2:21 Paul contrasts Timothy's willingness to sacrifice himself with the self-centeredness of some other Christians who are at Rome. Paul's criticism is blistering and recalls his harsh judgment in 1:15, 17 against the "minority" group of Roman Christians. Paul now excoriates these Christians: "**they all look after their own interests, not those of Jesus Christ**" (*hoi pantes gar ta heautōn zētousin ou ta Iēsou Christou*).

The universality of Paul's criticism may be partially mitigated if it is understood that he is focusing on the subgroup of Christians who might actually be able to undertake such a journey (Reumann 2008, 441). The range of this criticism is also restricted by Paul's words in 4:21-22 when he indicates that a number of Christians at Rome send greetings to the Christians at Philippi.

Timothy has no firm departure date for Philippi. Paul's own situation is extremely uncertain. It evidently is not possible for him to predict the responses of Nero's various officials and judges. Actual shifts in Paul's judicial process are probably what account for Paul's disparate comments about his situation within this letter.

Paul's remarks regarding Timothy's possible mission are bracketed with two expressions of hope. In 2:19a: "**I hope** (*elpizō*) **in the Lord Jesus to send Timothy to you soon.**" In 2:23a, "**I hope** (*elpizō*) **therefore to send him.**" Again it remains possible that Timothy will *not* be sent. In 2:23b Paul qualifies his hope with the words: "**just as soon as I see how it will go with me**" (*hōs an aphidō ta peri eme exautēs*).

In his final sentence of this section, Paul returns to a more hopeful projection (2:24): "**and I trust in the Lord that soon I shall come also**" (*pepoitha de en kyriō hoti kai autos tacheōs eleusomai*). This sentence reflects Paul's deep communion with the Philippians as well as his abiding communion with the Lord.

Writing to the Roman Christians from Corinth, Paul projects in Rom 15:24 that, after his stopover in Rome, he would undertake a westward mission to Spain; now, however, he envisions an eastward journey back to Philippi.

Throughout his letter Paul's deep concern for the well-being of the Philippians is evident. His communion with the Philippian Christians is what makes it especially attractive for him to send Timothy back to them. In 2:20 Paul has noted that Timothy "**will be genuinely anxious for your welfare**" (*hostis gnēsiōs ta peri hymōn merimnēsei*). Paul also indicates that Timothy will reliably report to Paul regarding the Philippians' situation (2:19b): "**so that I may be encouraged by knowing about you.**" Paul's abiding concern for the Philippians explains, at one level, his desire to revisit them. A more determinative explanation can be found in the fact that the Philippian church is a church under persecution.

Various factors pertaining to this persecution have been treated in the Introduction and in the commentary on 1:30. It now emerges that Paul desires to stand firm with his beloved Philippians in facing their persecution once he is released from his own chains! Paul does not indicate that he will travel from Philippi to any of his other congregations in the eastern provinces. Philippi appears to be his central focus because of the persecution of the colony conducted by the Roman authorities.

In 2:24 Paul expresses trust "in the Lord" that he will return to Philippi soon. The use of "Lord" (*kyrios*) recalls the ultimate sovereignty that Jesus received from the Father in the final scene of the passion play of 2:6-11. Paul relates every aspect of his own situation to the sovereign position of Jesus. Paul hopes "in the Lord" to send Timothy to Philippi. He is confident "in the Lord" that he himself will be able to come. Paul does not know for certain whether either visit will take place. However, Paul does know that Jesus, in his sovereignty, will provide for Paul's comings and goings.

Philippians 2:25-3:1
IX. The Mission of Epaphroditus

Introductory Comments

Epaphroditus, referenced in this section of the letter and again at 4:18, is an emissary who travels with the deep trust of the Philippians and of Paul. The Philippian Christians have selected him to travel over land and sea to bring a monetary gift to Paul. Paul may now be selecting him for the mission of bringing this letter back to Philippi.

Further, as discussed above regarding Timothy, Epaphroditus may have responsibility for the performance of the letter. If this commentary's analysis of 2:6-11 as a drama to be performed is correct, Epaphroditus might have been Paul's ideal choice for arranging this performance.

The next section will consider the character of Epaphroditus's various roles at Philippi. With Timothy, or independently of Timothy, Epaphroditus may have been able to arrange a clandestine performance of these verses utilizing Christian actors and performers from Philippi's resident theater groups.

One additional preliminary comment regards the inclusion of 3:1 within the section now to be treated. The rationale for doing so is that Paul is concluding his positive exposition regarding Epaphroditus with a general encouragement for rejoicing in the Lord.

Tracing the Train of Thought

Paul now informs the Philippians regarding Epaphroditus's return (2:25a): "**But I think it necessary to send back to you Epaphroditus.**" As in the case of Timothy, Paul makes clear his high esteem for Epaphroditus. As a member of their community, Epaphroditus is obviously well known to the Philippians.

The name *Epaphroditus* references the goddess Aphrodite and commonly has such meanings as "lovely, "charming," "amiable." This name is among the most common Roman slave names and is thus common among freed slaves. It is also a name used extensively for those who were citizens at their birth (Weaver 1994, 468).

Taking the position that Epaphroditus was a freed slave, Krytatas conjectures that Epaphroditus was connected to the *familia caesaris* (2011, 589). In contrast, commentators such as Fee (1995, 274n11) and O'Brien (1991, 329) assume that Epaphroditus was never a slave; rather, his name was given him by his natural parents.

If Epaphroditus was free born, he would have been eligible for civic office. Weaver underscores the inscriptional evidence indicating that over twenty *decuriones* from Asia, Achaea, and Macedonia were named *Epaphroditus* (1994, 468n3). It is thus possible that Epaphroditus might have had civic standing at Philippi.

The possibility that Epaphroditus might have been a legionary or praetorian veteran (or descended from veterans) should also be considered. Such military credentials would have given him access to praetorian-guarded Paul once he reached Rome. If Epaphroditus was a member of the *familia caesaris,* this credential would also facilitate his access. Penetrating the cordon around Paul in order to deliver a significant financial gift was no easy matter.

It is noteworthy that in 2:25b Paul employs *five* positive appellatives in characterizing Epaphroditus. Ephaproditus is "**my brother, my co-worker, my companion-in-arms.**" Further he is "**your apostle**" and "**your public servant for my need.**"

Since "brother" (*adelphos*) is Paul's favorite synonym for "a Christian" (Hawthorne 1983, 116), Paul's use of this term here indicates that Epaphroditus is one with him in the faith.

The second appellative, "co-worker" (*synergōn*), is a distinctive Pauline term. He uses it to characterize Euodia, Synteche, and Clement in 4:3, and he used it elsewhere to characterize such collaborators as Timothy (1 Thess 3:2 and elsewhere), Apollos (1 Cor 3:9), Titus (2 Cor 8:23), Priscilla and Aquila (Rom 16:3), Urbanus (Rom 16:9), Philemon (Phlm 1). Its use here may imply that Epaphroditus worked with Paul at the time of Paul's initial visit(s) to Philippi.

Paul's use of *systratiōtēn* ("companion-in arms"—NAB, NJB) may connote that Epaphroditus had stood with Paul during a time of duress. The only other use of this term in the New Testament is Phlm 2, where Paul uses it in reference to Archippus. If Epaphroditus was present at the time of Paul's flogging and imprisonment at Philippi, he possibly played a role in supporting Paul during those events. He evidently is now Paul's comrade in the conflict that Paul is experiencing as a prisoner in Rome.

Paul's final two terms express appreciation for the standing that Epaphroditus has in the Philippian church. As "your apostle" (*hymōn apostolon*), Epaphroditus has come to Paul's side as a quasi-official representative of the Philippian church.

The following questions may be posed regarding the character of the church at Philippi and Epaphroditus's mission from this community: Was the decision to send him made by "the bishops and deacons" mentioned at 1:1? Were Euodia and Synteche and Clement involved in this decision? Was Lydia, prominent in Acts 16, possibly involved? If Epaphroditus was himself one of the deacons of the Philippian church (Reumann 2008, 442n13), could that have been the basis on which he undertook his mission?

Ideally, the person the Philippian community designated for this mission would be familiar with the route between Philippi and Rome and familiar with Rome itself. To navigate in the complex surroundings of a city with one million inhabitants and no street signs or directional markers was no easy task (Murphy-O'Connor 1996, 359–60). In 2 Tim 1:17 Paul is depicted as deeply grateful for the steadfastness that Onesiphorus manifested in searching *diligently* for the location of Paul's custody in Rome.

Paul's fifth term for characterizing Epaphroditus is **"your public servant for my need"** (*leitourgon tēs chreias mou*). The term *leitourgon* suggests benefaction as well as priestly service. If Epaphroditus possessed wealth, he might have contributed personally to the monetary gift that he was bringing to Paul (Reumann 2008, 443).

Since *leitourgos*, in the Septuagint, has sacrificial connotations, Paul may view Epaphroditus's mission as a priestly endeavor (Hawthorne 1983, 117). In 4:18 Paul refers to the gift that Epaphroditus brought him as "a sacrifice" (*thysia*).

Paul indicates that the Philippians already know of Epaphroditus's severe illness. Epaphroditus himself **"has been distressed because you heard that he was ill"** (2:26b). Did the illness occur during the course of his travel to Rome or after he arrived? If it occurred en route, someone traveling in the direction of the colony presumably notified the Philippians regarding this development.

If the illness had occurred after Epaphroditus reached Rome, it still could have been communicated back to Philippi by someone traveling to the colony. Nevertheless, such a report would have lacked Paul's own assessment of the situation. Paul thus now provides his own commentary regarding what has occurred.

Epaphroditus was indeed **"close to death"** (2:27a; cf. 2:30a). However, God had mercy on both Epaphroditus and Paul **"in order that I might not have sorrow upon sorrow"** (2:27b). This is probably a reference to the sorrow (*lypēn*) that Paul experiences from his present custody and from the mean-spirited response by a minority of the Roman Christian community.

Paul is **"therefore the more eager to send"** Epaphroditus back to Philippi (2:28a). He foresees two benefits that will follow from this step. First (2:26a), Epaphroditus himself longs to be reunited with the Philippians. Second (2:28), Paul anticipates the joy that the Philippians will derive from being reunited with Epaphroditus, and the thought of this joy makes Paul himself **"more free from grief"** (*alypoteros*).

In 2:29 Paul indicates the welcome that Epaphroditus deserves: **"So receive him in the Lord** (*en kyriō*) **with all joy** (*meta pasēs charas*) **and hold such people in high esteem."** In this verse (as previously at 2:17b-18) a connection between "joy" and "being in the Lord" can be seen (O'Brien 1991, 340).

Paul now relates three aspects of Epaphroditus's conduct (2:30). First, in his mission, Epaphroditus **"risked his life"** (*paraboleusamenos tē psychē*) for Paul. Second, in an expression that echoes 2:7, Paul states that

Epaphroditus "**came near to death**" (*mechri thanatou ēngisen*) in fulfilling his mission. Third, Epaphroditus persevered to present the Philippians' **service** (*leitourgias*) to Paul.

The scenario that Paul envisions may be as follows. The Philippians collected a considerable amount of money for Paul (see on 4:10-20). In order to get this gift to the prisoner, they selected Epaphroditus as their chosen "minister" (*leitourgan*, 2:25). The transport of a large sum of money over land and sea for circa thirty days was a formidable task (see commentary on 4:10-20). Epaphroditus faced dangers but he "risked his life" (Deissmann 1978, 88; Moulton-Milligan 1930, 480) in order to complete his mission. He eventually reached Paul with the Philippians' gift intact.

As with Timothy's departure date, the specific time of Ephaphroditus's departure is not determined. The opening words of 2:28 are translated by Bruce (1991, 100) and others as "Therefore I am all the more eager to send him." Paul is indeed eager to send Epaphroditus, but he does not indicate that Epaphroditus's departure will occur in the *immediate* future.

Ephaphroditus's departure may, in fact, be tied to Timothy's departure. Conceivably, Paul's two highly esteemed co-workers might undertake the arduous journey to Philippi together. Presumably they would not be traveling with a chest of money; the trip back to Philippi should thus not be as dangerous as Epaphroditus's initial journey.

Still the journey to Philippi would not be without its perils, and Timothy might have been pleased to travel with Epaphroditus. The inns (*mansiones*) where travelers stayed were located about one day's journey apart (Forbes 1955, 153). Many of these inns were in a half-ruinous condition (Ramsay 1906, 393). From his own experience, Epaphroditus could alert Timothy regarding potential danger spots and guide him to the safest venues.

As noted, Timothy had traveled as Paul's "official delegate" at least twice before—from Athens to Thessalonica and from Ephesus to Corinth. Neither of these journeys was as complex as the journey from Rome to Philippi. Also so far as can be determined (from Paul's letters and from Acts), Timothy was not a Roman citizen. In contrast, Epaphroditus was almost certainly a citizen; and, as discussed above, he may have had a military background or membership in the *familia caesaris*.

The verse with which Paul closes this section (3:1) has proved another "interpreter's cross" (*crux interpretum*). As noted in the Introduction, *to loipon*, the first words of the verse, have been translated "finally" by commentators who hold that Paul is bringing a letter fragment to a close. However, *to loipon* may be taken as having inferential meaning (O'Brien 1991, 348; BDAG 2000, 603) and be translated "therefore." This translation is adopted here.

The meaning of *chairete* in 3:1a is also debated. Based on her analysis of the use of *chairete* in ancient letters, Loveday Alexander concludes (1989, 87) that "rejoice" not "farewell" is the appropriate translation for *chairete* here. Paul's meaning in this verse is thus to urge rejoicing "in the Lord" (*en kyrio*) over Epaphroditus's steadfast service to Paul and his projected return to Philippi in good health: "**Therefore, my brothers and sisters, rejoice in the Lord.**"

Because Paul recognizes that he has urged rejoicing earlier in the letter (2:17-18) and even in the preceding verses (2:28), he now offers an explanation for this repetition (3:1b): "**To write the same things to you is not irksome for me and is a safeguard for you.**"

How is a repeated emphasis on "joy in the Lord" a "safeguard" (*asphales*) for the Philippians? Bockmuel (1998, 181) proposes that Paul understands "joy in the Lord" as "a bulwark against all manner of dangers." As noted above, Paul's emphasis that Jesus is the true grounds for joy refutes claims by imperial propagandists that the emperor is the source of joy (see section 15 of the Introduction).

Philippians 3:2-7
X. Paul's Response to a Threat from "the Circumcisers"

Introductory Comments

Paul abruptly switches to a new topic in 3:2-7, the irrationality of circumcision for Gentile Christians. His sharp opening words in 3:2 are seemingly in response to information that has just reached him about "circumcisers."

Whether these adversaries are active at Philippi, at Rome, or some other location, Paul launches a vigorous attack on them lest the Philippians be influenced by this subversion of the gospel. He vigorously refutes these opponents with a variety of arguments in 3:2-7 before returning to the main themes of the letter in 3:8. The adversaries Paul castigates here are *not* the adversaries he decries in 3:18-19.

Tracing the Train of Thought

Paul's phrasing in 3:2 is staccato-like. He characterizes the proponents of circumcision for Gentile Christians with three unflattering terms that each begin with the Greek letter *kappa*. Further, he employs the imperative "beware" (*blepete*) three times. In the translation of Bruce (1991, 104; cf. Martin 1976, 140), the intensity of Paul's warning is unmistakable: "**Beware the dogs** (*tous kynas*), **beware the evil-workers** (*tous kakous ergatas*), **beware the mutilators of the flesh** (*tēn katatomēn*)."

Paul has previously dealt forcefully with the advocates of circumcision. In Gal 5:12 his finale is, "I wish those who unsettle you would mutilate themselves" (RSV). It is far from certain whether these long-standing adversaries have made their way to Philippi or possibly to Rome (Fee 1995, 294; O'Brien 1991, 354). Wherever they are now active, Paul takes them seriously and provides the Philippians with a forceful, sharp-edged warning about them.

In 3:3 he reminds the Philippians, "**we are the true circumcision who worship God in spirit and glory in Christ Jesus and put no confidence in the flesh.**" In 3:4-7 he then lists his own credentials only to minimize their value in comparison with his identity *in Christ*.

Paul's approach in 3:4-6 is reminiscent of his "Fool's Speech" in 2 Cor 11:21ff. He lists seven credentials to establish that his own Jewish standing is second to none. He places his own circumcision at the head of the list. His parents fulfilled the law by having him "**circumcised on the eighth day**" (cf. Lev 12:3). He was raised to speak Hebrew (3:5; cf. 2 Cor 11:22; Acts 21:40; 22:2). As a member "**of the tribe of Benjamin**," he may have received his Hebrew name after Saul, Israel's first king, also a Benjamite (Martin 1976, 146).

In 3:6a Paul states that he was "**a Pharisee as to the law**" and so ardent that he became "**a persecutor of the church.**" Paul here uses "church" (*ekklēsian*) to refer to the Christians of a region, that is, Judea and Syria (cf. Acts 8:3; 9:1-2; 26:11). In 4:25 he will use *ekklēsia* precisely for the church of Philippi.

In earlier letters Paul has adverted to his efforts to persecute the followers of Christ (1 Cor 15:9; Gal 1:13; cf. 1 Tim 1:13). He now references his persecutor's role for the purpose of establishing his zeal (*zēlos*) for the Jewish religion, including its laws. By doing this he relativizes the claims of his opponents that they are the exclusive representatives of "zealousness." Paul concludes this listing of his attributes by stating at 3:6b that **"as to righteousness in the sphere of the law"** (*dikaiosynēn*; used also at 3:9), he was **"blameless"** (*amemptos*). He then emphasizes in 3:7 that any **"gain"** (*kerdē*) conferred by these credentials he now counts as **loss** (*zēmian*) **"for the sake of Christ"** (*dia ton Christon*).

Again, the proponents of circumcision for all Christians may not yet be active in Philippi. Paul is proactive regarding any such activity. He is extremely agitated over this "proselytizing." As soon as it comes to his attention, he attacks the proselytizers forcefully.

Philippians 3:8-16
XI. Paul's Communion with Christ in Life and Death

Introductory Comments

Having dealt decisively with those advocating circumcision for Gentile Christians, Paul returns to his reflections regarding allegiance to Christ within the setting of his Roman custody. How much time has elapsed between the composition of the preceding section on circumcision and the new section regarding Paul's embrace of Christ's form of death is impossible to say.

Tracing the Train of Thought

In 3:8 Paul reemphasizes the idea expressed in 3:7 regarding what he now counts as loss for the sake of Christ: **"What is more"** (Martin 1976, 148, so translates *alla menounge*) **"I count everything as loss because of the ultimate value of the knowledge of Christ Jesus, of my Lord."**

Paul employs three genitives to modify "ultimate value" (Hawthorne 1983, 137, so translates *hyperechon*). They may be translated: "of the knowledge," "of Christ Jesus," "of my Lord." The last genitive, "of my Lord," clearly adds intensity to "of Christ Jesus."

Paul refers to Jesus as "Lord" (*kyrios*) fifteen times in Philippians (also in 1:2, 14; 2:11, 19, 24, 29; 3:1, 20; 4:1, 2, 4, 5, 10, 23). Yet here his *personal communion* with Jesus as Lord is highlighted. Elsewhere Paul has frequently named Jesus as "the Lord" and as "our Lord," but only here is Jesus "*my* Lord."

In 3:8b Paul uses the expression "**to gain Christ**" (*hina Christon kerdēsō*). Gaining Christ is so important to him that he counts everything else as so much "**rubbish**" (*skybala*). Paul does not gain Christ through his own righteousness (*dikaiosynēn*) but rather through "**the righteousness from God that depends on faith**" (*tēn ek theou dikaiosynēn epi tē pistei*). Regarding this clause Hawthorne comments: "In this one verse Paul distils his great fundamental doctrine of justification by faith" (ibid., 142).

In 3:9 Paul states his desire "**to be found in him**" (*heurethō en autō*). In 3:10b he expresses his concern "**to have communion in his sufferings**" (*kai koinōnian pathēmatōn autou*), and in 3:10c he dramatically specifies that his communion will involve "**sharing the form of his death**" (*symmorphizomenos tō thanatō autou*).

This last phrase is significant in disclosing how Paul now visualizes the ultimate outcome of his earthly journey with Christ. Paul, the Roman prisoner, now apprehends that his own form of death could well be in close correspondence with *the form of death* that Jesus embraced. Paul has previously reflected that, in the suffering he endured during the course of his ministry, he was approximating Jesus's sufferings and death. Consider, for example, 2 Cor 4:7-12, especially 4:10a: "always carrying in the body the death of Jesus." Now, at a later stage of his journey, one in which he experiences sustained Roman custody, Paul's reflections regarding Jesus's death, and his own, are deepening.

The presence of the root *morph-* ("form") in *symmorphizomenos* at 3:10c is significant in terms of the "echo" it provides for Paul's description of Jesus taking the form of a slave (*morphēn doulou*) in 2:7b and accepting the slave's form of death in 2:8. Jesus embraced the slave's form of death; Paul is now anticipating his own conformity to Jesus' form of death.

Paul indicated his willingness to embrace death in 1:21, and in 2:17 he indicated that his death could have a sacrificial quality to it. He now provides new insight into the parallel between Jesus's form of death and his own.

The following similarities can be identified: (1) Paul, like Jesus before him, is being held as a Roman prisoner. (2) He, like Jesus, is charged with a capital offense. (3) Paul, like Jesus, will face a Roman judge who possesses the power to release or condemn him. (4) Paul, like Jesus, could have the experience of having his own testimony rejected. (5) If condemned, Paul, like Jesus, will be executed by Roman military personnel. (6) Paul, like Jesus, will have his execution carried out according to officially authorized Roman procedures. (7) As was the case for Jesus, the grounds for Paul's execution will presumably be conduct hostile to the emperor/empire, in other words, "treason" (*maiestas*).

The apostle visualizes a connection between his allegiance to Jesus as *Lord* and his Roman execution. Paul is now facing a death sentence from an ersatz "lord." Yet he embraces this travesty of justice because, through it, he is being conformed to the death of Jesus—"*my* Lord."

If Paul is executed by imperial decree, the Philippian Christians will find themselves facing a potentially dispiriting "scandal." They have professed Christian faith in the face of the scandal of Jesus's Roman crucifixion. They will now be asked to profess their allegiance to Christ in the face of Paul's own "scandalous" death. In light of these factors, Paul may now be striving to "innoculate" the Philippian Christians against any potential "propaganda benefits" that the Philippian magistrates might seek to derive from Paul's execution. Paul's Roman imprisonment and his chains were already, for some, the occasion of scandal. (Recall the analysis at 1:15, 17 regarding the response of the minority of Roman Christians.) An imperial death sentence, followed by execution, had the potential for generating still greater scandal.

Further, the situation of the Christians of Philippi could well become more perilous if Paul were to be condemned and executed. Already persecuted by the Philippian magistrates, the Philippian Christians could be subjected to additional harassment in the light of any capital verdict against their founder. Paul thus desires to strengthen the Philippian

Christians for continuing in their allegiance to Jesus as "Lord," despite his impending execution.

Paul mentions Christ's resurrection and his own projected resurrection just before and right after he notes the possibility that he might share the form of Christ's death. In 3:10 he refers to **"the power of his resurrection"** (*tēn dynamin tēs anastaseōs autou*). In 3:11 he expresses his expectation that he himself will gain the resurrection of Christ: **"so that I may attain the resurrection from the dead"** (*ei pōs katantēsō eis tēn exanastasin tēn ek nekrōn*)

Paul's insight regarding "the power" exercised by Jesus in 3:10, and implicitly in 3:11, is enhanced when it is recalled that, in 2:9-11, he emphasized *the Father's* power in taking Jesus from the cross to the highest place. The Father had been present during the stages of Jesus's self-emptying unto death by crucifixion, and the Father then intervened decisively to vindicate Jesus from the unjust verdict and the degradation that Roman personnel had visited on him.

Here in 3:10-11 the emphasis falls on the power that now accrues to the risen Jesus by reason of the resurrection. Ultimately there is no conflict between the power exercised by the Father and the power that Jesus exercises from "the highest place." Nevertheless, here and especially in 3:21, Paul accentuates the "power" (*dynamin*) possessed by the risen Jesus.

The RSV and other translations render Paul's Greek in 3:11 to the effect that Paul has some degree of uncertainty as to whether he will attain the life of the resurrection. In the translation proposed by Sumney (2007, 82), the two particles, *ei pōs*, do not express doubt but rather expectation: "*so that* I may attain the resurrection from the dead."

Discussing Paul's use of these two particles in Rom 1:10 and 11:44, Judith Gundry (1990, 254–58) reaches a similar conclusion: Paul is expressing the *expectation* not the doubt that he will attain the resurrection. In 3:10-11 Paul relates being conformed to Christ's death and attaining the resurrection. By the sovereign power of his Lord, Paul expects resurrection to follow from being conformed to Christ's death.

In 3:12-13a Paul uses forms of the verb *lambanō* four times to identify additional facets of his embrace of the death and resurrection of Christ. It is helpful to repeat the word "obtain" in translating these four forms: **"Not that I have already *obtained* it or am already perfected, but**

I persevere to *obtain* it because I have been *obtained* by Christ Jesus. Brethren I do not consider that I have *obtained* it." The translation just given follows Sumney (2007, 83) in supplying "it" as the object of *elabon* in 3:12a: "Not that I have already obtained *it*." Sumney indicates that the antecedent of the supplied pronoun is probably everything that is included in knowing Christ. Paul has not yet attained the resurrection because he has still to pour out his life in death.

There is a propitiousness in Paul's expression "because I have been *obtained* by Christ Jesus" (*katelēmphthēn hypo Christou Iēsou*). Christ has taken the initiative of calling Paul, and Christ is the sovereign Lord who has made Paul his own. Indeed, it is because of Jesus's sovereign role over him that Paul has referred to Jesus as *my* Lord in 3:8 and characterized himself as Christ's slave in 1:1a and 2:22.

Although Paul is not yet perfected, he perseveres toward this goal. In 3:13b and 3:14 he uses athletic imagery to express this perseverance: "**but I do this one thing: forgetting the things that are behind me, stretching forward to what is ahead, I press on to the finish line for the prize of the upward call of God in Christ Jesus.**" The participle *epekteinomenos*, translated "stretching forward" by Vincent (1902, 110), conveys the image of a runner bending forward toward the finish marker with eyes fastened on it. *Skopon*, translated here as "finish line," might also be translated more broadly as "goal." "Prize" (*to brabeion*) is also used by Paul in 1 Cor 9:24 to refer to the prize for which runners in a race compete.

Paul's use of spatial imagery in his phrase "the *upward* call of God in Christ Jesus" (*tēs anō klēseōs tou theou en Christō Iēsou*) looks backward to his spatial imagery in 2:9 and forward to his spatial imagery in 3:20. In 2:9 the Father exalted Jesus to "the highest place." In 3:20 Paul anticipates the arrival on earth of Savior Jesus "from heaven." Jesus is now in heaven, and Paul eagerly awaits the "upward" call that will bring him to heavenly communion with Jesus.

In the two verses concluding this section Paul counsels unity in embracing the insights he has just presented. He uses the term "this" (*touto*) twice without explicitly indicating its antecedent. In 3:15a he writes: "**Let all of us who are mature, therefore, think *this* together.**" In 3:15b he writes, "**if you think differently about anything, God will reveal** *this* **to you."** Sumney notes that the *touto* in the second clause may well have the same antecedent that it does in the first clause (2007, 88).

In the interpretation now proposed, Paul is referring to what he has written in 3:10 regarding sharing the form of Jesus's death. He is urging the Philippians to share his own new perspective about the similarities between the death of Jesus and Paul's own death.

With Paul, the Philippians are to contemplate their call to communion with Jesus in the manner of his death. As discussed with regard to 3:10, two dimensions of Jesus's death are central. First, Jesus' embrace of crucifixion represented his embrace of the slave's form of death. Second, the form of death that Jesus embraced was authorized by Rome and inflicted on him by Rome.

In addition to having in view what he has written in 3:10 regarding the possibility of his own Roman-decreed death, Paul may also be envisioning what he is about to write in 3:18-19, where he decries the aberrational conduct of Nero and his confederates (see below). In both instances, Paul shares perspectives with the Philippians that broadly challenge any positive estimation of Rome's leading officials.

Paul surely wants the Philippians to embrace the perspectives that he is proposing. In 3:15a he urges those who are "mature" (*teleioi*) to adopt them. Nevertheless, Paul appears to recognize that it may take time for the perspectives he is advocating to be embraced by everyone.

In 3:15b he continues as follows: "if you think differently about anything, God will reveal this to you" (*kai ei ti heterōs phroneite kai touto ho theos hymin apokalypsei*). In other words, Paul leaves it to God, in God's good time, to bring the "other-minded" Philippians to embrace the new view of "Christ's things" and "things Roman" that Paul is delineating.

As the process for embracing Paul's full proclamation is underway, backsliding must be guarded against (3:16): **"However, regarding that which we have already attained, let us hold fast to it."** The verb *stoichein*, "hold fast," can connote military discipline in keeping to a line (Fee 1995, 360). Paul wants to preclude any retreat regarding the bedrock elements of the worldview that he has articulated. The line must hold!

A possible illustration of Paul's meaning is that there can be no retreat from the confession that Jesus is Lord. In the matter of participation in the various observances of the emperor cult and the cults of deities such as Artemis, Silvanus, and Isis, time may be needed for "maturity." It may also take time for the Philippian Christians to accept Paul's radical devaluing of Roman citizenship. Even more time may be required for the free Christians of Philippi to walk according to the light of Jesus's self-sacrificing love for slaves. Once again, 2:15 affirms that the maturity that God desires in these matters will be God's own work.

Philippians 3:17-4:1
XII. Paul's Response to a Threat from "the Enemies of the Cross of Christ"

Introductory Comments

This section features a carefully composed critique of the Roman authorities. Paul uses coded language in 3:18-19 to denounce them as "enemies of the cross of Christ" who will face annihilation. In 3:20-21, he contrasts the situation of Christians who await Jesus as their Lord and Savior and that of these enemies. Paul bookends this teaching regarding Christ by encouraging the Philippians to be imitators of Paul in 3:17 and to stand firm with him in the Lord in 4:1b.

There is an important link between the adversaries critiqued in 1:28 and those now indicted in 3:18-19. In 1:28 the opponents are the imperial authorities *at Philippi*. Here in 3:17-19 the adversaries are Nero and his confederates *at Rome*. Both groups are bound together in one and the same imperial system. Paul uses the same term in 1:28 and 3:19 to indicate that the Christians' enemies at both locations are headed for "annihilation" (*apōleias*).

The interpretation just proposed for this passage is distinctive. One searches in vain among the existing commentaries to find any reference that the Roman authorities constituted "the enemies of the cross of Christ." For example, O'Brien (1991, 453–54) does not advert to the Roman authorities in considering six groups to whom Paul might be referring when he uses the expression "the enemies of the cross of Christ."

Tracing the Train of Thought

As just noted, in the first verse of this section (3:17) Paul asks the Philippians to take him as an example: **"Brethren, be imitators together of me and observe those who live according to the pattern you have from us"** (*symmimētai mou ginesthe, adelphoi, kai skopeite tous houtōs peripatountas kathōs echete typon hēmas*).

The term, "imitators together" (*symmimētai*) is not found elsewhere in the New Testament or in other Greek literature. However, Paul has used the simple word "imitators" (*mimētai*) in 1 Cor 4:16 and 11:1 (cf. 1 Thess 1:6). Both in 1 Corinthians and here in Philippians, Paul does not hesitate to present himself as a model to be imitated. Paul encourages the members of both communities to imitate his complete dedication to Christ Jesus. The Philippians have the further dimension of imitating Paul's example *as someone persecuted by the Roman authorities*.

In 3:18 Paul pivots to decry those who are **"the enemies of the cross of Christ"** (*tous echthrous tou staurou tou Christou*). He remarks that there are **"many"** (*polloi*) who fall into this camp and that Paul has warned the Philippians about them **"many times"** (*pollakis*). He does so **"now even with tears"** (*nyn de kai klaiōn*).

Paul's potential conversations with his praetorian guards may have brought him to the perspective that "the enemy of the cross of Christ" fittingly designates Nero. If Paul has become well informed regarding Nero's murderousness and wantoness, he could have learned at the same time of Nero's near impregnable power. For there is simply no tribunal anywhere in Rome where Nero can be brought to judgment. Paul thus gives vent, even in tears of frustration, to the fact that Nero's behavior knows no human boundaries.

To be an enemy of the cross of Christ is metonomy for being an enemy of Christ himself. For Christ never grasped at "status" and "glory." Yet Paul now recognizes that Nero and his allies do not cease from grasping at "honor" and "glory." Nero and his confederates at Rome and elsewhere live in a grasping, self-glorifying manner that knows no bounds.

If Paul, in iron chains, knew of Nero's episodes in golden chains, Paul's deriding of "the enemies of the cross of Christ" might have been become still more focused upon the emperor. In his theater performances, Nero insisted on playing all of the leading roles, including roles that required his submission. In roles that required him to be chained, however, only golden chains could bind him.

Nero did not consider it proper for a "lord" such as himself to be bound in iron shackles (Dio, *Epitome of Book 62* 9.4.6; cf. Suetonius, *Nero* 23.2-14). Such an "actor lord," perpetrator of iron chains but bound only with chains of gold, was indeed an enemy of the cross of Christ. He will be brought into complete and lasting subjection to Christ. That Paul has previously reflected regarding Christ's enemies is indicated by 1 Cor 15:25: "For he must reign until he (Christ) has put "all his enemies (*pantas tous echthrous*) under his feet."

In 3:19, Paul proceeds with a bill of particulars against those who are the enemies of the cross of Christ. Philippians 3:19 is remarkable for its staccato character. No finite verb appears in any of these indictments (O'Brien 1991, 454). Paul is so outraged over this abusive behavior that he hurls his indictments on to the written page without concern for grammatical form.

Verse 3:19b presents the first and most damning charge: "**their god, their sexual organ**" (*hōn ho theos hē koilia*). Some interpreters opt to translate *hē koilia* as "visceral appetite" (for example, Bockmuel 1998, 231, referring to Rom 16:18). However, in the Septuagint, *koilia* can refer to the male sex organ (Behm 1964, 3:786), and Marshall (1992, xxiv) suggests that Paul's use of the word in 3:19 is euphemistic. (Note, however, that Marshall considers Paul's comment to be directed against advocates of circumcision and not Nero and his allies.)

From his contacts in Rome Paul may have been gained information regarding Nero's sexual conduct that previously was not accessible to him. The following description may typify the reports that reached Paul (Tacitus, *Annals* 15.37): "First came obscene gestures and dances; then, as darkness advanced, the whole of the neighboring grove together with the dwelling-houses around, began to echo with song and glitter with lights. Nero himself, defiled by every natural and unnatural lust had left no abomination in reserve with which to crown his vicious existence."

Paul uses *ho theos* ("God") more than twenty times throughout Philippians. His use of *theos* in 3:19b is the single instance in which he uses this word to indicate idolatry. Nero and his confederates worship their own "gods," that is, their own sexual organs!

Nero and his accomplices also **glory in their shame** (*hē doxa en tē aischynē autōn*). The "shame" or "shameful conduct" (*aischynē*) that Paul denounces here is precisely the exploitative sexual misconduct that he decried in the preceding clause. Link (1978, 3:564) observes that Paul here condemns the immoral sexual practices that characterize pagan life. The enemies of the cross are so inverted in their perspective that they publicly indulge in their disgraceful conduct. In a twisted way they seek to derive a certain "reputation" (*doxa*) from doing so.

Paul's third indictment of these adversaries is that "**their minds are set on earthly things**" (*hoi ta epigeia phronountes*). Their focus is entirely on what is temporal and transient. In the next two verses Paul will contrast the eternal realities of heaven with the ephemerality of these earthly things.

Before proceeding to 3:20-21, however, attention should be given to the judgment that Paul announces at 3:19a. Paul previously used *apōleia* in 1:28a to describe the ultimate outcome that the Philippians' opponents (*tōn antikeimenōn*) would face. Paul contrasted their "annihilation" with the Christians' coming salvation (*sōtērias*) bestowed by God (1:28a). The imperial authorities *at Philippi* had orchestrated the persecution of Christians, and they were the ones who would face obliteration. Paul now predicts that "annihilation" (*apōleia*) will be the same outcome for Nero and the imperial authorities *at Rome*: "**their end is annihilation.**"

Paul's words in 3:18-19 can be taken as an example of what James Scott terms (1990, passim) "a hidden transcript." While the concepts embedded in 3:18-19 are obscure to hostile outsiders, they illuminate and encourage insiders who grasp their meaning.

In these verses Paul makes disguised reference to a group of oppressors, indicts them for egregious practices, and announces their demise. Paul demonstrates great skill in formulating and linking five rhetorical concepts. He first derides the Philippians' opponents for four violations, and then, via a fifth slogan, he announces their destruction.

Here the crucial role played by Epaphroditus and/or Timothy as the presenter(s) of the letter should be referenced. It is possible that these two delegates or other designated performers of the letter might have invited the Philippian Christians to chant in unison each concept after it has been presented. Christian actors from Philippi's theater might have provided guidance for such a performance. By means of such modulated chanting, the denunciations that Paul intended through his words could become still more evident. Thus:

(1) "They are enemies of the cross of Christ." *Repeated in unison by the assembly.*
(2) "Their gods, their sexual organs." *Repeated in unison by the assembly.*
(3) "They glory in their shame." *Repeated in unison by the assembly.*
(4) "Their minds are set on earthly things." *Repeated in unison by assembly.*
(5) "Their end is annihilation." *Repeated in unison by the assembly.*

Such chanting by the Philippians at Philippi could have been a resource for them in their resolve to stand firm against the threats of the Roman magistrates. In evolving such techniques for encouraging those persecuted by opponents whose power seems invincible, Paul is formulating a textbook example of "dis-praise."

The interpretation that Paul intentionally formulated phrases that were well suited for chanting has not been previously proposed. A corollary to this interpretation is that Paul potentially learned this technique from Nero himself.

Recall that Paul was being guarded by members of Nero's praetorian guard for an extended period of time. During this period Nero and his confederates orchestrated public chanting on Nero's behalf, and this practice surely became known throughout the praetorian camp. Nero's praetorians may have been involved in the "production" of such chanting.

Dio Cassius reports that the contrived chants were proclaimed on Nero's return from Greece in AD 67. Nevertheless, the episode detailed below was far from the first instance of Nero seeking to provide for his own adulation:

> The whole population, the senators themselves most of all, kept shouting in chorus: "Hail, Olympian Victor! Hail Pythian Victor! Augustus! Augustus! Hail to Nero, our Hercules! Hail to Nero, our Apollo! The only Victor of the Grand Tour, the only one from the

beginning of time! Augustus! Augustus! O Divine Voice, blessed are they that hear thee." (Dio Cassius, *Roman History, Epitome of Book 62* 20.5).

After projecting judgment against the Roman authorities in 3:18-19, Paul contrasts in 3:20-21 the situation of Christians. Paul's words at 3:20a, **"for our citizenship is already in heaven"** (*hēmōn gar to politeuma en ouranois hyparchei*), direct attention to a citizenship that is eternal. The conferral of this eternal citizenship is far beyond the competence of any Roman official. Further, this heavenly citizenship has been bestowed without regard for the prerogatives of those who confer Roman citizenship. The citizenship pertaining to heaven is manifestly outside the reach of all Roman officials.

Three situations regarding citizenship characterize the situation in Philippi at the time of Paul's letter. First, a significant number of the Philippian Christians hold Roman citizenship. Second, slaves at Philippi, including those who are Christians, have no connection whatever with Roman citizenship. Third, all of the Philippian Christians, including Christian slaves, hold heavenly citizenship and anticipate the coming of the Lord Jesus Christ from heaven.

Paul's use of *politeuma* in 3:20 is noteworthy. He has previously used the cognate form, *politeuesthe,* in 1:27. In his undisputed letters these are the only two occurrences of this term. Depending on the given secular context, *politeuma* may have such meanings as "commonwealth," "government," "state" (LSJ 1968, 1434). It may also have the meaning of "citizenship" (Moulton-Milligan 525; Ruppel 1927, 268–312 and 433–54). Further, in Macedonian cities such as Philippi, *politeuma* denotes the *citizen body* (Hatzopoulos 2011, 240).

When *politeuma* is understood as "citizenship," Paul is stating, in effect, that the true "citizenship" of Christians lies in heaven. What meaning does this heavenly citizenship in heaven have for Roman citizenship? If their true citizenship is in heaven, what is the value of the Roman citizenship that Paul and a goodly number of Philippian Christians hold on earth?

Before proposing an answer to this question, it is useful to reflect that members of the Philippian Christian community who were present at the time of Paul's initial visit to the colony might have "anticipated" a clarification from Paul regarding the value of Roman citizenship.

According to Acts 16, Paul initially refrained from any mention of his Roman citizenship. The owners of the clairvoyant slave girl derided Paul and Silas because they were *not* Roman citizens (literally, that they subscribed to practices illicit for *us* Romans). Despite such taunts, Paul remained silent. He and Silas actually accepted a severe beating with rods rather than disclose their Roman citizenship and perhaps have their status as Christ's missionaries overshadowed by their Roman status.

At the time of his public beating, no one present knew that Paul was a Roman citizen. Only out of public view did Paul declare to the jailer (Acts 16:37) that he and Silas were "Roman citizens" (*anthrōpous Rōmaious hyparchontas*). He then asked that this information be transmitted to the magistrates. The magistrates came *publicly* to the prison at Paul's request. A further implication is that news of this surprising turn of events then circulated publicly in Philippi.

Perhaps Paul provided the Philippians with the rationale for his approach during his subsequent visit(s) to the colony. Now in Rome, as a Roman citizen in chains for Christ, he offers a definitive assessment of the worth of Roman citizenship.

In 3:20 Paul's implied meaning is that Roman citizenship is worthless! Bormann (1995, 219) correctly expresses that Paul here identifies *die Bedeutunglosigkeit des römischen Bürgerrechts*, "the meaninglessness of Roman citizenship." Roman citizenship is worthless because it has no actual power to save anyone. Those who confer it are the enemies of the cross of Christ and have no real power. Only Jesus has the power to confer a citizenship that is truly salvific, the citizenship of heaven.

Paul's teaching is "good news" for the Philippian Christians, even if his words are initially surprising to them. The Philippians "already" hold title (*hyparchei*) to a heavenly citizenship that is beyond any earthly citizenship. Heavenly citizenship gives Christians the standards for their conduct. They are protected from "the enemies of the cross of Christ" who are present at Philippi as well as at Rome by Lord Jesus, the true savior, whom they eagerly await.

Active chanting of 3:18-19 by the Philippian Christians has been discussed in the paragraphs above. Paul may have envisioned a similar chanting of 3:20, especially the first clause: "but our citizenship is in heaven."

As discussed in section 6 of the Introduction, Augustus may have conferred Roman citizenship universally at Philippi, slaves excepted. If this was the case, then the chanting of "our citizenship is in heaven" by the Christians who were Roman citizens would have constituted a defiant proclamation to the effect that citizenship, the highest benefit the Roman system could confer, was *inconsequential*.

Attention must also be given to the participation in this chanting by Christian slaves. On the one hand, such chanting implies that, because of Christ's sovereign power, the slaves' lack of Roman citizenship does not demean them. On the other hand, the chanting slaves are presenting an enobling claim. They are proclaiming, salutarily, that in heaven they possess citizenship along with everyone else. As with 3:18-19, the verses immediately preceding, the chanting of 3:20 would doubtlessly occur only in clandestine settings.

The conjecture that the Christian slaves of Philippi participated in chants affirming their citizenship in heaven is a startling one. A more startling historical fact regarding the status and aspirations of Christian slaves is the governor Pliny's report regarding his torture of women slaves who were Christians. As discussed in section 11 of the Introduction, in order to gain information regarding the burgeoning Christian movement in Bithynia-Pontus, Pliny tortured two women slaves who ministered as deacons within this province. Conceivably, Paul's words in Philippians about slaves' noble citizenship may have paved the way for *women slaves* to serve the Christian community as deacons in Bithynia-Pontus.

Once again, for the Christian slaves of Philippi, Paul's words in 3:20a are fundamentally encouraging. Within the Roman system, slaves were degraded. Their status was approximately that of property. Yet by the standards of the Lord Jesus Christ, they are honored citizens with all of the saints of heaven.

There are parallels between Paul's approach at 3:1-7 and his words in 3:17–4-1. In responding to the advocates of circumcision, Paul recited his credentials as a circumcised and observant Jew, stressing his lineage as a member of the tribe of Benjamin. However, he then discredited these credentials, indicating that, in comparison to the worth of knowing Christ, these credentials were *skybala* ("refuse, offscouring"). Paul now employs a comparable approach against a different set of opponents: Nero and the Roman authorities. Paul possesses Roman citizenship, the primary benefit that these authorities can confer. Yet he now disparages this credential on the grounds that it is eclipsed by the citizenship of heaven. In 3:20b Paul continues to refer to heaven, stating that it is from heaven that **"we await a savior, the Lord Jesus Christ"** (*sōtēra apekdechometha kyrion Iēsoun Christon*).

Paul's attribution of "savior" to Jesus occurs within the context of the widespread use of *sōtēr* by Augustus and his successors, including Claudius and Nero. Claudius was hailed as "god, savior, and benefactor" (*theos sōtēr kai euergetēs*) in an inscription from Aesani and as "savior of the world" (*sōtēr tas oikēmenas*) in an inscription from Eresi (Tellbe 2001, 253). Nero was hailed as "savior of the world" (*sōtēr tēs oikoumenēs*) in Egypt and as "benefactor and savior of the world" (*ton euergetan kai sōtēra tas oikēmenas*) at Eresi (ibid.). According to Deissmann (1978, 364), Nero also coined the adjectival form "world-saving" or "belonging to the world savior" (*sōsikosmios*).

In 3:20 "savior (*sōtēr*) is linked with both "lord" (*kyrios*) and "Christ" (*Christos*). This is the sole instance in which *sōtēr* appears linked with *kyrios* in Paul's undisputed letters, and the combination with *Christos* represents an unsurpassed acclamation of Jesus. Bornhauser (1938, 14) holds that *Christos* encompasses the meaning of "king" in this verse and asserts that Paul is attributing to Jesus three of Nero's most highly prized titles: "lord," "savior," and "caesar"="king."

In 3:21 Paul indicates a precise way in which Jesus will save. He **"will change the body of our weakness to be similar in form to his body of glory"** (*metaschēmatisei to sōma tēs tapeinōseōs hēmōn symmorphon tō sōmati tēs doxēs autou*). When *symmorphon* in 3:21 is translated as "similar in form," the following pattern of usage then is evident:

2:6 "the *form* of God" (*morphē theou*)
2:7 "the *form* of a slave" (*morphēn doulou*)
3:10 "taking the *form* of his death" (*symmorphizomenos tō thanatō autou*)
3:21 "similar in *form* to his body of glory" (*symmorphon tō sōmati tēs doxēs autou*)

Conceptually there is a link between Paul's being "conformed" to Christ's death and then being conformed to Christ's body of glory.

In addition to "body of our weakness," another possible rendering for *sōma tēs tapeinōseōs* is "our fragile body." Whatever the precise translation, Paul is emphasizing that, while the existing weak human body can be degraded (and killed) by those who glory in their shame, Jesus alone has the power to effect a transformation of the present fragile human body into a "body of glory" like his own.

Once again, Paul is claiming unsurpassed power for Jesus, who is Lord and Savior. This power enables him "**to subject *all* things to himself**" (*hypotaxai autō ta panta*). There is *nothing* that is not subject to Christ's power.

What Paul states regarding Christ in 3:18-21 corresponds in three ways with what he states regarding the Father in 2:9-11. (Reumann 2008, 602, regards these two passages as "the two peaks" of the letter.) First, in 2:9-11 the Father manifests power in bringing the self-emptied, Roman-crucified Jesus to a position of unsurpassed glory. In 3:21a, Jesus himself is portrayed having the power to transform the fragile and vulnerable human body into a body of glory like his own.

Second, just at the Father's power in 2:9-11 is universal in scope, so is Jesus's power universal in scope. In 3:21b, Jesus has the power to subject "all things" (*panta*) to himself. In 2:11, the Father requires that "every tongue" (*pasa glōssa*) confess Jesus as sovereign Lord.

Third, in 3:18-21 and 2:9-11 Jesus and the Father exercise their power positively and negatively. In 2:9-11 the Father effects the exaltation of Jesus and (implicitly) the saving of those who generously confess that Jesus is Lord. In 3:18-21 Jesus confers a body of glory by reason of his sovereign power.

As for the negative consequences, 2:9-11 portrays the Father bringing those who carried out Jesus's crucifixion into eternal prostration. In 3:19 those who have degraded the human body and perpetrated other evils are subject to "annihilation."

Paul closes this section with a sentence that expresses his deep affection for the Philippians (4:1): "**And so, brethren, my beloved, my longed for, my joy and crown, in this way stand firm in the Lord, my beloved.**" The words "and so" (*hōste*) at the beginning of 4:1 recall Paul's preceding characterization of the opponents' destruction and the Christians' salvation from Christ. Paul is now moving to exhort the Philippians to stand firm. Hearkening back to his words in 3:17, the Philippians are to be imitators of Paul in doing so. The salvation and annihilation Paul has just mentioned are motivations for their conduct.

Paul uses the vocative "my beloved" (*agapētoi*) at the beginning of his sentence and at the very end (4:1a and 4:1c). These terms bracket the related term "my longed for" (*epipothētoi*). Paul is asking great self-sacrifice from the Philippian Christians in this letter. He formulates his requests in the context of his abiding love for them.

Further signs of his affection are expressed in the terms "joy" (*chara*) and "crown" (*stephanos*) in 4:1b. Paul has previously linked these two entities in 1 Thess 2:19. *Stephanos* references the woven crown, a wreath of wild olive, green parsley, bay, or pine awarded to the victors at athletic contests (Vincent 1902, 129). The Philippians are, in effect, Paul's victory crown. Elsewhere in this letter, Christ is the principal source of Paul's joy (see on 2:17-18). Here the Philippians themselves constitute a reason for his joy.

The verb "stand firm" (*stēkete*) has appeared earlier in 1:27. It is modified here by "in the Lord" (*en kyriō*). (Paul uses *en kyriō* over forty times in Philippians.) The Philippians are to view themselves as standing firm *in communion* with the Lord. They are to see themselves joining with Paul and *with Christ* in maintaining a line of formation.

Philippians 4:2-3
XIII. Entreaty to Euodia and Synteche

Introductory Comments

Paul's emphasis in this section is on encouragement. Two subsections constitute this section. In 4:2-3, Paul is specifically concerned to encourage two prominent Philippian women in the cause of unity, and in 4:4-9, he encourages the Philippian community as a whole in noblemindedness and prayer.

Tracing the Train of Thought

Paul begins to draw his letter to a close by attending to a specific pastoral matter. In 4:2-3 he attempts to reconcile a dispute between two women who are prominent in the life of the community: "**I encourage Euodia and I encourage Synteche to think the same thing in the Lord**" (*Euodian parakalō kai Syntychēn parakalō to auto phronein en kyriō*).

Paul evidently appreciates both of these women and the role that they have played in the community at Philippi. He addresses each by name. Their dispute is evidently a matter of grave concern to him; he gives *public* encouragement to them for its resolution.

The name Euodia is derived from *eu*, "well," and *hodos*, "way," and has the meaning "Prosperous Journey" (Fee 1995, 390). The name Synteche is derived from *syn* "with" and *Tyche*, the proper name of the goddess of Fortune. The probable meaning is "Fortunate" or "Lucky." Such a name might be given to a slave. It is remotely possible that Synteche might have been the name of the slave girl from whom Paul expelled the demonic spirit in Acts 16.

If either of these prominent women was a slave or former slave, this would represent an additional dimension of Paul's response to the circumstances of slaves in this letter. As just noted for 3:20, the phenomenon of a slave playing a prominent role in a Christian community is not without historical parallel. Pliny identified two slave women as "ministers" (*ministrae*) within the Christian community of Bithynia-Pontus before he tortured them.

In 4:3a, Paul asks another associate to help reconcile the dispute between Euodia and Synteche: "**And I ask you also, genuine companion, to help these women**" (*nai erōtō kai se gnēsie syzyge syllambanou autais*). The word translated here as "companion" (*syzygos*) has been taken to be a proper name, but such a proper name is unattested in the ancient world (Marshall 1991, 109). Paul has close bonds with the companion whom he addresses here since *syzygos* means literally "with a yoke."

Paul is probably referring to Timothy in using this term, but it is possible that he is referring to Epaphroditus. In 2:20 Paul used the adverbial form "genuinely" (*gynēsiōs*) in speaking of Timothy. Further, if the dispute between Euodia and Synteche involves their attitudes toward the imperial authorities (see below) Timothy would be familiar with Paul's own perspective and thus well qualified to mediate.

Paul addresses both women with appreciation. He repeats the word "encourage" (*parakalō*) for each woman. Paul's entire phrasing indicates that these women have high standing with him. In 4:3a he states that they have **"struggled together with me for the gospel"** This is high praise: to be *with Paul* in struggling for the gospel (Christ).

Paul also states that their names **"are recorded in the book of life along with Clement and my other co-workers."** Here Paul implies that the specific service these two women and Clement have rendered for Christ is recognized in heaven. Bruce (1991, 139) uses the term "the burgess roll of the heavenly commonwealth" in striving to capture what Paul envisions when he writes "book of life." Paul acclaims Clement by name without giving additional background. Two other "co-workers" (*synergōn*) not identified by name are also acclaimed.

In urging that Euodia and Synteche "think the same thing in the Lord" Paul implies that they do not have a unified outlook. What is the issue of their dispute? Reumann (2008, 628–33) discusses six areas in which a dispute between these two women co-workers might have emerged. The subject of their disagreement is impossible to determine. Nevertheless, one of Reumann's suggestions (that the conflict regards appropriate conduct vis-à-vis the imperial authorities) merits particular consideration in light of an earlier passage in Philippians.

The expression that Paul uses at 4:3a, "struggled together for the gospel with me" (*en tō euangeliō synēthlēsan moi*), is very similar to his wording previously in 1:27. At 1:27c when Paul wrote, "struggling together for the faith of the gospel" (*synathlountes tē pistei tou euangeliou*), he had in view a struggle involving the Roman authorities at Philippi. In that context, he recommended unity: "with one mind" (*mia psychē*). Now in 4:3, Paul specifically implores Euodia and Synteche to reach unity ("to think the same thing in the Lord"). Perhaps this is a further instance in which unity is needed so that the threat posed by the Roman authorities can be withstood. It is also possible that unity is needed because the dispute revolves around the status of slaves who are Christians at Philippi.

Philippians 4:4-9
XIV. Encouragement to Rejoice and Be Grounded in Christ

Introductory Comments

In the verses that follow Paul moves beyond the matter of the reconciliation of Euodia and Synteche to provide encouragement for the community as a whole. Philippians 4:4-9 can be analyzed in terms of two subsections, 4:4-7 and 4:8-9. Each of these subsections ends with encouraging words regarding peace.

Tracing the Train of Thought

Paul begins his first subsection with two imperatives (4:4-5a): **"Rejoice in the Lord always and again I say it, rejoice. Let your gentleness be evident to all."** An indicative affirmation follows (4:5b): **"The Lord is near."** An extended imperative then follows (4:6): **"Do not be anxious about anything, but let your requests about everything be made known to God through prayers and petition made with thanksgiving."** Paul then concludes with an indicative sentence regarding peace (4:7): **"And the peace of God which surpasses all understanding will garrison your hearts and minds in Christ Jesus."**

In his first imperative, Paul urges the Philippians to rejoice always "in the Lord" (*en kyriō*). One dimension of Paul's meaning here is that the Philippians have the Lord as an *object* of their rejoicing. Moreover, the Philippians are also *in communion* with their Lord as they rejoice.

With his second imperative, Paul urges "gentleness" (*epieikes*). The meaning of this rare term is illumined by Paul's use of its cognate noun in 2 Cor 10:1, where Paul refers to "the gentleness of Christ" (*epieikeias tou Christou*).

Paul similarly affirms two dimensions of meaning in his brief but decisive indicative statement (4:5b): "The Lord is near" (*ho kyrios engys*). Paul affirms to the Philippians that their Lord is near to them in terms of his presence. Even now the Philippians have close communion with him. Yet the time of the Lord's ultimate arrival is also near. Christ's arrival with full power and majesty is close at hand. This temporal dimension in Paul's meaning hearkens back to 3:20-21. In 3:20 *apekdechometha* was used to express that Paul and the Philippians *"eagerly await"* the decisive arrival of Lord Jesus. Paul now affirms that Christ's arrival is "near."

It is useful to identify what Paul visualizes regarding Jesus's portentous advent. His words in 1 Thess 4:16-17 are suggestive: "For the Lord himself will descend from heaven with a cry of command, with the archangel's call, and with the sound of the trumpet of God . . . and so we shall always be with the Lord."

The Philippians' familiarity with the ceremonies heralding the arrival of Roman imperial figures undoubtedly constituted the context for their appreciation of what Paul was affirming regarding Jesus's arrival. An inscription that was erected at Cos commemorating the inflated arrival of Gaius Casear, Augustus's adopted son, may have been known at Philippi. The exact day of an imperial arrival became the first day of a new year (Deissmann 1978, 370). The date at which any emperor arrived in a given city could occasion a proclamation of that date as a "holy" day (Price 1984a, 105).

To commemorate the vainglorious arrival of Nero at Corinth and Patras during his Greek tour in AD 67, special "arrival" coins were minted in each city. In honor of his imperial visit, the city of Acraephiae published a decree acclaiming Nero as "the lord of the entire world" (*ho tou pantos kosmou kyrios Nerōn*) (Deissmann 1978, 354). In addition to his praetorians, a considerable number of upper echelon officials traveled with Nero on this grand tour.

As noted previously, Nero gained victories in all the events held at six festivals. His lieutenants enforced the cooperation of each festival's organizers and judges. They also secured the subservience of all who ventured to compete against Nero (Champlin 2003, 58–61).

Further Nero's guards wantonly committed murder on the emperor's behalf. According to Dio Cassius (62.11.1), Nero ordered the murder of numerous inhabitants of the sites he visited and many of the prominent Romans who had accompanied him to Greece. Dio (62.11.4) states that Nero's couriers "hurried back and forth bearing no other communication than 'Put this man to death' or 'So-and-so is dead.'" To the degree that Dio's reports are credible, the arrival of Nero in the cities of Greece was the advent of a *kakourgos kyrios*, "a crime lord."

Paul's third imperative in this passage occurs in 4:6 when he urges: "Do not be anxious about anything" (*mēden merimnate*). Facing persecution, Paul's readers have, on one level, much to be anxious about. Yet Paul counsels prayer made with thanksgiving" (*meta eucharistias*) and "petition" (*tē deēsei*) as well as "requests" (*aitēmata*). In 4:7 Paul characterizes the result of such prayers: "the peace of God (*hē eirēnē tou theou*) which surpasses all understanding will garrison their hearts and minds in Christ Jesus" (*kai he eirēne tou theou he hyperechousa panta noun phrourēsei tas kardias hymōn kai ta noēmata hymōn en Christō Iesou*).

In virtually every Roman province, the *pax Augustana* was heralded as Augustus's most enduring achievement. Philo remarks (*Embassy* 147) that in Egypt Augustus was esteemed as "the guardian of peace" (*ho eirēnophylax*). In contrast, Paul now stresses the decisiveness of "the peace of God." Paul also employs a term with a military nuance that would have easily been grasped at Philippi. He emphasizes that God's peace will "garrison" (*phrourēsei*) the Philippians' hearts and minds.

Paul begins his second subsection in 4:8 by encouraging the Philippians to "think on" (*tauta logizesthe*) six specific virtues and then to aspire to all that is virtuous: "whatever is true (*hosa estin alēthē*), whatever is noble (*hosa semna*), whatever is just (*hosa dikaia*), whatever is pure (*hosa hagna*), whatever is lovely (*hosa prosphilē*), whatever is honorable (*hosa euphēma*)." He then invites the embrace of all other virtues: "if there is anything of moral excellence or praise" (*ei tis aretē kai ei tis epainos*).

Various commentators have noted that the positive qualities listed here are similar to concepts that occur in contemporary Stoic moral exhortations. Bockmuel considers this an example of how Paul takes over familiar concepts of ethics and integrates them in his overall catechesis (1998, 250). In 2:1, Paul's encouragement for the "mindset" the Philippians are to adopt is similarly structured but permeated more deeply by virtues proper to Christ and the Spirit.

In 4:9 Paul proposes his own practice as a model for the Philippians: "and practice the things you have learned and received and heard and seen in me" (*ha kai emathete kai parelabete kai ēkousate kai eidete en emoi tauta prassete*). This counsel echoes 3:17, where Paul advocated that the Philippians jointly "imitate" (*symmimētai*) him. Clearly Paul is not "ashamed" to present such counsels from the "shameful" condition of his Roman chains. Indeed, Paul's invitation implies that he considers himself an example of how to testify boldly that Jesus is Lord within hostile Roman surroundings.

When the Philippians imitate Paul's practice, they will experience the God of peace overshadowing them: "and the God of peace will be with you" (*kai ho theos tēs eirēnēs estai meth' hymōn*). Paul has used "the God of peace" previously in 1 Thess 5:23; 2 Cor 13:11; Rom 15:33; 16:20. This term is close in meaning to "the peace of God," the phrase Paul used just above at 4:7a (O'Brien 1991, 512). As with "the peace of God," the phrase "God of peace" counters the *pax Augustana* heralded at Philippi and beyond.

Philippians 4:10-20
XV. Response to the Philippians' Gift

Introductory Comments

In 4:10-20 Paul makes his response to the gift that the Philippians have sent to him in care of Epaphroditus. His response is highly nuanced. Remarkably, Paul never *explicitly* thanks the Philippians for this gift, nor does he indicate how it will be of use to him. In careful language Paul characterizes the Philippians' gift as an offering that is highly pleasing to God, an offering that credits the Philippians themselves.

The exposition that follows will focus on the monetary character of the Philippians' gift. The very *form* of this gift is what caused Paul to be so measured and restrained in responding to it.

Tracing the Train of Thought

Paul begins his response to the Philippians' gift with a reemphasis on the joy he has in the Lord and with a review of the Philippians' patterns of concern and support for him (4:10): **"I greatly rejoiced in the Lord that now at length you have renewed your concern for my affairs about which you were concerned but had no opportunity."**

Paul probably uses the aorist *echarēn* ("rejoiced") at the outset of 4:10a to indicate the joy that he felt when Epaphroditus first arrived.

Paul had presumably experienced a break in contact with the community at Philippi (4:10b). This break may have been a consequence of Paul having become a chained prisoner in the imperial capital.

Paul shares that during the interval in which he did not receive support from the Philippians he still continued well. In 4:11 he writes, "**I do not complain of want because I have learned to be content in whatever circumstances I find myself**" (*ouch hoti kath' hysterēsin legō egō gar emathon en hois eimi autarkēs einai*). An alternative translation for Paul's first affirmation regarding his situation would be, "Not that I speak because of want" (Zerwick/Grosvenor 1988, 601).

To indicate that he is "content" in all circumstances, Paul uses the term *autarkēs*. This word was used by Socrates as well as other Stoics in reference to someone who was fully self-sufficient. Bruce (1991, 150) observes that Paul uses this term to express that he is not so much self-sufficient as "Christ-sufficient."

In 4:12 Paul uses three contrasting word pairs to indicate his ability to maintain his equilibrium in diverse circumstances. He has learned "**how to be abased** (*tapeinousthai*) **and how to abound** (*perisseuein*)." He has learned the secret of "**facing plenty** (*chortazesthai*) **and hunger** (*peinan*), **whether abounding** (*perisseuein*) **or needy** (*hystereisthai*)." In effect, if Paul is abased, he can cope. If he faces hunger, he can subsist. If he is needy, he can manage.

What might have influenced Paul to state so emphatically that limitations in his circumstances do not impact his ability to cope well? Paul may be following such a course with a view to preparing the Philippians for his decision *not* to utilize their gift. He will still be "sufficient" without utilizing the money that Epaphroditus has brought.

In 4:13 Paul forswears any credit for having learned the meaning of sufficiency. It is Christ who empowers (*endynamounti*) him: "**I can do all things in him who empowers me.**" In 3:10, Paul used the cognate form *tēn dynamin* to refer to the "power" of Christ's resurrection.

In 4:14 Paul focuses on the gift that the Philippians have sent to him. As noticed by Peterlin (1997, 121–61) and others, Paul does not use *eucharisteō* ("I thank you") or otherwise express his gratitude directly. Rather, Paul comments that it was good of the Philippians to keep communion with him in his current travail: "**Nevertheless you did well in keeping communion with me in my affliction.**"

As noted, an important theme of the letter is the communion (*koinōnia*) that exists between Paul and the Philippians. Paul here uses a compound term, "keeping communion" (*synkoinōnēsantes*), to indicate that the Philippians have communion with him in his present situation. His present situation is that of "affliction" (*thlipsei*). He has used *thlipsis* with a similar meaning in 1:17.

Paul then reviews the history of his "communion" (*koinōnia*) with the Philippians, highlighting the fact that he has previously accepted financial support *only* from them (4:15-16): "**Now you yourselves, Philippians, know that from the beginning of the gospel, when I first set out from Macedonia, no church maintained communion with me as to an account of giving and receiving except you only and that even in Thessalonica you sent support for my needs now and again.**"

Paul here uses the vocative *Philippēsioi* ("Philippians") in addressing the community members. The spelling of this word may reflect that he has taken the Latin word *Philippenses* and rendered it into Greek. To use this Latin-based word instead of the more usual *Philippeis* may mean that Paul is acknowledging the Roman orientation of many at Philippi (O'Brien 1991, 531).

Paul's affirmation is that he has accepted financial support for his ministry *only* from the Philippians. Only with them does he have an "account" (*logon*) for giving and receiving. (In 2 Cor 11:7-12 Paul emphasizes that he did not take support from the Corinthians because he was supplied by brethren who came "from Macedonia.") Indeed, Paul has *repeatedly* received such support from the Philippians. The Greek adverbial phrase *hapax kai dis* means "now and again" (Sumney 2007, 116). The giving and receiving that Paul references here is a manifestation of the communion (*koinōnia*) that Paul shares with the Philippians in Christ.

Paul's use of *ekklēsia* in 4:15 indicates that the Philippians do not support Paul as a loosely defined Christian group. Rather they support him as a defined entity, the "church" of Philippi. Paul uses *ekklēsia* to refer to the Christian congregation of a given city in 1 Thess 1:1, 1 Cor 1:2, 2 Cor 1:1, Gal 1:2, and Phlm 2. He employs *ekklēsia* with this meaning here. This usage contrasts with Phil 3:6, where Paul uses *ekklēsia* more broadly in reference to his persecution of the Christians of Judea and Syria.

In Greek secular literature as well as in the Septuagint, *ekklēsia*'s fundamental meaning is that of "assembly" (O'Brien 1991, 377). In Macedonia the citizen body (*polituema*) met as a popular assembly (*ekklēsia*) (Hatzopoulos 2011, 240). In Philippi itself there is reference to the *ekklēsia* of the *dēmos* (the "assembly" of the "populace") (Koukouli-Chrysanthaki 2011, 444).

Having affirmed the past generosity of the Philippian congregation, Paul proceeds to give his response to the new gift that Epaphroditus has brought (4:17): "**Not that I seek the gift, but I seek the interest that accrues to your account.**" Paul's use of several commerce-related terms is notable in 4:17. First, "gift" (*doma*) may have the meaning of "money" or "payment" (LSJ 1968, 44). Commentators such as Bormann (1995, 27), Marshall (1992, 122), Walter, Reinmuth, and Lampe (1998, 70, 99–100), and Fee (1995, 278) hold that Epaphroditus has brought a *monetary* gift to Paul. Philippi possessed an imperial mint (Kremydi 2011, 177–78; cf. Levick 1967, 161), and it is likely that the Philippians' gift consisted of the imperial coins minted there, coins on which the countenances of Nero and other Julio-Claudians were represented along with their authorized titles. [See examples of such coins in this book's appendix on Roman imperial coinage.]

Paul's second commerce-related term is "interest" (*karpon*), a term that also occurs in 1:11 and 22. Paul's third mercantile term is "accrues" (*pleonazonta*). Martin (1976, 167) asserts that it is a regular banking term for financial growth. O'Brien (1991, 538) holds that *pleonazonta* has commercial nuances in the present passage. Paul's fourth "commercial" term is *logon*. He uses it here (as above in 4:15) in the sense of "account." *Logos* with such a monetary meaning is frequently encountered in extant papyri (Moulton-Milligan 1930, 379).

Paul uses *epizēteō* twice in 4:17 to express what he desires and what he does not desire. In the introductory dependent clause *epizēteō* is preceded by *ouch hoti* and has the meaning: "Not that I seek." In other words, Paul's introductory clause proclaims: I *do not seek* this gift.

His principal clause then discloses the following: "But I *do seek* the interest that accrues to your account." O'Brien (1991, 538) underscores the adversative force of *alla*, "but," at the beginning of this second clause. Paul is emphatic about what he is seeking and what he is *not* seeking.

Fundamentally, Paul is declining the Philippians' gift. Nevertheless, he is quite careful to indicate his appreciation for their generosity. Because he is not accepting their gift, Paul has no need to indicate possible uses to which it might be put. His outlook on their gift does not prevent him from being deeply appreciative of what the Philippians *intended* to do for him.

Before proceeding to conjecture regarding Paul's motive for rejecting the Philippians' offering, it is useful to review the scope of Epaphroditus's commitment to get this gift to Paul in Rome. Each of the following steps required Epaphroditus's self-sacrifce and perseverance. Epaphroditus himself may have contributed money to the collection for Paul. This collection was probably taken up surreptitiously to avoid interference from the colony's magistrates. Epaphroditus was then designated to transport these funds. On the model of 2 Cor 11:9 (cf. 1 Cor 16:13; 2 Cor 8:16-24), Epaphroditus was probably accompanied on his mission by other Philippian Christians. If Fee is correct in surmising that Epaphroditus was transporting "a considerable sum of money" (1995, 278), the need for Epaphroditus to be accompanied by others from Philippi was all the more compelling.

If Epaphroditus was a praetorian veteran or a member of the *familia caesaris* (see on 4:22), the potential for difficulties with the Roman soldiers on the Via Egnatia and at the ports of Dyrrhachium and Brundisium would have been diminished. Nevertheless, the transportation of money across provincial boundaries was still a risky proposition, even though the Via Egnatia was a guarded Roman road. Nickle (1966, 83) cites the Babylonian Talmud in reference to paid security guards who assisted in the transportation of the annual collection for the Jerusalem temple.

On his arrival in Rome, Epaphroditus might have faced obstacles and even danger in penetrating the security perimeter around Paul. Walter (1998, 70) reflects that it might have been necessary for Epaphroditus to "smuggle" (*schmuggeln*) the gift into Paul's quarters. Alternately, Epaphroditus might have brought only a few sample coins into Paul's place of custody.

Epaphroditus, Paul's truly valued and truly loyal co-worker, conceivably experienced a severe shock when Paul rejected the Philippians' gift! In the interpretation now proposed, Paul expressed his rejection of the Philippians' gift as soon as he learned that it consisted principally of coins bearing imperial images and titelature. In effect, Paul considered that the coins Epaphroditus brought were contaminated by the Julio-Claudian propaganda engraved on them! Despite the Philippians' generosity and despite Epaphroditus's valiant efforts to bring their gift to him, Paul could not accept the proffered gift.

The power of Roman coins for conveying imperial propaganda should not be underestimated. Paul himself may earlier have used coins with the visages of Roman emperors and their titles of acclaim (Koukouli 1998, 23). He might have accepted such tender from the Philippians themselves when they previously sent financial assistance to him.

Paul, however, has now become hypersensitive to the imperial propaganda advanced by these coins. Because Paul now regards Nero as an enemy of the cross of Christ, as an imposter "savior" and as a charlatan "lord," he can have nothing to do with coins that promote this emperor and his idolatrous claims.

The writings of the Stoic philosopher Epictetus indicate that Paul's putative reaction to Nero's coins corresponds with the position that Epictetus himself adopted. Epictetus lived circa AD 55 to AD 135 (von Fritz 1970, 324). He was once a slave owned by the Epaphroditus who served as Nero's trusted and powerful lieutenant. After gaining his freedom, Epictetus gained renown and fame as a Stoic philosopher.

In his *Discourses* (4.5.17), Epictetus gave the following counsel regarding any coin bearing Nero's countenance: "Throw it out, it will not pass, it is rotten" (*ripson, exō, adokimon estin, sapron*). In the first century, Epictetus was heralded for his concern to promote moral character. His familiarity with Nero's depravity may have led him to reject all trafficking in Nero's coins.

If Epictetus adopted a radical stance toward Nero's coins because of his own moral probity, how much more might Paul adopt such a stance on the grounds of his personal allegiance to Jesus. For Nero was not *merely* morally depraved. He was also blasphemously claiming to be "*lord*" and "*savior*"!

Epaphroditus's presumed shocked reaction to Paul's rejection of the Philippians' gift might have alerted Paul to the need for careful wording when he acknowledged the gift in his letter. Paul could speak with Epaphroditus in person and gradually bring him to an appreciation of Paul's perspective regarding these imperial coins. In his letter, Paul must find a way to affirm the Philippians' generosity to him (and to God) while simultaneously conveying to them that he would not make use of their gift.

Paul's next verses (4:18-19) accomplish both of these objectives. He first acknowledges the Philippians' gift and then characterizes it as spiritually beneficial *for them*: "**I am full to overflowing; now that I have received the things sent from you through Epaphroditus, I am abundantly provided for. They are a fragrant offering, an acceptable sacrifice pleasing to God. And my God will provide for all of your needs in accordance with his riches in glory through Christ Jesus.**"

The loving rapport that Paul feels toward the Philippians must be kept in view. He cannot use their monetary gift, yet their generosity (4:18a) has "filled him to overflowing" (*peplērōmai*). As a result of what they have sent through Epaphroditus (4:18b), Paul is "abundantly provided for" (*perisseuō*). Their generosity is "an acceptable sacrifice pleasing to God" (*thysian dektēn euareston tō theō*), who will supply their every need (4:18c).

At the time of the Philippians' *earlier* gift to him, Paul seemingly did not express any reservation about using imperial coins (2 Cor 11:8-9). Also he presumably did not express such a reservation when he asked the Philippians to contribute to the funds that he was collecting for the church in Jerusalem (2 Corinthians 8 and 9).

Paul's perspective has now been fully transformed. He has been deeply radicalized to the implications of his conviction that Jesus *alone* is Lord. Throughout Philippians, Paul testifies consistently to his new insights regarding Roman imperial practices. Yet the good-faith generosity of the Philippians toward him must still be affirmed.

Consider also the delicateness of the task that Epaphroditus and/or Timothy will have as Paul designates them to oversee the reading/performance of his letter. Perhaps it is because of this complexity that Paul presents his comments on the Philippians' gift only at the end of the letter.

Paul concludes this section with a doxology (4:20): "**To our God and Father be glory for ever and ever. Amen.**" *Doxa* ("glory") is now used for the second time in two verses. In 4:19b Paul has indicated that the Philippians will be supplied from "the Father's riches *in glory* in Christ Jesus" (*to ploutos autou en doxē en Christō Iēsou*).

Philippians 4:21-23
XVI. Concluding Greeting and Benediction

Introductory Comments

Paul ends his letter with two verses imparting greetings and a final verse imparting grace. Paul begins with an imperative to greet "all the saints" at Philippi (4:21a), followed by greetings from Paul's immediate companions and greetings from the others at his present location (4:21b-22). The final verse then imparts the grace (*charis*) of Christ (4:23).

Tracing the Train of Thought

Paul uses three forms of *aspazomai* ("to greet") in two verses. In 4:21a Paul's writes "every saint" (*panta hagion*), seemingly to indicate that his greetings should be given to every saint, women as well as men, slave as well as free: "**Greet every saint in Christ Jesus.**" In 4:21b he continues, "**The brethren who are with me greet you.**" Presumably this greeting comes from Timothy, Epaphroditus, and others in Paul's circle of co-workers. Then in 4:22a he broadly indicates that "**all the saints**" (*pantes hoi hagioi*) send greetings. These latter words represent a generous gesture on Paul's part when it is recalled that a minority of the Roman Christian community has been working to marginalize him (1:15, 17).

In 4:22b Paul then specifies that greetings come from "**especially the members of Caesar's household**" (*malista hoi ek tēs Kaisaros oikias*). This last greeting deserves to be examined from several vantage points.

Beginning with Augustus, the term *domus Caesaris* (literally "house of the emperor") was a term encompassing the emperor's family and friends. In addition, it encompasses the *libertini/ae* and slaves who served in the emperor's households in various locations as well as those who functioned as staff in the various departments that Augustus created for the administration of the empire. The bureaucracy established by Augustus expanded dramatically under Claudius (Millar 1984, 74–76).

Weaver (1972, 6–7) treats the titles and functions of those who served in the the emperor's domestic staff as well as those who served in his various administrative departments. Domestic staff positions included food preparation, wardrobe oversight, gardening and entertainment. Lightfoot (1888, 172) lists the grades, subgrades, and Latin titles of the domestic staff. Abbott (1911, 362) identifies *a rationibus* (financial matters), *ab epistulis* (imperial correspondence), *a libellis* (petitions), *a cognitionibus* (juridical inquiries), and *a memoria* (imperial speech preparation) as the emperors' leading administrative bureaus.

The great majority of *familia caesaris* members were concentrated in Rome. However, they served also at imperial sites throughout the provinces. At least some members or former members of the *familia caesaris* were present at Philippi. Bockmuel (1998, 27) notes that a public inscription was erected in Philippi in AD 36 or 37 by three of Augustus's *libertini*.

Because his letter to the Philippians is preeminently about the lordship of Jesus, Paul's reference to those who are in the service of "lord" Caesar deserves careful consideration. Paul use of the plural *hoi* ("those") indicates that more than one member of Caesar's "family" is in his view. Presumably those whom Paul mentions are Christians or catechumens. Were they Christian prior to Paul's arrival or did he evangelize them while in chained custody? If these members of the *familia caesaris* became Christians prior to Paul's arrival, they must have aligned themselves with the majority who supported Paul despite his chains (1:14, 16).

Some members of the *familia caesaris* might have first become attracted to Christianity when they investigated Paul's custody. Officials of the imperial *a cognitionibus* (literally "inquiry") department were charged with collecting information and preparing assessments for judicial cases awaiting the emperor's determination (Abbott 1911, 362). Conceivably staff from other imperial departments might also have had direct contact with Paul. If any of the *familia caesaris* members who lived at Philippi were Christians, it is possible that they might have advised their counterparts at Rome to seek out Paul.

As noted above, Christians who held positions in the *familia caesaris* could have been a source of information regarding Nero's depravities and his gangsterism. The praetorian guards were not Paul's only source of information regarding the emperor.

The importance of the greetings given by the Christians who are members of the *familia caesaris* is underscored by Paul's use of the adverb "especially" (*malista*) in 4:22b. Their greetings afford support for Paul's claim at 1:12 that what has happened to him has served to advance the cause of Christ. If Paul evangelized the members of this group himself, then clearly his ministry in Rome was bearing fruit, despite his chains. Even if he did not evangelize them, Paul still is able to appreciate the fact that these members of the imperial household are maintaining *communion* with him.

More importantly, they have communion with Paul's *Lord*. They are in the service of "lord" Nero, but their fundamental allegiance is to Lord Jesus. This itself offers encouragement to the Christians at Philippi suffering persecution from the imperial officials there. Not all imperial officials disdain the lordship of Jesus. There are actually members of the imperial staff at Rome who profess that Jesus *is* Lord.

These Christians from Nero's bureaus are presumably willing to have Paul advert to their allegiance to Jesus in general terms. Their situation may be extremely delicate. In the event that Paul's letter is intercepted by those guarding him, Nero's agents will presumably act quickly to learn the names of those within Nero's household who are partisans of Jesus. It may be for security concerns that Paul, in writing this letter, does not identify a single *Roman* Christian by name.

Paul's conclusion now follows (4:23): "**The grace of the Lord Jesus Christ be with your spirit.**" In its form and vocabulary the verse is exactly the same as Phlm 24 and closely resembles 1 Thess 5:28 and Gal 6:18. Harrison observes that the letters of the Pauline corpus, disputed as well as undisputed, all close with some form of the *charis* benediction (2003, 242).

In his letters prior to Philippians, Paul may not have employed *charis* as a counter to the emperor cult. In those letters Paul's concern may have been solely to close with an affirmation that the "benevolent power" of Christ and the Father be bestowed on the recipients of the letter. As a result of his communications with the Christians of Rome and his interactions with the praetorians who guarded him, Paul has now become aware of the ways in which *charis* ("power") was being attributed to such emperors as Claudius and Nero. Under these new circumstances, Paul's use of *charis* in his concluding verse would have a dimension of meaning over and beyond the meaning present when he used this term in his earlier letters.

In AD 63, Gaius Tuscus, the prefect of Egypt, informed military veterans disgruntled over their compensation that their concerns would be resolved according to *hē charis tou kyriou*, according to the "favor" or "power" of the lord (Harrison 2003, 88; Arzt-Grabner 2011, 4, both citing P. Fouad. 21). Since he is the regnant emperor, Nero is "the lord" mentioned in this edict, and he holds the "power" (*charis*) to resolve the veterans' concerns benevolently.

Claudius predated Nero, but an edict reporting a key decision by Claudius apparently was not published in Egypt until AD 68. In this edict, the new prefect of Egypt, Tiberius Alexander, formally proclaimed that a reduction in taxes had earlier been effected *tou theou Klaudiou charitie*, "according to the 'favor' or 'power' of the god Claudius" (Harrison 2003, 48, citing OGIS 669). Here again, *charis* ultimately pertains to imperial *power*.

An additional example in which *charis* is attributed to the ruling emperor comes from an inscription at Ephesus recounting that several cities of Asia enjoyed their free status as a result of the *charis* of the emperor (Friesen 1993, 38). In this inscription the emperor's power is proclaimed to have been exercised benevolently on behalf of these Asian cities.

In the light of such attributions of *charis* to the emperor, Paul's use of *charis* at the close of Philippians takes on an added dimension of meaning. Paul's benediction affirms that Christ *alone* is the source of benevolent power. His benediction implicitly *denies* that the Roman emperor is an authentic source of *charis*.

The claims of Claudius and Nero to have authentic majesty and wield benevolent power are a sham. That they or any Julio-Claudian actually intends benevolence for the subjected peoples of the empire is a hoax. Contrary to the AD 68 inscription, Claudius is *not* "the god" (*ho theos*); contrary to the AD 63 inscription, Nero is *not* "the lord" (*ho kyrios*).

When they present the closing verses of this momentous letter, Timothy and Epaphroditus will be called on to communicate, by their diction and their gestures, Paul's deeply counter-imperial meaning. As Paul's trusted co-workers, schooled in the meaning of what this slave of Jesus has just written, they will presumably proclaim faithfully and emphatically that Jesus Christ and the Father possess and manifest *all power, all benevolence, all majesty, all glory*.

Appendix I
CARTOGRAPHY

Map of the Route between Philippi and Rome.

Erich Gaba's brilliant rendering of the entire route from Philippi to Rome by land over the Via Egnatia, by ship across the Adriatic Sea, and then by land over the Via Appia makes it possible to see with a glance the entire route Epaphroditus would have traveled in bringing Paul's gift from Philippi to Rome (Phil 4:18).

Cartographer Gaba has most graciously adopted and enhanced his previous map for use within the present commentary. Not only is the route of Epaphroditus's impressive journey illuminated. This modified map also clarifies the route that Paul traveled from Neapolis to Philippi and then from Philippi to Thessalonica (Acts 16:11-12; 17:1).

Conjecture regarding Epaphroditus's challenge in traversing the Via Egnatia, the Adriatic Sea, and then the Via Appia is provided in the commentary proper. The speed with which imperial documents could be sent over this same route is a factor that deserves careful consideration. The *cursus publicus*, the imperial postal service, commonly transmitted a document a distance of 75 kilometers per day. However, special dispatches could be transmitted via the *cursus velox*, at double this distance per day.

The ease of potentially ominous imperial communications between Rome and Philippi has implications for the trial of Paul in Rome and the persecution of Christians at Philippi. Queries about Paul could be sent expeditiously to the magistrates of Philippi by those charged with administering Paul's case in Rome. Conversely, the Philippian magistrates could also use the *cursus velox* in order to gain information about prisoner Paul with a view to undermining the Christians of Philippi.

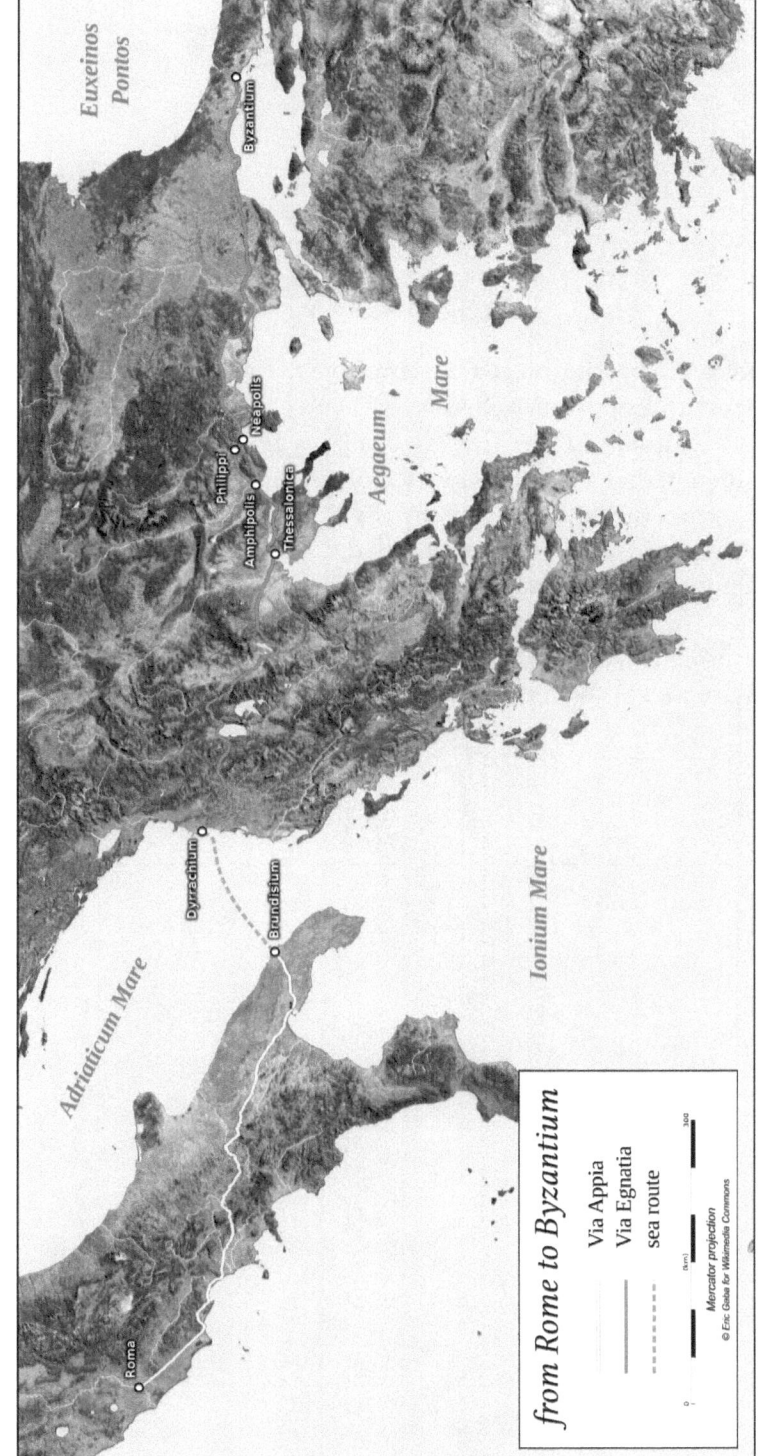

Figure I-2
Via Egnatia near Neapolis

As indicated by the preceding large map, the Via Egnatia connects Philippi with its port of Neapolis on the Aegean Sea. According to Acts 16:11-12 Paul sailed from Troas to Neapolis and then proceeded by land to Philippi perhaps over these very stones. Paul would have approached Philippi from the east, entering the city through the Neapolis Gate.

The Roman military constructed the Via Egnatia and other roads according to standardized code, sometimes impressing slaves to do so. The costs of the Via Egnatia were born by the Roman treasury, by the lands through which it passed, and by those traveling the road. (This photo licensed by Wiki Commons.)

Figure I-2

Figure I-3
Via Egnatia Bordering Philippi's Forum

Philippi owed its strategic and commercial significance to its location straddling the Via Egnatia. Vendors and traders from as far away as Byzantium could make their way to Philippi and ultimately to Rome with *relative* ease and security.

In this westward facing photo, Amphipolis and Thessalonica (Paul's next two stops according to Acts 17:1) are over the horizon, but Paul only needed to stay on the Via Egnatia in order to reach them. Much later, in bringing the Philippians' gift to Paul in Rome (Phil 2:25-30; 4:18), Epaphroditus himself presumably traveled westward over the Via Egnatia. (This photo licensed by WikiCommons.)

Figure I-3

Figure I-4
The City Plan of Philippi

The city plan of Philippi identifies the relative location of Philippi's gates and its principal buildings. The Neapolis Gate and the Gate of Crenides have particular importance as the gates by which the Via Egnatia entered and exited the city. Within the city this road cut a nearly straight line and was designated the Decumanus Maximus.

From the east, Paul would have entered Philippi through the Neapolis Gate, perhaps turning to the right to view Philippi's impressive theater. Traveling west toward Thessalonica, Paul would have departed through the Crenides Gate. (Image used with permission of Samuel Provost and Michael Boyd.)

APPENDIX I: CARTOGRAPHY | 155

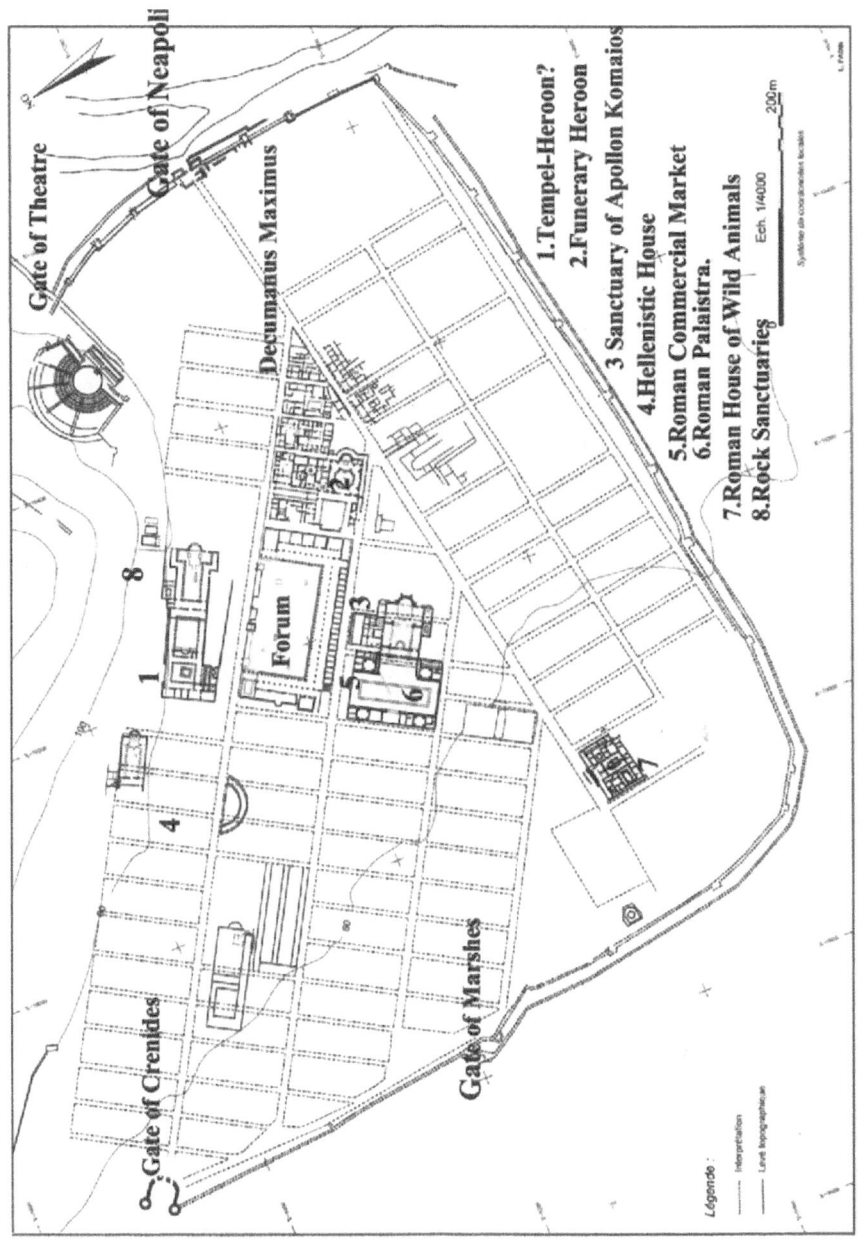

Figure I-4

Figure I-5
Map of the Forum and Commercial Market of Philippi

This map indicates the prominence of Philippi's forum. The forum was centrally positioned within the city and was bordered on the north by the Via Egnatia. Occupying 10 percent of the city's surface area, the forum was the center of the colony's political life and its cult of the emperor.

Of particular note is the Curia building at the northwest corner of the forum. The colony's Roman magistrates and their lieutenants operated from this building. According to Acts 16, Philippi's magistrates had Paul stripped of his clothes and beaten with rods in the public setting of the forum. Later, in writing back to the Philippian Christians, Paul referenced this earlier persecution (Phil 1:30). (Image used with permission of Michael Sève.)

Appendix I: Cartography

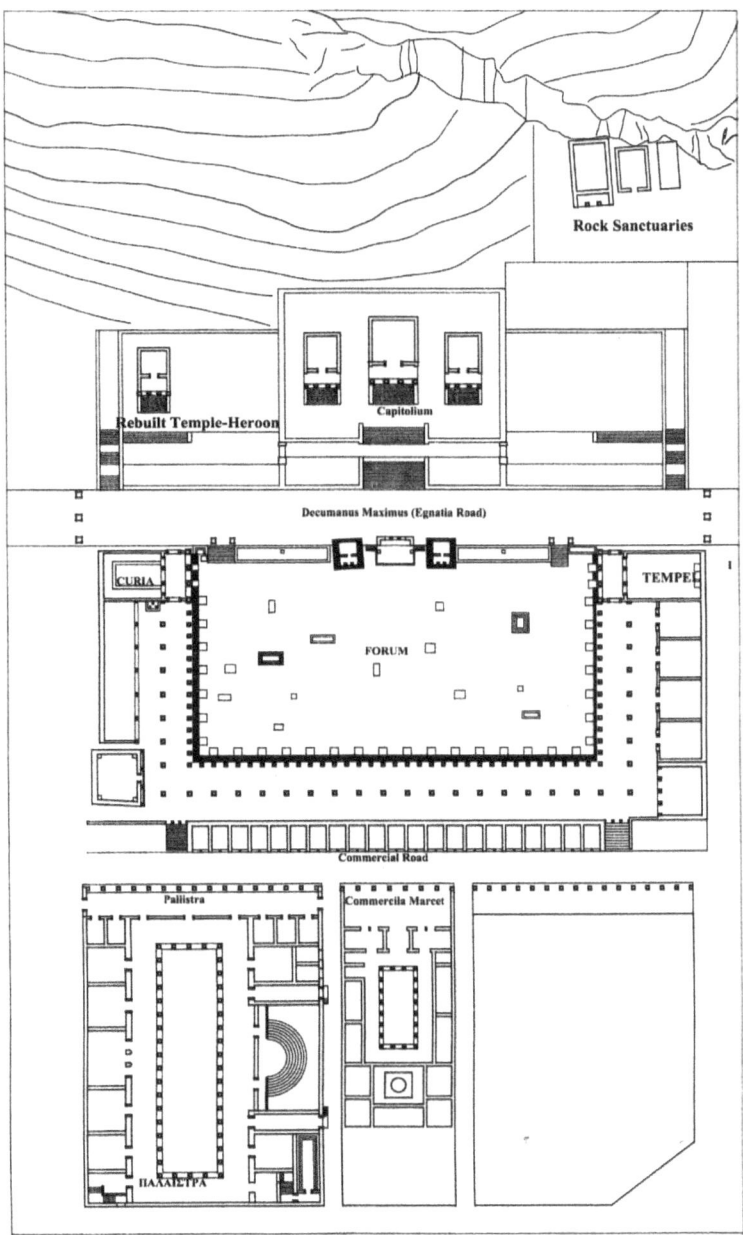

Figure I-5

Figure I-6
Philippi's Buildings in Three Dimensions

Balage Balogh has evolved a technique for the presentation of the buildings of many ancient cities in three dimensions. His presentation of Philippi's buildings illustrates this technique as does his presentation of Philippi's walls and gates. Certainly, many of Philippi's official, commercial, and residential buildings had more than one story, and Balogh's rendering conveys a sense of residential and commercial buildings in close proximity.

Balogh's approach also effectively delineates Philippi's situation as a city constructed at the base of a hilly outcropping from the Lekani Mountain range. The eastern wall of Philippi extended up the slope of this hill to the acropolis of the city. The lands outside of the city walls are evidently stylized in Balogh's rendering. These fertile lands were the prized awards that both Antony and Augustus granted to their Praetorians in appreciation for dedicated and loyal service. (This photo licensed by Wiki Commons.)

APPENDIX I: CARTOGRAPHY | 159

Figure I-6

Appendix II
ROMAN PROVINCIAL AND IMPERIAL COINS

Introduction

The ten coins presented in this appendix, five from Greece and five from Rome, testify in different ways to the conditions at Philippi and at Rome under the Julio-Claudian emperors. These coins are held within the collection of the Münzkabinett of the Staatliche Museen zu Berlin and are presented here courtesy of the Münzkabinett.

The remarkable contribution to this study made by Dr. Karsten Dahmen, vice-director of the Munzkabinett, must be emphasized here. Dr. Dahmen has guided me through the complex process of identifying these coins, and he has authorized their reproduction in this commentary. These coins have required precise, technical photography, and that photography, as is indicated for each coin, has been provided by Dr. Dahmen and other members of his staff.

The coins from Philippi attest to the importance of Philippi to Augustus and his successors and conversely to the extolment of these emperors by the Roman magistrates at Philippi, some presumably reflecting their own Praetorian Guard heritage. These coins span the first eight decades of Roman imperial rule from the victory of Augustus at Philippi in 42 BC to the suicide of Nero in Rome in 68 AD. The additional coin from Greece documents the solemnity with which Patras prepared for the arrival (*adventus*) of Nero at the time of his Greek tour.

Three of the Rome-minted coins testify to the importance that Claudius and Nero attached to the Praetorian Guards during their respective regimes. The third Roman coin pertaining to Nero indicates that, prior to his matricide, young Nero recognized the important imperial role of his mother, Agrippina. The fourth Nero coin evidences Nero's desire to be recognized as a great artist, even an incarnate Apollo, the god of music.

Philippi Coin #1: The abbreviated words on the obverse proclaim the victory of Augustus at Philippi. The goddess Victoria extends the victory wreath and there is no reference to Anthony's role. The reverse acclaims the role of the Praetorian cohorts at Philippi by displaying three Praetorian standards.

    Münzkabinett, Staatliche Museen zu Berlin, 18234171
    Photographs by Reinhard Saczewski
    https://ikmk.smb.museum/object?id=18234171

Philippi Coin #2: The obverse presents the laureated head of Augustus and part of the inscription indicates that this coin is issued under Augustus's authority. The reverse shows Julius Caesar in a toga standing on a cippus next to Augustus who is depicted in military garb. The message conveyed is that Caesar's heritage is transmitted to Augustus at Philippi and beyond.

    Münzkabinett, Staatliche Museen zu Berlin, 18215890
    Photographs by Karsten Dahmen
    https://ikmk.smb.museum/object?id=18215890

Philippi Coin #3: The obverse depicts Claudius's countenance bordered by the abbreviated words: Colony Augustus Julius Philippi. The reverse retains the design used for the preceding coin, i.e., images of the divine Julius and the divine Augustus standing next to each other on a *cippus*.

        Münzkabinett, Staatliche Museen zu Berlin, 18234172
        Photographs by Reinhard Saczewski
        https://ikmk.smb.museum/object?id=18234172

Philippi Coin #4: The obverse images the laureated head of Nero. The reverse depicts the divine Julius (in toga) and the divine Augustus with outstretched arms standing next to each other on a *cippus*. This design is a carryover from the earlier coins of Augustus and Claudius.

        Münzkabinett, Staatliche Museen zu Berlin, 18234173
        Photographs by Reinhard Saczewski
        https://ikmk.smb.museum/object?id=18234173

APPENDIX II: ROMAN PROVINCIAL AND IMPERIAL COINS | 163

Patras Coin: The obverse depicts the head of Nero with the bordering words: Nero Caesar Augustus Germanicus Imperator. The reverse depicts a ship arriving at Patras with the inscription "Arrival (*adventus*) of Augustus." These coins were minted in anticipation of Nero's ignoble tour of Greece. Paul's words at Phil 3:20-21 stand as a counter to Nero's "advent" propaganda.

    Münzkabinett, Staatliche Museen zu Berlin, 18266830
    Photographs by Karsten Dahmen
    https://ikmk.smb.museum/object?id=18266830

Roman Coin #1: The obverse presents the head of Claudius bordered by his name and abbreviated titles. The reverse depicts Claudius clasping the hand of the Prefect of the Praetorian Guard, holding the praetorian standards. The two bordering words identify the event as the Praetorian Reception.

    Münzkabinett, Staatliche Museen zu Berlin, 18219441
    Photographs by Dirk Sonnenwald
    https://ikmk.smb.museum/object?id=18219441

Roman Coin #2: The obverse represents a young Nero and his mother, Agrippina, as virtually co-equal rulers. One interpretation of the scene depicted on the reverse is that Nero and Agrippina are seated together, regally guiding a chariot drawn by four elephants. The existence of this coin made Agrippina's subsequent murder all the more shocking.

> Münzkabinett, Staatliche Museen zu Berlin, 18202642
> Photographs by Lutz-Jürgen Lübke (Lübke und Wiedemann)
> https://ikmk.smb.museum/object?id=18202642

Roman Coin #3: The obverse presents a laureated Nero with his titles bordering. The reverse depicts Nero with outstretched arm delivering a formal address (adlocution) to the Praetorians, identified by their standards. The Prefect of the Praetorians stands at Nero's side.

> Münzkabinett, Staatliche Museen zu Berlin, 18220852
> Photographs by Dirk Sonnenwald
> https://ikmk.smb.museum/object?id=18220852

Roman Coin #4: The obverse presents Nero's countenance with his names and titles bordering. The reverse depicts Nero astride a stallion, boldly setting forth with a less noble rider, a Praetorian, in the *Decursio*, a traditional Praetorian parade.

>Münzkabinett, Staatliche Museen zu Berlin, 18220883
>Photographs by Dirk Sonnenwald
>https://ikmk.smb.museum/object?id=18220883

Roman Coin #5: The obverse is again Nero's laureated head bordered by his names and titles. The reverse identifies Nero through his title *pontifex maximus*, and associates him with the god Apollo, who is signified by his flowing robes and musical zither. In addition to vaunting his instrumental skills, Nero also vaunted his "celestial voice."

>Münzkabinett, Staatliche Museen zu Berlin, 18204251
>Photographs by Dirk Sonnenwald
>https://ikmk.smb.museum/object?id=18204251

Appendix III
IMAGES OF SLAVES

Figure III.1
Funeral Stele

This stele was discovered in 1939 by Jacques Roger in a cemetery at Amphipolis, not far from Philippi. This stele was more than seven feet high when Roger discovered it and made the photograph that is presented here. Unfortunately, during WWII, the stele was battered and broken.

Various features internal to the design of this stele suggest that it existed by the middle of the first century CE, when Paul journeyed in the vicinity of Amphipolis. Also, as described in the commentary proper, the slave trade between Thrace and other parts of the Roman Empire was fully underway at the time of Paul's travels elsewhere. Paul could have easily encountered processions of slaves such as the one depicted in the stele's lower panel.

Four sections comprise the stele. Noted in passing are the top panel portraying a funeral banquet and the inscription below it which commemorates Aulus Caprilius Timotheus and his achievements as a slave trader, *sômatemporos*. The center panel depicts slaves carrying bronze amphora of wine. The wine and the bronze containers may represent the payment that the slave merchant has received for selling his slaves.

The bottom panel, with its imaging of chained slaves, is highly consequential for the present study. Eight male slaves are marching in chained procession behind their hooded overseer. In this procession each male slave is constrained with a metal collar. For security or for punishment, the collars worn by the first and last slaves are significantly larger. Two women and two children who are not harnessed by chains follow after the eight males.

APPENDIX III: IMAGES OF SLAVES | 167

Figure III-1

Figure III.2
Naked Slaves

In the previous photo the male slaves were garbed in short tunics and the women and children were fully dressed. In the photo now presented, the stark nakedness of the two chained slaves is shocking. This sculpture is now located in the Museum of Mainz. This particular photo is by Robert Clark.

In addition to encountering processions of minimally clad slaves, Paul may also have encountered slaves who were completely naked, just as Jesus was stripped naked at his crucifixion. This degrading aspect of Jesus's crucifixion may now have registered more deeply with Paul. The naked slaves in this photo may have already been programmed for crucifixion, "the slave's form of death." (Image with the permission of Robert Clark.)

APPENDIX III: IMAGES OF SLAVES | 169

Figure III-2

Appendix IV
LATER IMAGES OF PAUL
AS AN IMPERIAL PRISONER

The two sarcophagus sculptures presented on the opposite page are three centuries removed from the time of Philippians, which is to say that both sculptures issue from the latter half of the fourth century AD.

The top sculpture is one panel of the sarcophagus of Junius Bassius, located now at the Vatican Museum. Bassius was a prefect of the city of Rome who became a Christian prior to his death. In this panel two Roman soldiers have Paul in their custody, the one soldier twisting Paul's arm behind him, the other ready to beat him with a military baton.

The bottom sculpture is one panel of the sarcophagus of the Resurrection, now located in the crypt of St. Victor Monastery in Marseilles. In this panel a Roman soldier has placed a security restraint around Paul's neck. The sculpture suggests that Paul is being taken against his will, perhaps to prison, perhaps to an administrative hearing, perhaps to execution.

As noted, both of these sculptures were created approximately three centuries after Philippians and also decades after Constantine's edict. Neither sculpture alludes to Paul's chains or to his praetorian guards. Notwithstanding, both sculptures express that Paul's situation as an imperial prisoner is dire.

APPENDIX IV: LATER IMAGES OF PAUL | 171

Appendix V
MATERIAL FACTORS IN THE PRODUCTION
OF THIS COMMENTARY

In the Reflection given in one of the front pages of this volume, I made mention of "the cloud of witnesses" whose affirmation, support, faith friendship, and other forms of intangible encouragement have so assisted me during the writing of this commentary. In this present appendix, I want to acknowledge those who have made material, that is, hands-on, contributions to the production of this book.

Gwendolin Herder, the publisher of U.S. Herder and Herder, is a descendant of the Herders who first began publishing theological books in Freiburg, Germany, at the end of the eighteenth century. Perspicaciously, Gwendolin has appointed Mr. Chris Myers as her delegated editor for books such as this one. Chris's team includes Ms. Julie Boddorf and Ms. Janaki Kagel as well as Mr. Fred Courtright, director of permissions, and Mr. Paul Kobelski, manuscript editor and editor for book design.

These professionals have overseen every facet of this book's production. In particular, Chris and Paul have both been extremely dedicated in bringing this book and its appendixes through to definitive publication.

For a commentary on Philippians, on-site experience with Philippi and its surroundings in Greece is vital. Ms. Bessie Mousoulea and her colleagues at Himalaya Travel were remarkable in the service they provided to me, Bessie through countless e-queries and responses. My personal guide, Ms. Maria Mouschou, was exceptional as she walked me through the ruins and the surroundings of Philippi. I also benefitted from the insights of Rev. Eduard Verhoef, a Dutch scholar with a particular passion for Philippi and the Via Egnatia. Eduard was referred to me by Dr. Martinus deBoer, who was already perusing my manuscript.

Because the 2018 Annual Meeting of SNTS (Society for the Study of the New Testament) was being held in Athens, I was able to engage positively with Professors Atonopoulos Athanasios, Sotirios Despotis, and Christos Karakolis from the local organizing committee. As a result of Professor Karakolis's personal intervention, Mrs. Liza Evert, an expert in photographing St. Paul's sites in Greece, authorized the use of her photo of Philippi for the cover of this book.

In addition to Philippi, imperial Rome is the other city of vital importance for this commentary. From my previous Herder book, *Paul in Chains*, I was familiar with Paul's situation in the capital. That being said, I want to recognize the perspectives that I gained regarding Nero's regime in the seminar led by Professor Hans Dieter Betz, assisted by Professor Margaret Mitchell at the 2012 SNTS Meeting in Leuven, Belgium. Professor Reimund Bieringer and PhD candidate Loretta Mann also rendered estimable assistance to me at this same meeting.

In regard to the reference works, articles, and images that occupy a central place within this commentary, the work of the library staff of Sacred Heart Major Seminary in Detroit has been invaluable. Mr. Christopher Spilker, Mr. Michael Nowicki, Mrs. Norma Forbes, and seminarian Samuel Waldron assisted in securing works not held by Sacred Heart and in identifying several of the images that now appear in the commentary. Chris Spilker's IT skills are also evident in the actual production of images for this commentary.

In a similar way, I am indebted to the staff of Christ the King Parish in Detroit for IT assistance pertaining to the manuscript and regarding the images that the manuscript now contains. Many staff members at Christ the King have assisted in this process. Here I recognize the particular contributions made by Fr. Victor Clore, PhD, Ms. Nancy Soisson, Mrs. Andrea Kovach, and Ms. Nicole Evans.

It is fitting to close this appendix by expressing gratitude for the contribution made on behalf of this commentary by Detroit Archbishop Allen Vigneron, PhD. Archbishop Vigneron has previously served as professor, academic dean, and rector of Sacred Heart Major Seminary. His material and moral support for me as a priest of the Detroit Archdiocese has undergirded the successful completion of this new Philippians commentary.

Bibliography

Abbott, F. 1911. *A History of and Description of Roman Political Institutions*. Third edition. Cambridge: Harvard University Press.

Abrahamsen, V. 1995. *Women and Worship at Philippi: Diana/Artemis and Other Cults in the Early Christian Era*. Portland, ME: Astarte Shell Press.

———. 1988. "Christianity and the Rock Reliefs at Philippi." *Biblical Archaeologist* 51:46–56.

———. 1987 "Women at Philippi: The Pagan and Christian Evidence." *Journal of Feminist Studies in Religion* 3:411–20.

Achtemeier, P. 1986. "An Elusive Unity: Paul, Acts, and the Early Church." *Catholic Biblical Quarterly* 48:1–26.

Addington, W. 1989. "Archaeology and Imperialism: Roman Expansion and the Greek City." *Journal of Mediterranean Archaeology* 2:87–135.

———. 1971. *The Golden Ass: Being the Metamorphoses of Lucius Apuleius*. Repr. ed. London: Heinemann.

Alcock, S. 1993. *Graecia Capta: The Landscapes of Roman Greece*. New York: Cambridge University Press

Alexander, L. 1989. "Hellenistic Letter-Forms and the Structure of Philippians." *Journal for the Study of the New Testament* 37: 87-101.

Alexander, S. 1999. *The Complete Odes and Satires of Horace*. Princeton, NJ: Princeton University Press.

Alfonsi, L. 1964. "Cittadini del cielo." *Rheinisches Museum für Philologie* 107:302–4.

Amandry, M. 1998. "Le Monnayage de la Res Publica Coloniae Philippensium." In *Stephanos Nomismatikos: Edith Schoenert-Geiss zum 65 Geburtstag*, 23–33. Edited by U. Peter. Berlin: Akademie Verlag.

Anderson, J. 1927. "Augustan Edicts from Cyrene." *Journal of Roman Studies* 17:33–48.

Ando, C. 2000. *Imperial Ideology and Provincial Loyalty in the Roman Empire*. Berkeley: University of California Press.
Arbandt, S., and W. Macheiner. 1976. "Gefangenschaft." In *Reallexikon für Antike und Christentum: Supplement* 9:318–45.
Armistead, J. 1987. "The Social Settings of the Early Christian Community at Philippi." Ph.D., University of Mississippi.
Arzt-Grabner, P. 2011. "Der 'Herr Jesus Christus' und 'Caesar, der Herr'—über die Anfänge einer Konfrontation." In *Kult und Macht*, 1-7. Edited by A. Lykke and F. Schipper. Tübingen: Mohr Siebeck.
———. 2003. *Papyrologische Kommentare zum Neuen Testament, Bd.1, Philemon*. Göttingen: Vandenhoeck & Ruprecht.
———. 2002. "'Brothers' and 'Sisters' in Documentary Papyri and in Early Christianity." *Rivista Biblica* 50:185–204.
———. 1994. "The 'Epistolary Introductory Thanksgiving' in the Papyri and in Paul." *Novum Testamentum* 36:29–46.
Ascough, R. 2003. *Paul's Macedonian Associations: The Social Context of Philippians & 1 Thessalonians*. New York: Mohr.
Aurelius Victor. 1994. *Liber de Caesaribus of Sextus Aurelius Victor*. Translated by H. Bird. Liverpool: Liverpool University Press.
Badian, E. 1982. "Figuring out Roman Slavery: Conquerors and Slaves by K. Hopkins." *Journal of Roman Studies* 72:164–69.
Bakirtzis, C., and H. Koester, eds. 1998. *Philippi at the Time of Paul and after His Death*. Harrisburg, PA: Trinity Press International.
Balsdon, J. 1979. *Romans and Aliens*. Chapel Hill: University of North Carolina Press.
Balsdon, J., and A. Lintott. 1996. "maiestas." In *Oxford Classical Dictionary*. Third edition. Oxford: Oxford University Press.
Balz, H., and G. Schneider, eds. 1990. *Exegetical Dictionary of the New Testament*, 3 volumes. Grand Rapids, MI: Eerdmans.
Barclay, J. 1991. "Paul, Philemon and the Dilemma of Christian Slave Ownership." *New Testament Studies* 37:161–86.
Barth, G. 1979. *Der Brief an die Philipper*. Zürcher Bibel Kommentare. Zurich: Theologischer Verlag.
Barth, K. 1962. *The Epistle to the Philippians*. Translated by J. Leitch. London: SCM.
Bauer, W., F. Danker, W. Arndt, and W. Gingrich. 2000. *A Greek-English Lexicon of the New Testament and Other Early Christian Literature*. Third edition. Chicago: University of Chicago Press.

Bauman, R. 1974. *Impietas in Principem: A Study of Treason against the Roman Emperor with Special Reference to the First Century, A.D.* Munich: Beck.
Beare, F. 1959. *A Commentary on the Epistle to the Philippians.* New York: Harper and Brothers.
Becker, J., and H. Conzelmann. 1976. *Die Briefe an die Galater, Epheser, Philipper, Kolosser, Thessalonicher und Philemon.* Göttingen: Vandenhoeck & Ruprecht.
Behm, J. 1965. "kollia." In *Theological Dictionary of the New Testament*, 3: 786–89. Edited by G. Kittel and G. Friedrich. Translated and edited by G. Bromily. Grand Rapids: Eerdmans.
Beker, J. 1991. *Heirs of Paul.* Minneapolis: Fortress Press.
Benjamin, A., and A. Raubitschek. 1959. "Arae Augusti." *Hesperia* 28:65–85.
Bergmann, M. 1998. *Die Strahlen der Herrscher.* Mainz: von Zabern.
Betz, H.-D., 2015. *Studies in Paul's Letter to the Philippians.* Tübingen: Mohr Siebeck.
———. 2013. *Der Apostel Paulus in Rome.* Julius Wellhausen-Vorlesung 4. Berlin: de Gruyter.
———. 1992. "Paul." In *Anchor Bible Dictionary*, 186–201. Edited by D. Freedman. New York: Doubleday.
Bieringer, R. 2000. "My Kingship Is Not of This World." Pp. 159–75 in *The Myriad Christ.* Edited by T. Merrigan and J. Haers. Leuven: Peeters.
Black, D. 1995. "The Discourse Structure of Philippians: A Study in Textlinguistics." *Novum Testamentum* 37:16–49.
———. 1988."The Authorship of Philippians 2:6-11: Some Literary-Critical Observations." *Criswell Theological Review* 2:269–88.
———. 1985. "Paul and Christian Unity: A Formal Analysis of Philippians 2:1-4." *Journal of the Evangelical Theological Society* 28:299–308.
Bloomquist, L. 2007. "Subverted by Joy: Suffering and Joy in Paul's Letter to the Philippians." *Interpretation* 61:270–82.
———. 1993. *The Function of Suffering in Philippians.* Sheffield: Sheffield Academic Press.
Bockmuel, M. 1998. *The Epistle to the Philippians.* Peabody, MA: Hendrickson Publishers.
Bodel, J. 2011. "Slave Labor and Roman Society." In *The Cambridge World History of Slavery,* 1:311–36. Edited by K. Bradley and P. Cartledge: Cambridge: Cambridge University Press.

———. 2005. "Caveat Emptor: Towards a Study of Roman Slave-Traders." *Journal of Roman Archaeology* 18:181–95.
Boettrich, C. 2004. "Verkündigung aus 'Neid und Rivalität': Beobachtungen zu Phil 1,12-18. *Zeitschrift für die neutestamentliche Wissenschaft* 95:84-101.
Bormann, L. 1995. *Philippi: Stadt und Christengemeinde zur Zeit des Paulus*. Leiden: Brill.
Bornhauser, K. 1938. *Jesus Imperator Mundi (Phil 3:17-21 and 2:5-12)*. Gütersloh: Bertelsmann.
Bousset, W. 1970. *Kyrios Christos*. Translated by J. Steely. Nashville, TN: Abingdon.
Bradley, K. 1994. *Slavery and Society at Rome*. Cambridge: Cambridge University Press.
———. 1989. *Slavery and Rebellion in the Roman World, 140 B.C.–70 B.C.* Bloomington: Indiana University Press.
———. 1984. *Slaves and Masters in the Roman Empire: A Study in Social Control*. New York: Oxford University Press.
———. 1978. *Suetonius' Life of Nero: An Historical Commentary*. Brussels: Latomus.
Brant, J. 1993. "The Place of Mimesis in Paul's Thoughts." *Studies in Religion* 22:285–300.
Braund, D. 1985. *Augustus to Nero: A Sourcebook on Roman History, 31 BC – AD 68*. Totowa, NJ: Barnes and Noble Books.
Brawley, R. 2015. "An Alternative Community and an Oral Encomium: Traces of the People in Philippi." Pp. 223–46 in *The People Beside Paul*. Edited by J. Marchal. Atlanta: SBL Press.
Brewer, R. 1954. "The Meaning of *Politeuesthe* in Philippians 1:27." *Journal of Biblical Literature* 73:76–83.
Brewster, E. 1972. *Roman Craftsmen and Tradesmen of the Early Empire*. Repr. ed. New York: Burt Franklin.
Brown, R. 1996. *An Introduction to the New Testament*. New York: Doubleday.
Bruce, F. 1991. *Philippians*. Peabody, MA: Hendrickson Publishers.
———. 1983. *Philippians*. San Francisco: Harper & Row.
———. 1980. "St. Paul in Macedonia 3. The Philippian Correspondence." *Bulletin of the John Rylands Library* 63: 260-84.
———. 1967. "St. Paul in Rome. 5. Concluding Observations." *Bulletin of the John Rylands Library* 50:262–79.
———. 1963. "St. Paul in Rome." *Bulletin of the John Rylands Library* 46:326–45.

Brunt, P., and J. Moore. 1967. *Res Gestae Divi Augusti.* 5th ed. Bristol: Oxford University Press.
Burnett, A., M. Amandry, P. Alegre, and M. Butcher. 1998. *Roman Provincial Coinage.* Vols. 1 and 2. London: British Museum Press.
———. 1984. "Nero's Visit to Greece: Two Numismatic Notes." *Schweizer Munzblatter* 136:81–85.
Burton, G. 1976. "The Issuing of Mandata to Proconsuls and a New Inscription from Cos." *Zeitschrift für Papyrologie und Epigraphik* 21:63–68.
Byrnes, M. 2003. *Conformation to the Death of Christ and the Hope of Resurrection: An Exegetico-Theological Study of 2 Corinthians 4,7-15 and Philippians 3,7-11.* Rome: Gregorian University Press.
Callahan, A. 1993. "Paul's Epistle to Philemon: Toward an Alternative Argumentum." *Harvard Theological Review* 86:357–76.
Calpurnius Siculus. 1968. "Ecologue IV." In *Minor Latin Poets.* Translation by J. Duff and A. Duff. Cambridge, MA: Harvard University Press.
Campbell, B. 1984. *The Emperor and the Roman Army 31 BC–AD 235.* Oxford: Clarendon.
———. 1978. "The Marriage of Soldiers under the Empire." *Journal of Roman Studies* 68:153–66.
Campbell, J. 1932. "KOINONIA and Its Cognates in the New Testament." *Journal of Biblical Literature* 51: 352–80.
Carls, P. 2001. "Identifying Syzygos, Euodia and Syntyche, Philippians 4:2f." *Journal of Higher Criticism* 8:161–82.
Cassidy, R. 2015a. *Jesus, Politics, and Society: A Study of Luke's Gospel.* New edition. Eugene, OR: Wipf & Stock.
———. 2015b *John's Gospel in New Perspective: Christology and the Realities of Roman Power.* New edition. Eugene, OR: Wipf & Stock.
———. 2014. *Society and Politics in the Acts of the Apostles.* Expanded edition. Eugene, OR: Wipf & Stock.
———. 2007. *Four Times Peter: Portrayals of Peter in the Four Gospels and at Philippi.* Collegeville, MN: Liturgical Press.
———. 2001a. *Christians and Roman Rule in the New Testament: New Perspectives.* New York: Crossroad/Herder.
———. 2001b. *Paul in Chains: Roman Imprisonment and the Letters of St. Paul.* New York: Crossroad/Herder.
Casson, L. 1974. *Travel in the Ancient World.* New York: HarperCollins.

Champlin, E. 2003. *Nero*. Cambridge, MA: Belknap Press.
Charlesworth, M. 1970. *Trade-Routes and Commerce of the Roman Empire*. 2d ed. New York: Cooper Square Publishers.
———. 1951. *Documents Illustrating the Reigns of Claudius and Nero*. Cambridge: Cambridge University Press.
Chisholm, K., and J. Ferguson. 1981. *Rome: The Augustan Age: A Source Book*. New York: Oxford University Press.
Chrysanthaki, C. and C. Bakirtzis. 1995. *Philippi*. Athens: Archaeological Receipts Fund.
Cicero, Marcus Tullius. 1967. *The Verrine Orations*. Translated by L. Greenwood. Cambridge, MA: Harvard University Press.
Clauss, M. 1999. *Kaiser und Gott: Herrscherkult im römischen Reich*. Stuttgart: Teubner.
Coarelli, F. 2005. "L' 'Agora des Italiens': lo statarion di Delo?" *Journal of Roman Archaeology* 18:196–212.
Collange, J.-F. 1979. *The Epistle of Saint Paul to the Philippians*. London: Epworth.
Collart, P. 1937. *Philippes, ville de Macédoine depuis ses origins jusqu'à la fin de l'époque romaine*. 2 vols. Paris: Boccard.
Collins, A. 2003. "Psalms, Philippians 2:6-11 and the Origins of Christology." *Biblical Interpretation* 11:362–72.
———, ed. 1996. *Ancient and Modern Perspectives on the Bible and Culture: Essays in Honor of Hans Dieter Betz*. Atlanta: Scholars Press.
Cook, Z. 2009. "Honor, Shame, and Social Status Revisited." *Journal of Biblical Literature* 128:591–611.
Cornell, T. and P. Rhodes. 1996. "*hetaireiai*." In *The Oxford Classical Dictionary*. Third edition. Oxford: Oxford University Press.
Cotter, W. 1994. "Women's Authority Role in Paul's Churches: Countercultural or Conventional?" *Novum Testamentum* 4:350–72.
———. 1993. "Our Politeuma Is in Heaven: The Meaning of Philippians 3.17-21." In *Origins and Methods,* 92–104. Edited by B. McLean. Sheffield: Sheffield Academic Press.
Craddock, F. 1985. *Philippians*. Atlanta: John Knox.
Croy, N. 2003. "'To Die Is Gain' (Philippians 1:19-26) Does Paul Contemplate Suicide?" *Journal of Biblical Literature* 122:517–53.
Culpepper, A. 1980. "Co-Workers in Suffering. Philippians 2:19-30." *Review and Expositor* 77:349–58.
Cumont, F. 1903. "Dendrophoroi." In *Paulys Real-encyclopädie der classischen Altertumswissenschaft*, 216–19. Stuttgart: Metzler.

Cuss, D. 1974. *Imperial Cult and Honorary Terms in the New Testament*. Fribourg: University Press.

D'Arms, J., and E. Kopff. 1980. *The Seaborne Commerce of Ancient Rome: Studies in Archaeology and History*. Rome: American Academy in Rome.

Dailey, T. 1990. "To Live or Die: Paul's Eschatological Dilemma in Philippians 1:19-26." *Interpretation* 44:18–28.

Daube, D. 1952. "Slave-Catching." *Juridical Review* 64:12–28.

deBoer, M. 1980. "Images of Paul in the Post-Apostolic Period." *Catholic Biblical Quarterly* 42:359–80.

Deissmann, A. 1965. *Light from the Ancient East*. Translated by L. Strachan. Grand Rapids: Baker.

———. 1901. *Bible Studies: Contributions Chiefly from Papyri and Inscriptions to the History of the Language, the Literature, and the Religion of Hellenistic Judaism and Primitive Christianity*. Translated by A. Grieve. Edinburgh: T. & T. Clark.

DeVogel, C. 1977. "Reflexions on Philippi 1:23-24." *Novum Testamentum* 19:262–74.

DeVos, C. 1999. *Church and Community Conflicts: The Relationships of the Thessalonian, Corinthian, and Philippian Churches with Their Wider Civic Communities*. Atlanta: Scholars Press.

———. 1999. "Finding a Charge That Fits: The Accusation against Paul and Silas at Philippi (Acts 16:19-21)." *Journal for the Study of the New Testament* 74:51–63.

Dibelius, M. 1956. "Rom und die Christen im ersten Jahrhundert." In *Botschaft und Geschichte* 2:177–228. Tübingen: Mohr.

———. 1937. *An die Thessalonischer I II und die Philipper*. Tübingen: Mohr.

Dio Cassius. 1969. *Dio's Roman History in Nine Volumes*. Translated by E. Cary. Cambridge, MA: Harvard University Press.

Doble, P. 2002. "'Vile Bodies' or Transformed Persons? Philippians 3.21 in Context." *Journal for the Study of the New Testament* 86:3–27.

Donderer, M., and I. Spiliopoulou-Donderer. 1993. "Spätrepublikanische und kaiserzeitliche Grabmonumente von Sklavenhaendlern." *Gymnasium* 100:254–66.

Donfried, K. 1997. "The Imperial Cults of Thessalonica and Political Conflict in 1 Thessalonians." In *Paul and Empire: Religion and Power in Roman Imperial Society*, 215–23. Edited by R. Horsley. Harrisburg, PA: Trinity Press International.

Doty, W. 1973. *Letters in Primitive Christianity*. Philadelphia: Fortress.

Doughty, D. 1995. "Citizens of Heaven: Philippians 3.2-21." *New Testament Studies* 41:102–22.
Duchene, H. 1986. "Sur la stèle d'Aulus Caprilius Timotheos Sômatemporos." *Bulletin de correspondance hellénique* 110: 513–30.
Dunn, J. 2003. *The Cambridge Companion to St. Paul*. Cambridge: Cambridge University Press.
–––––. 1996. *The Epistles to the Colossians and to Philemon: A Commentary on the Greek Text*. Grand Rapids, MI: Eerdmans.
Durry, M. 1938. *Les cohortes prétoriennes*. Paris: E. De Boccard.
Ehrenberg, V. and A. H. M. Jones. 1983. *Documents Illustrating the Reigns of Augustus and Tiberius*. Oxford: Clarendon.
Eastman, S. 2010. "Philippians 2:6-11: Incarnation as Mimetic Participation." *Journal for the Study of Paul and His Letters*. Sample Issue: 1–22.
Edson, C. 1972. *Inscriptiones Thessalonicae et Viciniae*. Berlin: Walter de Gruyter.
Ellis, E. 1971. "Paul and His Co-Workers." *New Testament Studies* 17:437–52.
Elsner, J. 1994. *Reflections of Nero: Culture, History, & Representation*. Chapel Hill: University of North Carolina Press.
Elsner, J., and J. Masters, eds. 1994. *Reflections of Nero*. London: Duckworth.
Engberg-Pedersen, T. 2003. "Paul, Virtues, and Vices." In *Paul in the Greco-Roman World: A Handbook*, 608–33. Edited by P. Sampley. Harrisburg, PA: Trinity Press.
Epictetus. 1966. *The Discourses as Reported by Arrian, the Manual and Fragments*. Translated by W. Oldfather. Cambridge, MA: Harvard University Press.
Ernst, J. 1974. *Die Briefe an die Philipper, an Philemon, an die Kolosser, an die Epheser*. Regensburg: Pustet.
Fee, G. 1999. *Philippians*. Downers Grove, IL: InterVarsity Press.
–––––. 1995. *Letter to the Philippians*. Grand Rapids: Eerdmans.
–––––. 1992. "Philippians 2:5-11: Hymn or Exalted Pauline Prose?" *Bulletin for Biblical Research* 2:29–46.
Feinberg, P. 1980. "The Kenosis and Christology: An Exegetical-Theological Analysis of Phil 2:6-11." *Trinity Journal* 1: 21-46.
Fentress, E. 2005. "On the Block: *catastae, chalcidica* and *cryptae* in Early Imperial Italy." *Journal of Roman Archaeology* 18:220–34.

Ferguson, W. 1913. *The Legal Terms Common to the Macedonian Inscriptions and the New Testament*. Chicago: University of Chicago Press.

Finley, M. 1968. *Aspects of Antiquity: Discoveries and Controversies*. New York: Viking.

———. 1962. "The Black Sea and Danubian Regions and the Slave Trade in Antiquity." *Klio* 40:51–59.

———. 1960. *Slavery in Classical Antiquity*. Cambridge: W. Heffer and Sons.

Fishwick, D. 1991. "Ovid and Divus Augustus." *Classical Philology* 86:36–41.

Fitzgerald, J. 2003. "Paul and Friendship." In *Paul in the Greco-Roman World: A Handbook*, 319–42. Edited by P. Sampley. Harrisburg, PA: Trinity Press.

———. 1996. *Friendship, Flattery, and Frankness of Speech: Studies on Friendship in the New Testament World*. Leiden: Brill.

Fitzmyer, J. 1987. *Paul and His Theology*. Second edition. Englewood Cliffs, NJ: Prentice-Hall.

Forbes, R. 1955. *Studies in Ancient Technology*. Volume 2. Leiden: Brill.

Fox, R., ed. 2011. *Brill's Companion to Ancient Macedon:* Studies in the Archaeology and History of Macedon, 650 BC – 300 AD. Leiden: Brill.

Friedrich, G. 1978. "Der Brief eines Gefangenen: Bemerkungen zum Philipperbrief." In *Auf das Wort kommt es an*, 224–35. Edited by J. Friedrich. Göttingen: Vandenhoeck & Ruprecht.

Friesen, S. 2005. "Satan's Throne, Imperial Cults and the Social Settings of Revelation." *Journal for the Study of the New Testament* 27:351–73.

———. 1993. *Twice Neokoros: Ephesus, Asia, and the Cult of the Flavian Imperial Family*. Leiden: Brill.

Fuhrmann, C. 2012. *Policing the Roman Empire: Soldiers, Administration, and Public Order*. Oxford: Oxford University Press.

Galitis, G. 2000. *Paulos Ho Apostolos Tōn Hellēnōn*. Athens: Asterismos-Liza Ebert.

Gardner, J. 1998. *Family and Familia in Roman Law and Life*. Oxford: Clarendon.

———. 1993. *Being a Roman Citizen*. London: Routledge.

Garland, D. 1985. "The Composition and Unity of Philippians: Some Neglected Literary Factors." *Novum Testamentum* 27:141–73.

———. 1980. "Philippians 1:1-26: The Defense and Confirmation of the Gospel." *Review and Expositor* 77:327–36.

Garnsey, P., and R. Saller. 1987. *The Roman Empire: Economy, Society and Culture*. Berkeley: University of California Press.

———. 1982. *The Early Principate: Augustus to Trajan*. London: Oxford University Press.

Geoffrion, T. 1993. *The Rhetorical Purpose and the Political and Military Character of Philippians*. Lewiston, NY: Mellen.

George, M. 2011. "Slavery and Roman Material Culture." In *The Cambridge World History of Slavery*. Volume 1: 385–413. Edited by K. Bradley and P. Cartledge. Cambridge: Cambridge University Press.

Gill, D. 1994. "Macedonia." In *The Book of Acts in Its Graeco-Roman Setting*, 397-417. Edited by D. Gill and C. Gempf. Grand Rapids, MI: Eerdmans.

Gillman, F. 1990. "Early Christian Women at Philippi." *Journal of Gender in World Religions* 1:59–79.

Glancey, J. 2011. "Slavery and the Rise of Christianity." In *The Cambridge World History of Slavery*. Volume 1: 456–81. Edited by K. Bradley and P. Cartledge. Cambridge: Cambridge University Press.

———. 2002. *Slavery in Early Christianity*. Oxford: Oxford University Press.

Glombitza, O. 1964. "Der Dank des Apostels zum Verständnis von Philipper iv 10-20." *Novum Testamentum* 7:135–41.

Gnilka, J. 1976. *Der Philipperbrief*. Freiburg: Herder.

———. 1965. "Die antipaulinische Mission in Philippi." *Biblische Zeitschrift* 9:258–76.

Gordon, M. 1964. "The Nationality of Slaves under the Early Roman Empire." In *Slavery in Classical Antiquity: Views and Controversies*, 171–89. Edited by M. Finley. Cambridge: Heffer and Sons.

Grant, M. 1974. *The Army of the Caesars*. 2nd ed. New York: Macmillan.

———. 1969. *From Imperium to Auctoritas: A Historical Study of Aes Coinage in the Roman Empire, 49 B.C.–A.D. 14*. New York: Cambridge University Press.

———. 1950. *Aspects of the Principate of Tiberius*. New York: American Numismatic Society.

Grayston, K. 1967. *The Letters of Paul to the Philippians and to the Thessalonians*. Cambridge: Cambridge University Press.

Grether, G. 1946. "Livia and the Roman Imperial Cult." *American Journal of Philology* 67:222–52.
Griffin, M. 1985. *Nero: The End of a Dynasty*. New Haven, CT: Yale University Press.
Gundry, J. 1990. *Staying and Falling Away: Paul and Perseverance*. Tübingen: Mohr Siebeck.
Guthrie, D. 1990. *New Testament Introduction*. Downers Grove, IL: InterVarsity Press.
Haenchen, E. 1971. *The Acts of the Apostles: A Commentary*. Philadelphia: Westminster.
Hajek, M. 1964. "Comments on Philippians 4:3—Who Was 'Gnesios Syzygo'?" *Communio Viatorum* 7:261–62.
Harrer, G. 1940. "Saul Who Was Called Paul." *Harvard Theological Review* 33: 19-34.
Harrill, J. 2006. *Slaves in the New Testament: Literary, Social, and Moral Dimensions*. Minneapolis: Fortress.
———. 2003. "Paul and Slavery." In *Paul in the Greco-Roman World: A Handbook*, 575–606. Edited by P. Sampley. Harrisburg, PA: Trinity Press.
———. 1995. *The Manumission of Slaves in Early Christianity*. Tübingen: Mohr Siebeck.
Harris, W. 1999. "Demography, Geography and the Sources of Roman Slaves." *Journal of Roman Studies* 89: 62-75.
———. 1980, "Towards a Study of the Roman Slave Trade." *Memoirs of the American Academy in Rome* 36: 117–40.
Harrison, J. 2003. *Paul's Language of Grace in Its Graeco-Roman Context*. Tübingen: Mohr Siebeck.
———. 2002. "Paul and the Imperial Gospel at Thessaloniki." *Journal for the Study of the New Testament* 25:71–96.
———. 1999. "Paul, Eschatology and the Augustan Age of Grace." *Tyndale Bulletin* 50:79–91.
Hatzopoulos, M. 2011. "The Cities." In *Brill's Companion to Ancient Macedon: Studies in the Archaeology and History of Macedon, 650 BC – 300 AD*, 235–41. Edited by R. Fox. Leiden: Brill.
Hawthorne, G. 1983. *Philippians*. Waco, TX: Word.
———, and R. Martin. 1993. *Dictionary of Paul and His Letters*. Downers Grove, IL: InterVarsity Press.
Hays, R. 1991. "Crucified with Christ: A Synthesis of the Theology of 1 and 2 Thessalonians, Philemon, Philippians, and Galatians." In

Pauline Theology, 1:227–46. Edited by J. Bassler. Minneapolis: Fortress Press.

———. 1989. *Echoes of Scripture in the Letters of Paul.* New Haven, CT: Yale University Press.

Heen, E. 2004. "Philippians 2:6-11 and Resistance to Local Timocratic Rule." In *Paul and the Roman Imperial Order,* 125–53. Edited by R. Horsley. Harrisburg, PA: Trinity Press International.

Hellerman, J. 2005. *Reconstructing Honor in Roman Philippi: Carmen Christi as Cursus Pudorum.* Cambridge: Cambridge University Press.

Hemer, C. 1985. "The Name of Paul." *Tyndale Bulletin* 36:179–83.

Hendrix, H. 1992. *Thessalonicans Honor Romans.* Ann Arbor, MI: University Microfilms International.

Hengel, M. 1997. *Crucifixion.* Translated by J. Bowden. Philadelphia: Fortress Press.

Herrmann, P. 1968. *Der römische Kaisereid.* Tübingen: Vandenhoeck & Ruprecht.

Hezer, C. 2011. "Slavery and the Jews." In *The Cambridge World History of Slavery* 1:438–55. Edited by K. Bradley and P. Cartledge. Cambridge: Cambridge University Press.

———. 2001. *Jewish literacy in Roman Palestine.* Tübingen: Mohr Siebeck.

Hirschfield, O. 1913. *Kleine Schriften.* Berlin: Weidmannsche Buchhandlung.

Holladay, C. 2017. *Introduction to the New Testament.* Reference Edition. Waco, TX: Baylor University Press

———. 1983. "Church Growth in the New Testament." *Restoration Quarterly* 26:85-102.

———. 1969. "Paul and His Opponents in Philippians 3." *Restoration Quarterly* 12:77-90.

Holloway, P. 2001. *Consolation in Philippians.* Cambridge: Cambridge University Press.

Horace. 1895. *The Works of Horace.* Translated by C. Smart. Philadelphia: McKay.

Horsley, R., ed. 2004. *Paul and the Roman Imperial Order.* Valley Forge, PA: Trinity Press International.

————, ed. 2000. *Paul and Politics: Ekklesia, Israel, Imperium, Interpretation.* London: Continuum.

————, ed. 1997. *Paul and Empire: Religion and Power in Roman Imperial Society.* Harrisburg, PA: Trinity Press International.

Howgego, C. 1995. *Ancient History from Coins*. New York: Routledge.
⎯⎯⎯⎯, V. Heuchert, and A. Burnett. 2005. *Coinage and Identity in the Roman Provinces*. Oxford: Oxford University Press.
Hugede, N. 1986. *Saint Paul et Rome*. Paris: Les Belles Lettres.
Hurst, L. 1986. "Re-Enter the Pre-Existent Christ in Philippians 2.5-11." *New Testament Studies* 32:449–57.
Jervis, A. 2007. *At the Heart of the Gospel: Suffering in the Earliest Christian Message*. Grand Rapids: Eerdmans.
⎯⎯⎯. 1991. *The Purpose of Romans: A Comparative Letter Structure Investigation*. Sheffield: Sheffield Academic Press.
Jewett, R. 1969. "Conflicting Movements in the Early Church as Reflected in Philippians." *Novum Testamentum* 11:362–90.
Jones, A. 1960. "Slavery in the Ancient World." In *Slavery in Classical Antiquity*, 1–15. Edited by M. Finley Cambridge: W. Heffer & Sons.
⎯⎯⎯. 1949. "The Roman Civil Service (Clerical and Sub-Clerical Grades)." *Journal of Roman Studies* 39, nos. 1 & 2:38–55.
Jones, D. 1980. "Christianity and the Roman Imperial Cult." In *Aufstieg und Niedergang der römischen Welt: Geschichte und Kultur Roms im Spiegel der neueren Forschung* 2, no. 23.2:1923–54.
Josephus. 1959. *The Jewish War*. Translated by G. Williamson. Baltimore, MD: Penguin Books.
⎯⎯⎯. 1930. *Jewish Antiquities*. Translated by H. St. J. Thackeray. Cambridge, MA: Harvard University Press.
⎯⎯⎯. 1926. *The Life and Against Apion*. Translated by H. St. J. Thackeray. Cambridge, MA: Harvard University Press.
Joshel, S. 2010. *Slavery in the Roman World*. New York: Cambridge University Press.
Judge, E. 2008. "'We Have No King but Caesar.' When Was Caesar First Seen as a King?" In *The First Christians in the Roman World*, 395–409. Tübingen: Mohr Siebeck.
⎯⎯⎯. 1971. "The Decrees of Caesar at Thessalonica." *Reformed Theological Review* 30:1–7.
Karakolis, C. 2013. "Church and Nation in the New Testament: The Formation of the Pauline Communities." *Saint Vladimir's Theological Quarterly* 57:361-380.
Käsemann, E. 1968. "A Critical Analysis of Philippians 2:5-11." In *God and Christ: Existence and Province*, 45–88. New York: Harper & Row.

Keay, S. 1996. "Emporion" In *Oxford Classical Dictionary*. Third edition, 524. Oxford: Oxford University Press.
Keller, M. 1995. "Choosing What Is Best: Paul, Roman Society and Philippians." Ph.D. diss., Lutheran School of Theology at Chicago.
Kennedy, D. 1978. "Some Observations on the Praetorian Guard." *Ancient Society* 9:275–301.
Keppie, L. 1984. *The Making of the Roman Army from Republic to Empire*. London: Batsford.
———. 1983. *Colonisation and Veteran Settlement in Italy 47–14 BC*. London, England: British School at Rome.
Klijn, A. 1965. "Paul's Opponents in Philippians 3." *Novum Testamentum* 7:278–84.
Koester, H. 1961. "The Purpose of the Polemic of a Pauline Fragment (Philippians III)." *New Testament Studies* 8:317–32.
Kolendo, J. 1978. "Les esclaves dans l'art antique: La stèle funeraire d'un marchand d'esclaves thraces découverte à Amphipolis." *Archeologia*, 29:24–34.
Koperski, V. 1996. *The Knowledge of Christ Jesus My Lord: The High Christology of "Philippians" 3, 7-11*. Kampen: Kok Pharos.
———. 1993. "The Early History of the Dissection of Philippians." *Journal of Theological Studies* 44:599–603.
———. 1992. "Feminist Concerns and the Authorial Readers in Philippians." *Louvain Studies* 17:269–92.
Koukouli-Chrysanthaki, C. 2011. "Philippi." In *Brill's Companion to Ancient Macedon: Studies in the Archaeology and History of Macedon, 650 BC – 300 AD*, 437–52. Edited by R. Fox. Leiden: Brill.
———, and C. Bakirtzis. 1995. *Philippi*. Athens: Archaeological Receipts Fund.
Krause, J.-W. 1996. *Gefängnisse im römischen Reich*. Stuttgart: Franz Steiner Verlag.
Kreitzer, L. 1996. *Striking New Images: Roman Imperial Coinage and the New Testament World*. Sheffield: Sheffield Academic Press.
Kremydi, S. 2011. "Coinage and Finance" In *Brill's Companion to Ancient Macedon: Studies in the Archaeology and History of Macedon, 650 BC – 300 AD*, 159–78. Edited by R. Fox. Leiden: Brill.
Krentz, E. 2003. "Paul, Games, and the Military." In *Paul in the Greco-Roman World: A Handbook*, 344–66. Edited by P. Sampley. Harrisburg, PA: Trinity Press International.

———. 1993. "Military Language and Metaphors in Philippians." In *Origins and Method*, 105–27. Edited by B. McLean. Sheffield: Sheffield Academic Press.

Kyrtatas, D. 2011. "Early Christianity in Macedonia" In In *Brill's Companion to Ancient Macedon: Studies in the Archaeology and History of Macedon, 650 BC – 300 AD*, 437–52. Edited by R. Fox. Leiden: Brill.

———. 1987. *The Social Structure of the Early Christian Communities*. London: Verso.

Lampe, P. 2003. "Paul, Patrons and Clients." In *Paul in the Greco-Roman World: A Handbook*, 488–523. Edited by P. Sampley. Harrisburg, PA: Trinity Press.

Lemerle, P. 1945. *Philippes et la Macedoine orientale à l'époque chrétienne et byzantine*. Paris: E de Boccard.

Lendon, J. E. 1997. *Empire of Honour: The Art of Government in the Roman World*. Oxford: Clarendon.

Lenski, N. 2006. "Servi Publici in Late Antiquity," In *Die Stadt in der Spätantike: Niedergang oder Wandel*, 335–57. Edited by J.-W. Krause. Stuttgart: Steiner.

Lentz, J. 1993. *Luke's Portrait of Paul*. Cambridge: Cambridge University Press.

Levick, B., and E. Breeze. 1996. "Colonization, Roman." In Oxford Classical Dictionary. Third edition, 364–65. Oxford: Oxford University Press.

Levick, B. 2000. *The Government of the Roman Empire: A Sourcebook*. 2nd ed. New York: Routledge.

———. 1979. "Poena Legis Maiestatis." *Historia: Zeitschrift für alte Geschichte* 28:358–79.

———. 1976. *Tiberius the Politician*. Plymouth, UK: Thames & Hudson.

———. 1967. *Roman Colonies in Southern Asia Minor*. Oxford: Clarendon Press.

Levie, J. 1963. "Le chrétien citoyen du Ciel (Phil 3,20)." *Analecta Biblica* 17–18:81–88.

Liddell, H., R. Scott, and H. Jones. 1968. *A Greek-English Lexicon*. Oxford: Clarendon Press.

Lightfoot. J. 1888/1961. *Saint Paul's Epistle to the Philippians*. Reprinted 1961. Grand Rapids, MI: Zondervan.

Lincoln, A., and A. Wedderburn. 1993. *The Theology of the Later Pauline Letters*. Cambridge: Cambridge University Press.

Link, H. 1978. "aischyne." In *The New International Dictionary of New Testament Theology,* 3: 564. Grand Rapids, MI: Zondervan.

Lintott, A., and J. Balson. 1996. "Maiestas." In *The Oxford Classical Dictionary,* 913–14. Third edition. New York: Oxford University Press.

Lohmeyer, E. 1974. *Der Brief an die Philipper.* 14th ed. Göttingen: Vandenhoeck & Ruprecht.

———. 1964. *Die Briefe an die Philipper, an die Kolosser und an Philemon.* Göttingen: Vandenhoeck & Ruprecht.

———. 1961. *Kyrios Jesus: Eine Untersuchung zu Phil. 2,5-11.* Darmstadt: Wissenschaftliche Buchgesellschaft.

———. 1919. *Christuskult and Kaiserkult.* Tübingen: Mohr.

Longenecker, R. 1995. *The Expositor's Bible Commentary: Acts.* Grand Rapids: Zondervan.

Longenecker, B., ed. 2002. *Narrative Dynamics in Paul.* Louisville, KY: Westminster John Knox.

Lüdemann, G. 1984. *Paul, Apostle to the Gentiles. Studies in Chronology.* Translated by S. Jones. Philadelphia: Fortress, 1984.

Luter, A. 1996. "Partnership in the Gospel: The Role of Women in the Church at Philippi." *Journal of the Evangelical Theological Society* 39:411–20.

———, and M. Lee. 1995. "Philippians as Chiasmus: Key to the Structure, Unity and Theme Questions." *New Testament Studies* 41:89–101.

Luther, M., and J. Stirewalt. 2003. *Paul, the Letter Writer.* Grand Rapids, MI: Eerdmans.

Magie, D. 1950. *Roman Rule in Asia Minor to the End of the Third Century after Christ.* Princeton, NJ: Princeton University Press.

Maier, H. 2005. "A Sly Civility: Colossians and Empire." *Journal for the Study of the New Testament* 27:323–49.

Malherbe, A. 1996. "Paul's Self-Sufficiency (Philippians 4:11)." In *Friendship, Flattery, and Frankness of Speech: Studies on Friendship in the New Testament,* 125–39. Edited by J. Fitzgerald. Leiden: Brill.

———. 1968. "The Beasts at Ephesus." *Journal of Biblical Literature* 37:71–80.

Malina, B. 1993. "Honor and Shame: Pivotal Values of the First-Century Mediterranean World," 28–62. In *The New Testament World.* Revised edition. Atlanta: Westminster John Knox.

———, and J. Pilch. 2006. *Social-Science Commentary on the Letters of Paul.* Minneapolis: Fortress Press.

Mann, J. 1983. *Legionary Recruitment and Veteran Settlement during the Principate.* Walnut Creek, CA: Left Coast Press.

Manson, T. 1958. "St. Paul in Ephesus: The Date of the Epistle to the Philippians." *Bulletin of the John Rylands University Library* 23:182–200.

Marrow, S. 1982. *Speaking the Word Fearlessly.* New York: Paulist.

Marshall, H. 1992. *The Epistle to the Philippians.* London: Epworth.

———. 1968. "The Christ-Hymn in Philippians." *Tyndale Bulletin* 19:104–27.

Martin, R. 1997. *A Hymn of Christ: Philippians 2:5-11 in Recent Interpretation & in the Setting of Early Christian Worship.* Downers Grove, IL: InterVarsity Press.

———. 1988. *The Epistle of Paul to the Philippians: An Introduction and Commentary.* Tyndale New Testament Commentaries. Valley Forge, PA: Trinity Press International.

———. 1988. *The Epistle of Paul to the Philippians.* Grand Rapids: Eerdmans.

———. 1976. *Philippians.* Grand Rapids: Eerdmans.

Matera, F. 1996. *New Testament Ethics. The Legacies of Jesus and Paul.* Louisville, KY: Westminster John Knox.

Mattingly, H. et al. 1984. *Roman Imperial Coinage: 31 BC–AD 69.* Revised edition. London: Spink.

———. 1965. *Coins of the Roman Empire in the British Museum.* London: Trustees of the British Museum.

McCasland, S. 1930. "The Origin of the Lord's Day." *Journal of Biblical Literature* 49:65–82.

McDermott, M. 1975. "The Biblical Doctrine of KOINONIA." *Biblische Zeitschrift* 19:64–77, 219–33.

McLaren, J. 2005. "Jews and the Imperial Cult: From Augustus to Domitian." *Journal for the Study of the New Testament* 27:257–78.

Mearns, C. 1987. "The Identity of Paul's Opponents at Philippi." *New Testament Studies* 33:194–204.

Meeks, W. 2003. *The First Urban Christians: The Social World of the Apostle Paul.* New Haven, CT: Yale University Press.

———. 1993. *The Origins of Christian Morality: The First Two Centuries.* New Haven, CT: Yale University Press.

———. 1990. "Equal to God." In *The Conversation Continues: Studies in Paul and John in Honor of J. Louis Martyn,* 309–22. Edited by R. Fortna and B. Gaventa. Nashville, TN: Abingdon.

———. 1982. "The Social Context of Pauline Theology." *Interpretation* 36:266–77.
Melick, R. 1991. *Philippians, Colossians, Ephesians*. Nashville, TN: Broadman.
Michael, J. 1928. *The Epistle of Paul to the Philippians*. London: Hodder & Stoughton.
Michaelis, W. 1925. *Die Gefangenschaft des Paulus in Ephesus*. Gutersloh: Bertelsmann.
Millar, F. 1984. *The Emperor in the Roman World 31 BC–AD 37*. New York: Cornell University Press.
———. 1973. "Triumvirate and Principate." *Journal of Roman Studies* 63:50–67.
Miller, E. 1982. "*Politeuesthe* in Philippians 1:27: Some Philological and Thematic Observations." *Journal for the Study of the New Testament* 15:86–96.
Mitchell, M. 1995. "John Chrysostom on Philemon: A Second Look." *Harvard Theological Review* 88:135–48.
———. 1993. *Paul and the Rhetoric of Reconciliation: An Exegetical Investigation of the Language and Composition of 1 Corinthians*. Louisville, KY: Westminster John Knox Press.
———. 1992. "New Testament Envoys in the Context of Greco-Roman Diplomatic and Epistolary Conventions: The Example of Timothy and Titus." *Journal of Biblical Literature* 111 (4): 641–62.
Momigliano, A. 1986. "How Roman Emperors Became Gods." *American Scholar* 55:181–93.
Morley, N. 2011. "Slavery under the Principate." In *The Cambridge World History of Slavery*, Volume 1: 265–86. Edited by K. Bradley and P. Cartledge. Cambridge: Cambridge University Press.
Morris, N., and D. Rothman. 1995. *The Oxford History of the Prison: The Practice of Punishment in Western Society*. New York: Oxford University Press.
Moule, C. 1978. *Philippian Studies*. London: Pickering & Inglis.
———. 1970. "Further Reflections on Philippians 2:5-11." In *Apostolic History and the Gospel: Biblical and Historical Essays Presented to F. F. Bruce on His 60th Birthday*, 264–76. Edited by W. Ward Gasque and R. Martin. Grand Rapids: Eerdmans.
Moulton, J., and G. Milligan. 1930. *The Vocabulary of the Greek Testament Illustrated from the Papyri and Other Non-literary Sources*. London: Hodder & Stoughton.

Moxnes, H. 1993. "BTB Readers Guide: Honor and Shame." *Biblical Theology Bulletin* 23:167–76.
Muller, J. 1976. *The Epistles of Paul to the Philippians and to Philemon.* Grand Rapids, MI: Eerdmans.
Muller, U. 1993. *Der Brief des Paulus an die Philipper.* Leipzig: Evangelische Verlagsanstalt.
Mullins, T. 1973. "Visit Talk in New Testament Letters." *Catholic Biblical Quarterly* 35:350–58.
Murphy-O'Connor, J. 1996. *Paul: A Critical Life.* Oxford: Clarendon Press.
———. 1995. *Paul the Letter-Writer: His World, His Options, His Skills.* Collegeville, MN: Michael Glazier Books.
———. 1976. "Christological Anthropology in Phil. II, 6-11." *Revue Biblique* 83:25–50.
Neuhaus, D. 2018. "Tra Nazaaret e Betlemme (Between Nazareth and Bethlehem)," *La Civiltà Cattolica* 44:525–31.
———. 2008. "Paul a 'Tentmaker.'" In *Saint Paul: Educator to Faith and Love*, 147–66. Edited by M. Ferrero and R. Spataro. Jerusalem: Studium Theologicum Salesianum.
Nickle, K. 1966. *The Collection: A Study in Paul's Strategy.* London: SCM Press.
Nock, A. 1952. "The Roman Army and the Roman Religious Year." *Harvard Theological Review* 45:187–252.
O'Brien, R. 1991. *The Epistle to the Philippians.* Grand Rapids: Eerdmans.
O'Sullivan. F. *The Egnatian Way.* Harrisburg, PA: Stackpole Books.
Oakes, P. 2007. *Philippians: From People to Letter.* Cambridge: Cambridge University Press.
———. 2005. "Re-mapping the Universe: Paul and the Empire in 1 Thessalonians and Philippians." *Journal for the Study of the New Testament* 27:301–22.
———. 2002. *Rome in the Bible and the Early Church.* Grand Rapids, MI: Baker.
Oliver, J. 1979. "Greek Applications for Roman Trials." *American Journal of Philology* 100:543–58.
Otto, W. 1910. "Augustus Soter." *Hermes* 45:448–60.
The Oxford Classical Dictionary. 1996 Third edition. Edited by S. Hornblower and A. Spawforth. Oxford: Oxford University Press.
Palmer, D. 1975. "'To die is gain.' (Philippians 1:21)." *Novum Testamentum* 17:203–18.

Parsons, M. 2008. *Acts*. Grand Rapids, MI: Baker.
Passerini, A. 1969. *Le cohorti pretorie*. Rome: Centro Editoriale Internazionale.
Pausanias. 1918. *Description of Greece*. Translated by W. Jones. Cambridge, MA: Harvard University Press.
Pekary, T. 1985. Das römische Kaiserbildnis in Staat, Kult und Gesellschaft: dargestellt anhand der Schriftquellen. Berlin: Mann Verlag.
Peppard, M. 2011. *The Son of God in the Roman World: Divine Sonship in Its Social and Political Context*. Oxford: Oxford University Press.
Perkins, P. 1991. "Philippians: Theology for the Heavenly *Politeuma*." In *Pauline Theology* 1:89–104. Edited by J. Bassler. Minneapolis: Fortress Press.
Peterlin, D. 1995. *Paul's Letter to the Philippians in the Light of Disunity in the Church*. Leiden: Brill.
Peterman, G. 1997. *Paul's Gift from Philippi: Conventions of Gift-Exchange and Christian Giving*. Cambridge: Cambridge University Press.
Philo. 1942. *The Embassy to Gaius*. Translated by F. Colson. Cambridge, MA: Harvard University Press.
Philostratus. 1912. *The Life of Apollonius of Tyana*. Translated by F. Conybeare. Cambridge, MA: Harvard University Press.
Pilhofer, P. 2000. *Philippi: Katalog der Inschriften von Philippi*. Tübingen: Mohr Siebeck.
———. 1995. *Philippi: Die erste christliche Gemeinde Europas*. Tübingen: Mohr Siebeck.
Pliny. 1969. *Letters and Panegyricus*. Translated by B. Radice. Cambridge, MA: Harvard University Press.
Plummer, A. 1919. *A Commentary on St. Paul's Epistle to the Philippians*. London: Robert Scott.
Plutarch. 1926. *Plutarch's Lives*. Translated by F. Babbit. Cambridge. MA: Harvard University Press.
Pobee, J. 1985. *Persecution and Martyrdom in the Theology of Paul*. Sheffield: Sheffield Academic Press.
Pollini, J. 1984. "Damnatio Memoriae in Stone: Two Portraits of Nero Recut to Vespasian in American Museums." *American Journal of Archaeology* 88:547–55.
Portefaix, L. 1988. *Sisters Rejoice: Paul's Letter to the Philippians and Luke-Acts as Seen by First-Century Philippian Women*. Uppsala: Almqvist & Wiksell.

Porter, S. 2016. *The Apostle Paul: His Life, Thought, and Letters*. Grand Rapids: Eerdmans.
———. 2009. "Did Paul Have Opponents in Rome and What Were They Opposing?" In *Paul and His Opponents*, 149–68. Edited by S. Porter. Leiden: Brill.
Pratscher, W. 1996. "Die Bewältigung von Leid bei Paulus." *Studien zum Neuen Testament und seiner Umwelt* 21:73–91.
———. 1979. "Der Verzicht des Paulus auf finanziellen Unterhalt durch seine Gemeinden: Ein Aspekt seiner Missionsweise." *New Testament Studies* 25:284–98.
Preuschen, E. 1901. "Die Rechtsverhaltnisse des Apostels Paulus." *Zeitschrift für die neutestamentliche Wissenschaft und die Kunde der alteren Kirche des Urchistentums* 2:81–96.
Price, S. 1984a. *Rituals and Power: The Roman Imperial Cult in Asia Minor*. Cambridge: Cambridge University Press.
———. 1984b. "Gods and Emperors: The Greek Language of the Roman Imperial Cult." *Journal of Hellenic Studies* 104: 79–95.
———. 1980. "Between Man and God: Sacrifice in the Roman Imperial Cult." *Journal of Roman Studies* 70:28–43.
Pucci, G. 2005. "'*detrahis vestimenta venalibus*': Iconografia della vendita di schiavi nell'antichità e oltre." *Journal of Roman Archaeology* 18:235–40.
Quinn, J. 1978. "'Seven Times He Wore Chains' (1 Clem 5.6)." *Journal of Biblical Literature* 97:574–76.
Raaflaub, K. 1990. *Between Republic and Empire: Interpretations of Augustus and His Principles*. Berkeley: University of California Press.
Ramelli, I. 2017. *Social Justice and the Legitimacy of Slavery*. Oxford: Oxford University Press.
———. 2007. "The Syntax of ἐν Χριστῷ in Thess 4:16." *Journal of Biblical Literature* 126:579–93.
Ramsay, W. 1906. *Studies in the History and Art of the Eastern Provinces of the Roman Empire*. Aberdeen: Aberdeen University Press
———. 1900. "Notes: The Philippians and Their Magistrates." *Journal of Theological Studies* 1:114–16.
———. 1893. *The Church in the Roman Empire before A.D. 170*. London: Hodder & Stoughton.
Rankov, B. 1994. *The Praetorian Guard*. London: Osprey Publishing.
Rapske, B. 1994. *The Book of Acts and Paul in Roman Custody*. Grand Rapids, MI: Eerdmans.

———. 1991. "The Importance of Helpers to the Imprisoned Paul in the Book of Acts." *Tyndale Bulletin* 42:3–30.
Reicke, B. 1970. "Caesarea, Rome, and the Captivity Epistles." In *Apostolic History and the Gospel: Biblical and Historical Essays Presented to F. F. Bruce on His 60th Birthday*, 277–86. Edited by W. Ward Gasque and R. Martin. Grand Rapids: Eerdmans.
Reid, B. 2017. "Editor's Introduction to Wisdom Commentary: 'She Is a Breath of the Power of God' (Wis 7:25)." Pp. xv–xxxiii in *Philippians, Colossians, Philemon*, by Elsa Tamez et al. Wisdom Commentary 51. Collegeville, MN: Liturgical Press.
Reumann, J. 2008. *Philippians*. New Haven, CT: Yale University Press.
———. 1997. "Philippians and the Culture of Friendship." *Trinity Seminary Review* 19:69–83.
———. 1993a. "Church Office in Paul, Especially in Philippians." In *Origins and Methods*, 82–91. Edited by B. McLean. Sheffield: Sheffield Academic Press.
———. 1993b. "Contributions of the Philippian Community to Paul and to Earliest Christianity." *New Testament Studies* 39:438–57.
———. 1984. "Philippians 3.20-21—A Hymnic Fragment?" *New Testament Studies* 30:593–609.
Rhoads, D. 2006. "Performance Criticism: An Emerging Methodology in Second Testament Studies. Parts I and II." *Biblical Theology Bulletin* 36: 118–33, 164–84.
Rich, J. 1992. *City and Country in the Ancient World*. New York: Routledge.
Riesner, R. 1998. *Paul's Early Period: Chronology, Mission, Strategy, Theology*. Translated by D. Stott. Grand Rapids: Eerdmans.
Rives, J. 1996. "Augustales." In *Oxford Classical Dictionary*. Third edition, 215. Oxford: Oxford University Press.
Riviere, Y. 1994. "Carcer et uincula: La détention publique à Rome sous la République et le Haut-Empire." *Mélanges de l'école française de Rome. Antiquité* 106:579–652.
Rolla, A. 1963. "La cittadinanza Greco-Romana e la cittadinanza celeste de Filippesi 3,20." *Analecta Biblica* 17–18:75–80.
Rudich, V. 1993. *Political Dissidence under Nero: The Price of Dissimulation*. London: Routledge.
Ruppel, W. 1927. "*Politeuma*: Bedeutungsgeschichte eines staatrechtlichen Terminus." *Philologus* 82: 268–312, 433–54.
Ryan, J, and B. Thurston. 2003. *Philippians and Philemon*. Collegeville, MN: Liturgical Press.

Saddington, D. 1996. "Roman Military and Administrative Personnel in the New Testament." Aufstieg und Niedergang der römischen Welt, Volume II.26.3, 2409–35.

Salmon, E. 1970. *Roman Colonization under the Republic*. Ithaca, NY: Cornell University Press.

Sampley, P., ed. 2003. *Paul in the Greco-Roman World: A Handbook*. Valley Forge, PA: Trinity Press International.

———. 1980. *Pauline Partnership in Christ: Christian Community and Commitment in Light of Roman Law*. Minneapolis: Fortress Press.

Sanders, J. 1969. "Dissenting Deities and Philippians 2:1-11." *Journal of Biblical Literature* 88:279–90.

Sarikakis, T. 1977. "Des soldats Macédoniens dans l'armée romaine." In *Ancient Macedonia II: Papers Read at the Second International Symposium Held in Thessaloniki, 19–24 August 1973*, 431–64. Thessaloniki: Institute for Balkan Studies.

Scheidel, W. 2011. "The Roman Slave Supply." In *The Cambridge World History of Slavery*. Volume 1: 287-310. Edited by K. Bradley and P. Cartledge. Cambridge: Cambridge University Press.

Schenk, W. 1984. *Die Philipperbriefe des Paulus: Kommentar*. Stuttgart: Kohlhammer.

Schlier, H. 1964. "parresia, parresiazomai." In *The Theological Dictionary of the New Testament*, 5: 871–76. Edited by G. Kittel and G. Friedrich. Translated and edited by G. Bromily. Grand Rapids: Eerdmans.

Schreiber, S. 2003. "Paulus im 'Zwischenzustand': Phil 1.23 und die Ambivalenz des Sterbens als Provokation." *New Testament Studies* 49:336–59.

Scodel, R., and D. Potter. 1993. "Martydom as Spectacle." In *Theater and Society in the Classical World*, 53–88. Edited by R. Scodel. Ann Arbor, MI: University of Michigan Press.

Scott, J. 1990. *Domination and the Arts of Resistance: Hidden Transcripts*. New Haven, CT: Yale University Press.

Scott, K. 1930. "Empire Worship in Ovid." *Transactions and Proceedings of the American Philological Association* 61:43–69.

———. 1929. "Plutarch and the Ruler Cult." *Transactions and Proceedings of the American Philological Association* 60:117–35.

Seeley, D. 1994. "The Background of the Philippians Hymn (2:6-11)." *Journal of Higher Criticism* 1:49–72.

Seneca. 1917. *Ad Lucilum Epistulae Morales*. Translated by R. Gummere. Cambridge, MA: Harvard University Press.

Sève, M., and P. Weber. 2012. *Guides du forum de Philippes*. Paris: De Boccard.

———. 1988. "Un monument honorifique au forum de Philippes." *Bulletin de Correspondance Hellenique* 112:467–79.

Shelton, J. 1988. *As the Romans Did: A Source Book in Roman Social History*. New York: Oxford University Press.

Sherk, R. 1988. *The Roman Empire: Augustus to Hadrian*. Translated Documents of Greece and Rome. New York: Cambridge University Press.

———. 1984. *Rome and the Greek East to the Death of Augustus*. Translated Documents of Greece and Rome. New York: Cambridge University Press.

———. 1969. *Roman Documents from the Greek East*. Baltimore, MD: Johns Hopkins Press.

———. 1957. "Roman Imperial Troops in Macedonia and Achaea." *American Journal of Philology* 78:52–62.

Sherwin-White, A. 1996. "Decuriones." In *Oxford Classical Dictionary*. Third edition, 437–38. Oxford: Oxford University Press.

———. 1985. *The Letters of Pliny: A Historical and Social Commentary*. Oxford: Clarendon.

———. 1980. *The Roman Citizenship*. Second edition. New York: Oxford University Press.

———. 1978. *Roman Law and Roman Society*. Grand Rapids: Eerdmans.

Silva, M. 1988. *Philippians*. Chicago: Moody Press.

Smallwood, M. 1967. *Documents Illustrating the Principates of Gaius, Claudius, and Nero*. Cambridge: Cambridge University Press.

Smith, R. 2006. *Roman Portrait Statuary from Aphrodisias*. Mainz: Verlag Philipp von Zabern.

———. 2000. "Nero the Sun God: Divine Accessories and Political Symbols in Roman Imperial Images." *Journal of Roman Archaeology* 13:532–42.

Smith, W. 1870. "Lesche." In *Dictionary of Greek and Roman Antiquities*. London: John Murray.

Snyman, A. 1993. "Persuasion in Philippians 4.1-20." In *Rhetoric and the New Testament*, 325–37. Edited by S. Porter and T. Olbricht. Sheffield: Journal for the Study of the New Testament Press.

Solin, H. 1996. "Names, Personal, Roman." In *Oxford Classical Dictionary*. Third edition, 1024-26. Oxford: Oxford University Press.

Speidel, M. 1970. "The Captor of Decebalus: A New Inscription from Philippi." *Journal of Roman Studies* 60:142–53.

Spicq, C. 1970. "L'imitation de Jésus-Christ durant les dernier jours de l'apôtre Paul." In *Mélanges Bibliques*, 313–22. Gembloux: Duculot.

Standhartinger, A. 2013. "Aus der Welt eines Gefangenen. Die Kommunikationsstruktur des Philipperbriefs im Spiegel seiner Abfassungssituation." *Novum Testamentum* 55 (2): 140–67.

———. 2013. "Eintracht in Philippi: Zugleich ein Beitrag zur Funktion von Phil 2,6-11 im Kontext." In *Paulus—Werk und Wirkung: Festschrift für Andreas Lindemann zum 70 Geburtstag*, 149–75. Edited by P. Klumbies and D. duToit. Tübingen: Mohr Siebeck.

———. 2006. "Die paulinische Theologie im Spannungsfeld römische-imperialer Machtpolitik: Eine neue Perspektive auf Paulus, kritische geprüft anhand des Philipperbriefs." In *Religion, Politik und Gewalt*, 364–82. Edited by F. Schweitzer. Gütersloh: Gütersloher Verlagshaus.

Staudinger, F. 1990. "desmos." In *The Exegetical Dictionary of the New Testament*, 1: 289. Edited by H. Balz and G. Schneider. Grand Rapids: Eerdmans.

Stevenson, G. 1949. *Roman Provincial Administration till the Age of the Antonines*. London: Blackwell.

Still, T. 1999. *Conflict at Thessalonica: A Pauline Church and Its Neighbours*. Sheffield: Sheffield Academic Press.

Stowers, S. 1991. "Friends and Enemies in the Politics of Heaven: Reading Theology in Philippians." In *Pauline Theology*, 1:105–21. Edited by J. Bassler. Minneapolis: Fortress Press.

———. 1986. *Letter Writing in Greco-Roman Antiquity*. Louisville, KY: Westminster.

Suetonius. 1913. *Suetonius: The Lives of the Caesars*. Translated by J. Rolfe. Cambridge, MA: Harvard University Press.

Sumney, J. 2007. *Philippians: A Greek Student's Intermediate Reader*. Peabody, MA: Hendrickson Publishers.

Sutherland, C. 1987. *Roman History and Coinage, 44 B.C.–A.D. 69: Fifty Points of Relation from Julius Caesar to Vespasian*. New York: Oxford University Press.

———, et al. 1984. *The Roman Imperial Coinage*. Revised edition. London: Spink.

Sydenham E. 1920. *The Coinage of Nero*. London: Spink and Son.

Syme, R. 1960. *The Roman Revolution.* New York: Oxford University Press.
Tacitus, Cornelius. 1969. *Tacitus in Five Volumes: The Histories Books IV–V. The Annals Books I–III.* Translated by C. Moore. Cambridge, MA: Harvard University Press.
Tajra, H. 1994. *The Martyrdom of St. Paul: Historical and Judicial Context, Traditions, and Legends.* Tübingen: Mohr.
———. 1989. *The Trial of Saint Paul.* Tübingen: Mohr.
Talbert, C. 1975. "The Concept of Immortals in Mediterranean Antiquity." *Journal of Biblical Literature* 94:419–36.
———. 1967. "The Problem of Pre-Existence in Philippians 2:6-11." *Journal of Biblical Literature* 86:141–53.
Tamez, E. 2017. "Philippians." In *Philippians, Colossians, Philemon.* Collegeville, MN: Liturgical Press.
Taylor, L. 1931. *The Divinity of the Roman Emperor.* Middletown, CT: American Philological Association.
Taylor, W. 2012. *Paul: Apostle to the Nations.* Minneapolis: Fortress Press.
Tellbe, M. 2001. *Paul between Synagogue and State: Christians, Jews, and Civic Authorities in 1 Thessalonians, Romans, and Philippians.* Stockholm: Almqvist & Wiksell.
———. 1994. "The Sociological Factors behind Philippians 3,1-11 and the Conflict at Philippi." *Journal for the Study of the New Testament* 55:97–121.
Thomas, D. 1972."The Place of Women in the Church at Philippi." *Expository Times* 83:117–20.
Thompson, A. 2002. "Blameless before God: Philippians 3:6 in Context." *Themelios* 28:5–12.
Thompson, F. 2003. *The Archaeology of Greek and Roman Slavery.* London: Duckworth.
Valerius Maximus. 1865. *Factorum et Dictorum Memorabilium Libri Novum.* Leipzig: Teubner.
Vanderpool, E. 1959, "Athens Honors the Emperor." *Hesperia* 28 (1): 86-90.
Verhoef, E. 2013. *Philippi: How Christianity Began in Europe.* London: Bloomsbury.
———. 2005. "The Church of Philippi in the First Six Centuries of Our Era." *Harvard Theological Studies* 61:565–92.
Vincent, M. 1902. *Epistles to the Philippians and to Philemon.* Edinburgh: T. & T. Clark.

Vittinghoff, F. 1951. *Römische Kolonisation und Burgerrechtspolitik unter Caesar und Augustus*. Wiesbaden: Steiner Verlag.

———. 1936. *Der Staatsfeind in der römischen Kaiserzeit; Untersuchungen zur "damnatio memoriae."* Berlin: Junfer und Dunnhaupt Verlag.

Von Fritz, K. 1970. "Epictetus." In *Oxford Classical Dictionary*. Second edition, 390. Oxford: Oxford University Press

Walter, N., E. Reinmuth, and P. Lampe. 1998. In *Die Briefe an die Philipper, Thessalonischer und an Philemon*. Göttingen: Vandenhoeck & Ruprecht.

Wansink, C. 1996. *Chained in Christ: The Experience and Rhetoric of Paul's Imprisonments*. Sheffield: Sheffield Academic Press.

Warmington, B. 1969. *Nero: Reality and Legend*. New York: W. W. Norton.

Watson, D. 1988. "A Rhetorical Analysis of Philippians and Its Implications for the Unity Question." *Novum Testamentum* 30:57–87.

Watson, G. 1981. *The Roman Soldier*. Ithaca, NY: Cornell University Press.

Watson, L. 1996. "Calpurnius Siculus," In *Oxford Classical Dictionary*. Third edition, 281. Oxford: Oxford University Press.

Weaver, P. 1994. "Epaphroditus, Josephus, Epictetus." *Classical Quarterly* 44: 468–79.

———. 1972. *Familia Caesaris: A Social Study of the the Emperor's Freedmen and Slaves*. Cambridge: Cambridge University Press.

Webster, G. 1969. *The Roman Imperial Army of the First and Second Centuries A.D.* New York: Funk & Wagnalls.

Weinstock, S. 1971. *Divus Julius*. Oxford: Clarendon.

Westermann, W. 1964. "Slavery and the Elements of Freedom in Ancient Greece." In *Slavery in Classical Antiquity*, 1-16. Edited by M. Finley. Cambridge: W. Heffer & Sons.

———. 1955. *The Slave System of Greek and Roman Antiquity*. Philadelphia: The American Philosophical Society.

Wiedemann, T. 1981. *Greek and Roman Slavery*. Baltimore, MD: Johns Hopkins University Press.

Williams, D. 2003. *Enemies of the Cross of Christ: The Terminology of the Cross and Conflict in Philippians*. Sheffield: Sheffield Academic Press.

Williams, D. J. 1995. *Acts*. Peabody, MA: Hendrickson Publishers.

Williamson, P. 2009. *Ephesians*. Grand Rapids, MI: Baker Academic.

Winter, B. 2003. *Roman Wives, Roman Widows: The Appearance of New Women and the Pauline Communities*. Grand Rapids, MI: Eerdmans.
Winter, S. 1987. "Paul's Letter to Philemon." *New Testament Studies* 33:1–15.
Witherington, B. 1994. *Friendship and Finance in Philippi*. Valley Forge, PA: Trinity Press International.
Wright, N. 2004. *Paul for Everyone: The Prison Letters: Ephesians, Philippians, Colossians and Philemon*. London: SPCK.
———. 2000. "Paul's Gospel and Caesar's Empire." In *Paul and Politics*, 160–83. Edited by R. Horsley. Harrisburg, PA: Trinity Press International.
———. 1986. "*harpagmos* and the Meaning of Philippians 2:5-11." *Journal of Theological Studies* 37:321–52.
Zerwick, M., and M. Grosvenor. 1988. *A Grammatical Analysis of the Greek New Testament*. Third edition. Rome: Pontifical Biblical Institute.

Index of Passages

Old Testament			Acts		20:6	25
			16	20, 21, 24, 110, 127, 132, 156	20:28	52
Exodus					21:33	57
16:2	101				21:40	114
			16:3	105	22:1	58
Leviticus			16:11-12	148, 150	22:2	114
12:3	114		16:12-40	105	22:24-29	21
			16:13	26	22:25-29	47
Numbers			2:23	92	24:10	58
15:8-10	103		5:31	92	24:27	32
			8:3	115	25:8	58
Deuteronomy			9:1-2	115	25:16	58
32:5	101		16:14-15	22	25:26	97
			16:15	20	26:1	58
Isaiah			16:16-21	22	26:2	58
42:8	94		16:18	20	26:11	115
45:23	94		16:19-39	21	26:24	58
45:24a	95		16:19-22	24	26:26	72
			16:22b-24	77	26:29	57, 72
Amos			16:23-24	22	28:14	51
5:20	56		16:33b	22	28:16	36, 57
			16:34	20	28:20	57
Joel			16:37-39	24	28:23	57
2:2	56		16:37-38	47	28:30	33, 36, 57, 58
			16:37	21, 127	28:31	72
New Testament			16:40	22, 24		
			17:1	49, 148, 152	Romans	
Mark					1:1	48
16:12	83		17:14	105	1:3	86
			18:11	49	1:9	60
John			19	49	1:10	118
13:4-5	88		19:22	105	1:11	60
15:15	88		20:1-6	20	1:29	68

INDEX OF PASSAGES | 203

2:8	79	11:1	122	13:4	59
3:23	76	11:25	29	13:11	137
5:9	29	11:27	29		
8:38	90	12:13	88	Galatians	
9:22	76	15:9	115	1:2	139
11:44	118	15:10	106	1:4	91
13:1-7	65, 66, 96	15:10a	106	1:10	48
14:4	76	15:20b	106	1:13	115
15:18-19	65	15:24	90	1:23	75
15:23	26	15:25	123	2:2c	102
15:24	107	15:32	32	2:19	75
15:25-27	25	16:13	76, 141	3:1	59
15:28	73	16:22	91	3:2	75
15:33	137			3:20	91
16:2	52	2 Corinthians		3:28	80, 88
16:3-15	31	1:1	139	4:4	85
16:3	110	1:14	56	5:11	59
16:9	110	1:23	60	5:12	114
16:18	123	4:7-12	116	5:20-21	68
16:20	137	4:10a	116	5:20	79
		5:2	60	5:26	79
1 Corinthians		5:7	79	6:14	59
1:2	139	7:4	71	6:18	146
1:6	59	7:11	58		
1:8	56	7:15	100	Ephesians	
1:13	59	8	143	3:1	57
1:21	59	8:2-4	25	4:1	57
1:23	59	8:16-24	141	6:19-20	72
1:30	89	8:23	110	6:20	57
2:2	59	9	143	6:24	91
2:3	100	9:2-4	25		
2:8	59	9:14	60	Philippians	
2:16	88	10:1	134	1:1–3:1	34
2:22	106	11:7-12	139	1:1-11	45, 46-61
3:5	52	11:8-9	143	1:1-2	45, 46, 69
3:9	110	11:9	25, 141	1:1	25, 47, 48, 49, 86, 106, 110
4:16	122	11:21	114		
4:17	105	11:22	114		
5:5	56	11:23	32	1:1a	51, 119
9:3	58	12:10	77	1:1b	51, 52
9:24	119	12:19	58	1:2	38, 53, 54, 60, 85, 93, 116
10:16a	29	12:20	79		

Index of Passages

Philippians (*continued*)		1:17	38, 56, 62, 67, 68, 69, 79, 106, 17, 139, 144	2:1-5	45, 78
1:2b	54			2:1-4	69, 78, 99
1:3-11	45, 46, 54			2:1	55, 60, 78, 79, 136
1:3	55				
1:4	46, 55, 61	1:18	67, 68, 69	2:2-4	40, 41, 101
1:5	54, 55, 61, 62	1:18b	69	2:2a	79
1:6	46, 54, 55, 61, 102	1:19-26	38, 45, 62, 70	2:2b	79
				2:3	69, 74, 75
1:7	46, 48, 53, 54, 55, 56, 58, 59, 68	1:19a	69	2:3a	79
		1:19b	70	2:3b-5	82
		1:20	30, 66, 70	2:3b-4	80
1:8	54, 60	1:20a	70	2:5	78, 80, 83
1:9-11	46	1:20b	70, 71	2:6-11	38, 39, 42, 43, 44, 45, 79, 81-99, 108
1:9	54, 61	1:21-25	62		
1:10-11	61	1:21-24	72		
1:10	46, 55, 102	1:21-22a	72	2:6-8	41, 48, 78, 81
1:11	54, 79, 98, 140	1:21	117		
		1:21a	72	2:6-7	89
1:12-26	45, 61-74	1:21b	72	2:6	79, 83, 84, 129
1:12-13	45, 62, 63	1:22	140		
1:12	146	1:22b-23a	73	2:7-8	39
1:12a	63	1:23b	73	2:7	46, 80, 83, 85, 86, 106, 111, 129
1:13	30, 38, 48, 56, 63	1:24-25	68, 73		
		1:24	73		
1:13a	64	1:25	73	2:7b	116
1:13b	65	1:26	62, 73	2:8	39, 90, 91, 95, 116
1:14-18	30, 31, 45, 62, 65, 67, 69	1:27-30	45, 74		
		1:27	40, 75, 78, 100, 126, 131, 133	2:8a	89
				2:8b	90
1:14-15b	37			2:9-11	35, 40, 60, 77, 81, 85, 88, 91, 92, 118, 130
1:14	38, 48, 56, 67, 71, 116, 145	1:27a	75		
		1:27b	41, 74, 75		
		1:27c	75, 133		
1:15	62, 106, 117, 144	1:28	70, 100, 121	2:9	49, 92, 94, 119
		1:28a	76, 124		
1:15a	38, 67, 68	1:28b	75, 76	2:9a	91
1:15b-16	38, 67	1:28c	75	2:9b	93
1:15b	67	1:29	76, 77	2:10-11	96
1:16	58, 145	1:30	26, 27, 73, 75, 77, 107, 156	2:10	90, 92, 95, 96
1:16a	68				
1:16b	67, 68			2:10a	92, 94

Index of Passages | 205

2:10b	94, 95	2:25-30	30, 64, 69, 104, 152	3:15a	119, 120
2:11	3, 61, 68, 71, 79, 94, 98, 116, 130	2:25	25, 53, 112	3:15b	119, 120
		2:25a	109	3:16	120
		2:25b	109	3:17–4:1	45, 121, 128
2:11a	96	2:26	60	3:17-19	121
2:11b	93, 98	2:26a	111	3:17	121, 122, 131, 136
2:12-16	45, 99, 102	2:26b	111	3:18-21	40, 130
2:12	70	2:27-30	40	3:18-19	64, 114, 120, 121, 124, 126, 127, 128
2:12a	100	2:27-28	38		
2:12b	100	2:27a	111		
2:12c	100	2:27b	111		
2:13	61	2:28	42, 111, 112, 113	3:18	122
2:14-18	40			3:19-21	44
2:14-16	101	2:28a	111	3:19	76, 80, 121, 123, 130
2:14	40, 101	2:29	111, 116		
2:15	90, 101, 121	2:30	111	3:19a	124
2:16	55, 101, 102	2:30a	111	3:19b	123
2:17-18	42, 45, 102, 103, 113, 131	3:1-7	128	3:20-21	35, 40, 42, 56, 121, 124, 126, 135, 160
		3:1	108, 113, 116		
2:17	30, 38, 72, 103, 104, 117	3:1a	113		
		3:1b	113	3:20	70, 77, 100, 116, 119, 126, 127, 128, 129, 132, 135
2:17b-18	103, 111	3:2–4:9	34		
2:19-30	102, 104	3:2–4:3	34		
2:19-24	37, 45, 99, 104, 105	3:2-7	45, 113, 114		
		3:2	34, 40, 101, 113, 114	3:20a	126, 128
2:19-22	64, 69			3:20b	129
2:19	116	3:3	114	3:21	72, 80, 118, 129
2:19a	107	3:10-11	118		
2:19b	107	3:10	30, 38, 39, 55, 72, 118, 120, 129, 138	3:21a	130
2:20	107, 132			3:21b	130
2:20a	106			3:30	75
2:21	106				
2:22-23	38			4:1	60, 76, 116, 130
2:22	48, 105, 106, 119	3:10b	116		
		3:10c	116	4:1a	131
2:22b	106	3:11	118	4:1b	121
2:23a	107	3:12-13a	118	4:1c	131
2:23b	104, 107	3:12	48	4:2-4	40, 69
2:24	73, 107, 108, 116	3:12a	119	4:2-3	41, 45, 101, 131, 132
		3:13b	119		
2:25–3:1	37, 45, 108	3:14	119		

Index of Passages

Philippians (continued)		4:20	79, 93, 98, 143	2 Timothy	
4:2	75, 116			1:8	67
4:3	110, 133	4:21-23	37, 45, 144	1:12	67
4:3a	25, 132, 133	4:21-22	106	1:16	57
4:4-9	45, 131, 134	4:21	52	1:16b-17	67
4:4-7	134	4:21a	144	1:17	110
4:4-5a	134	4:21b-22	144	4:8	71
4:4	42, 116	4:21b	64, 144	4:16	58
4:5	116	4:22	31, 64, 141		
4:5b	55, 134	4:22a	144	Titus	
4:6	134, 136	4:22b	144, 145	3:1	52
4:7	42, 53, 134, 136	4:23	53, 54, 97, 116, 144, 146	Philemon	
4:7a	137	4:25	115	1	57, 110
4:8-9	134			2	110, 139
4:8	136	Colossians		7	60
4:9	42, 53, 136	4:18	57	9	57
4:10-20	34, 45, 78, 112, 137			12	60
				20	60
4:10	116, 137	1 Thessalonians		24	146
4:10a	137	1:1	139		
4:10b	138	1:6	122	**Philo and Josephus**	
4:11	138	2:2	71		
4:12-18	58	2:5	60	Philo	
4:12	138	2:10	60	*Embassy to Gaius*	
4:13	138	2:19	131	15	42
4:14-19	58	3:2	105, 110	19	42
4:14	55, 138	3:6	60	147	136
4:15-16	139	3:8	76	353	2
4:15	25, 30, 52, 55, 139, 140	4:16-17	135		
		5:2	56	Josephus	
4:16	25	5:23	137	*Jewish Antiquities*	
4:17	36, 53, 140	5:28	146	18:6	57
4:18-19	143			18.6.5	63
4:18	108, 111, 148, 152	1 Timothy		18:7	58
		1:13	115	18:10	57
4:18a	143	3:2	52	*Jewish Wars*	
4:18b	143	3:8	52	4.10.7	66
4:18c	143	3:10	52	*Vita*	
4:19	79	3:12	52	3	30
4:19b	143	3:13	52		

Index of Passages

Greek and Latin Sources

Appian
Punic Wars
136 11

Aurelius Victor
Epitome de Caesaribus
3.7 2
3.8 96

Cicero
Second Oration against Verres
5.169 87

Dio Cassius
Epitome
9.4.6 123
20.5 126
62.11.1 135
62.11.4 135

Roman History
44.6 13
57.19 4
59.4 4
62.5.2 84
62.18 4

Epictetus
Discourses
4.5.17 142
Essays
4.13.5 36

Horace
Epode V 87

Ovid
Metamorphoses
15:858-66 95

Pausanias
Description of Greece
7.18.7 11

Philostratus
Life of Apollonius
7.27 37

Pliny
Letters
10.34.1 28
10.96.1-10 27
10.96.7 28
10.96.8 23
10.96.9 23

Plutarch
Galba
2:1-2 64

Seneca
De clementia
1:2 42
Epistles
5.7 36
9.9 67

Suetonius
Claudius
34 87

Domitian
21 3
Nero
23:2-14 123
35.5 4
36.2 57
Tiberius
14.3 13

Tacitus
Annals
2.32 87
14.48-49 4
14:48 36
15:37 123
15.67 64
16.21.1 5
16:22 36
6.39 36
Histories
2.72 87
4.11 87
15.60 87

Tertullian
De pallio
i 11

Valerius Maximus
Factorum ac dictorum memorabilium libri IX
2.7.12 87

Index of Authors and Contributors

Abbott, F., 65, 145
Alcock, S., 11
Appian, 11
Arndt, W., 24, 52, 54, 68, 69, 76, 91, 92, 113

Arzt-Grabner, P., 97, 147
Athanasios, A., 172
Aurelius Victor, 2, 96

Bakirtzis, C., 13, 14, 16
Balogh, B., 158
Balsdon, J., 3
Bauer, W., 24, 52, 54, 68, 69, 76, 91, 92, 113
Baumann, R., 3, 5
Behm, J., 123
Betz, H.-D., 44, 173
Bieringer, R., 173
Bockmuel, M., 30, 34, 46, 51, 53, 70, 74, 79, 82, 92, 95, 96, 98, 104, 113, 123, 136, 145
Boddorf, J., 172
Bormann, L., 13, 127, 140
Bornhauser, K., 129
Böttrich, 68, 173
Bradley, K., 19, 50
Braund, D., 2
Breeze, E., 12
Brown, R., 33

Bruce, F., 31, 64, 86, 95, 98, 112, 114, 133, 138

Calpurnius Siculus, 84, 85, 98
Campbell, J., 55
Cassidy, R., 4, 20, 21, 31, 42, 51, 66, 71, 72, 88, 90, 95, 96
Cicero, 35, 87, 104
Clark, R., 168
Clore, V., 173
Collange, J.-F., 72, 97, 101
Collart, P., 6, 8, 9, 10, 12, 13, 14, 15, 17, 53
Cornell, T., 28
Courtright, F., 172

Dahmen, K., 161, 163
Danker, F., 24, 52, 54, 68, 69, 76, 91, 92, 113
deBoer, M., 172
Deissmann, A., 2, 3, 52, 56, 58, 59, 84, 97, 112, 129, 135
Despotis, S., 172
DeVos, C., 7
Dickens, C., 42
Dio Cassius, 3, 4, 5, 13, 84, 123, 125, 126, 135
Doty, W., 35
Duchene, H., 50
Duff, J. and A., 84

Index of Authors and Contributors | 209

Ehrenberg, V., 2
Elsner, J., 3
Epictetus, 36, 37, 142
Evans, N., 173
Evert, L., 172

Fee, G., 40, 48, 52, 55, 64, 68, 70, 73, 75, 92, 93, 101, 109, 114, 120, 132, 140, 141
Feinberg, P., 86
Finley, M., 11, 50
Fitzmyer, J., 33
Forbes, R., 112
Forbes, N., 173
Friesen, S., 147
Fuhrmann, C., 9, 10, 17

Gaba, E., 148
Garnsey, P., 5
George, M., 17
Gill, D., 6
Gingrich, W., 24, 52, 54, 68, 69, 76, 91, 92, 113
Glancey, J., 22
Gordon, M., 50
Grant, M., 6, 14
Griffin, M., 33
Grosvenor, M., 65, 68, 71, 85, 91, 96, 103, 138
Gundry, J., 118
Guthrie, D., 33

Haenchen, E., 22
Harrer, G., 47
Harrill, J., 29, 50, 51
Harris, W., 17, 22, 50, 97, 146, 147
Harrison, J., 53, 97, 146, 147
Hatzopoulos, M., 126, 140
Hawthorne, G., 53, 54, 67, 70, 71, 85, 86, 91, 94, 102, 109, 111, 116
Heen, E., 84, 98

Hellerman, J., 86
Hemer, C., 47
Herder, G., 172
Hirschfeld, O., 36
Horace, 87

Jones, A., 2
Jones, H., 22, 26, 52, 59, 75, 79, 94, 126, 140
Josephus, 30, 33, 57, 58, 63, 66
Joshel, S., 17, 18, 19

Kagel, J., 172
Karakolis, C., 172
Keay, S., 12
Kobelski, P., 172
Koester, H., 16
Koperski, V., 55, 58
Koukouli, C., 142
Koukouli-Chrysanthaki, C., 8, 9, 13, 14, 26, 140, 142
Kovach, A., 173
Kremydi, S., 8, 140
Krytatas, D., 109

Lampe, P., 140
Lenski, N., 17
Levick, B., 3, 6, 8, 11, 12, 13, 14, 140
Liddell, H., 22, 26, 52, 59, 75, 79, 94, 126, 140
Lightfoot, J., 30, 31, 97, 104, 145
Link, H., 124
Lintott, A., 3
Longenecker, R., 22, 57
Lübke, L.-J., 164
Lüdemann, G., 32, 33

Magie, D., 50
Mann, L., 173
Marcion, 31
Marrow, S., 71

Marshall, H., 65, 80, 123, 132, 140
Martin, R., 20, 34, 42, 103, 114, 115, 140
Masters, J., 3
McDermott, M., 55
Meeks, W., 23, 25
Millar, E., 65, 144
Milligan, G., 53, 77, 112, 126, 140
Mitchell, M., 105, 173
Morley, N., 17, 19, 21
Moule, C., 86
Moulton, J., 53, 77, 112, 126, 140
Mouschou, M., 172
Mousoulea, B., 172
Murphy-O'Connor, J., 34, 35, 110
Myers, C., 172

Nickle, K., 141
Nicolaus of Damascus, 84
Nowicki, M., 173

Oakes, P., 7, 21, 22
O'Brien, R., 20, 31, 54, 63, 75, 81, 82, 86, 92, 94, 95, 109, 111, 113, 114, 121, 123, 137, 139, 140
Oliver, J., 58
Ovid, 95

Parsons, M., 22
Pausanias, 11
Peterlin, D., 8, 23, 26, 138
Philo, 2, 42, 136
Philostratus, 37
Pilhofer, P., 13
Pliny, 23, 24, 27
Plutarch, 64
Price, S., 12, 14, 15, 16, 28, 56, 84, 135
Pseudo-Demetrius, 34, 35
Publius Syrus, 51
Ramelli, I., 49

Ramsay, W., 26, 33, 104, 112
Rapske, B., 21, 22, 35, 57
Reicke, B., 31
Reinmuth, E., 140
Reumann, J., 7, 23, 52, 53, 67, 68, 76, 106, 110, 111, 130, 133
Rhoads, D., 37, 44, 104, 105
Rhodes, P., 28
Riesner, R., 20, 33
Rives, J., 13
Roger, J., 166
Ruppel, W., 126

Saczewski, R., 161, 162
Saddington, D., 9
Saller, R., 5
Scheidel, W., 17, 50
Schlier, H., 71
Scott, J., 44, 124
Scott, R., 22, 26, 52, 59, 75, 79, 94, 126, 140
Seneca, 36, 42, 67
Sève, M., 156
Sextius Paconianus, 35
Sherwin-White, A., 10, 11, 47
Smallwood, M., 2, 3
Smart, C., 87
Soisson, N., 173
Solin, H., 47
Sonnenwald, D., 163, 164, 165
Spilker, C., 173
Standhartinger, A., 37, 42
Staudinger, F., 56
Stevenson, G., 9, 12
Stowers, S., 34, 35
Strabo, 22
Suetonius, 3, 4, 13, 57, 87, 123
Sumney, J., 56, 65, 73, 76, 77, 79, 80, 81, 92, 94, 103, 118, 119, 120, 139
Syme, R., 4, 6

Tacitus, 3, 4, 5, 36, 64, 87, 123
Tamez, E., 25, 35
Tellbe, M., 2, 9, 129
Tertullian, 11
Thompson, A., 50, 51

Valerius Maximus, 87
Vanderpool, E., 2
Verhoef, E., 172
Vigneron, A., 173
Vincent, M., 8, 27, 77, 83, 119, 131

Waldron, S., 173
Walter, N., 140, 141
Watson, G., 64
Watson, D., 84
Weaver, P., 31, 109, 144
Westermann, W., 11, 17, 18
Williams, D., 6, 21, 78

Zerwick, M., 65, 68, 71, 85, 91, 96, 103, 138

Subjects

a cognitionibus (Roman
 department), 64, 65, 145
administrative fees, for civil appeals
 to emperor's court, 58
advent
 of Christ, 55, 119, 126, 135
 of imperial figures, 135, 163
aediles, 8, 9
Aemilius Paullus, 6
agoranomoi, 10
Agrippina, 4, 164
 depiction on coin, 164
altars, and emperor cult at Philippi,
 13, 14
Amphipolis, as center of slave trade,
 22, 50
animal sacrifice, and emperor
 worship, 28, 29
annihilation, of persecutors, 76, 77,
 121, 124, 130
Antistius, charge of *maiestas*, 36
apologia, 58, 59, 60
apostles of churches, 25
Appian Way, 104
archimimus, 9
Artemis, 14, 121
augur, at Philippi, 12, 14
augustales, 19
 and cult of Augustus, 12, 13
Augustus
 character of rule, 5–6
 conferral of Roman citizenship, 11,
 12, 128

depiction on coins, 161, 162
 as founder of Philippi, 6, 7
 as god, 2
 as holding sway over the earth, 95
 and *pax Augustana*, 136
 as savior, 2, 129
 use of *maiestas*, 3, 4
 use of Philippi as settlement for
 military veterans, 6, 63
 victory at Philippi, 161
Aulus Caprilius Timotheus, as slave
 trader, 50, 166
authorities
 as enemies of the cross of Christ,
 121–31
 Paul's critique of, 121–31
 See also magistrates

bacillae, 10
Battle of Actium, 6, 7, 16
Battle of Philippi, 6, 7, 13, 16
bebaiō, 59
bishops and deacons, at Philippi, 25,
 52, 53, 110
blood
 of animal sacrifices, 28, 29
 of Christ, 29
 of Paul, 103
book of life, 133

Caesar's household. *See familia
 caesaris*
Calpurnian drama, 98, 99

Calpurnius Siculus, on Nero as god, 84, 85
chains
  as engendering shame, 66, 67
  Paul in, 46, 48, 56, 57, 63, 64, 66, 67, 68, 102, 104, 122. *See also* Paul, as slave; Paul, as slave of Christ
  response of Christians to, 65, 66, 67, 68, 69
chanting
  on behalf of Nero, 125, 126
  and performance of letter to the Philippians, 125, 126, 128
  by Philippian slaves, 128
charis, 41, 53, 54, 55, 60, 144, 146, 147
  of ruling emperor, 146, 147
choragiarius, 9, 10
Christ
  as equal to the Father, 83–85, 130
  in the form of a slave, 85, 86, 129
  in the form of God, 83, 85, 86, 129
  as savior, 70
  as slave, 48, 49
  See also Jesus
Christ drama, 43, 44, 61, 78, 79, 81–99, 108
Christ Jesus, Paul's use of, 51
Christian community, as *hetaeria*, 27, 28
Christians, in household of Caesar, 145, 146. *See also* Philippians (community)
chronology, of Paul's writings, 66
circumcisers, 113–15, 128
circumcision
  of Gentile Christians, 113–15
  proponents of, 101
citizenship, heavenly, 126–29
  of slaves, 128
citizenship, Roman, at Philippi, 11–12, 126, 127. *See also* Paul, Roman citizenship of
Claudius
  as benefactor, 2, 129
  depiction on coin, 162, 163
  as god, 2, 129, 147
  as lord, 96, 97
  and *maiestas*, 4
  as savior, 2, 129
Clement (Paul's co-worker), 110, 133
coin(s)
  altars depicted on, 14
  and history of Philippi, 6, 7, 8
  imperial, and Philippians' gift to Paul, 140, 141, 142
  minted at Philippi, 41
  minted to celebrate arrival of emperor, 135
  from Patras, 163
  from Philippi, 161, 162
  Roman, 163, 164, 165
  roman provincial and imperial, 160–65
Colonia Victrix Philippensium, 6
Corinth
  provision for Paul's ministry, 25
  slave trading at, 50
crucifixion
  of Jesus, and court proceedings, 59
  of slaves, 18, 87
  as slave's form of death, 39, 87, 90, 116, 117, 168
cursus publicus (imperial postal service), 148
cursus velox, 148
Cybele, 14

day of Christ, 55, 56, 102
death, similarities between Paul's and Jesus's, 117–20, 130

214 | INDEX OF SUBJECTS

decuriones, 8, 10, 14
dendrophorus, 15
diakonos, 52, 53
discipleship, at Philippi, 99–102
division, because of Paul's chains, 62, 65–70
Domitian, and *maiestas*, 3
douloi, 48
doxology, 143
duumviri, 8, 9, 10, 14

ekklēsia, 52, 114, 115, 139, 140
emperor cult, 56, 101, 121
emperor day, 15, 16, 56
emperors, as gods, 84
Epaphroditus, 18, 31, 36, 37, 38, 41, 43, 44, 45, 53, 58, 64, 69, 78, 99, 102, 104, 124, 132, 137, 138, 140, 141, 142, 143, 144, 147, 148, 152
  as apostle, 25
  as "brother" and co-worker of Paul, 109–11
  civic standing, 109–11
  as freed slave, 109
  illness of, 111
  meaning of name, 109
  mission of, 108–13
  Paul's description of, 109–11
Ephesus, slave trade at, 50
Epictetus, rejection of coins bearing image of Nero, 142
episkopos, 52, 53
Esquiline Hill as site for crucifixion of slaves, 87
Euodia, 41, 45, 110, 131–34
  meaning of name, 132
Euodia and Synteche, Paul's encouragement to unity, 131–33
exaltation, of Jesus, following death, 91–96

familia caesaris, 19, 30, 31, 64, 109, 112, 141, 144–46
farewell supper, and Jesus's beneficence toward slaves, 88
fasces, 10
festivals, honoring emperors, 15, 16
flamines, for Augustus and Claudius at Philippi, 12, 14
forum
  at Philippi, 8, 156, 157
  emperor cult in, 13

Gaius
  as god, 2
  as lord, 2, 96
  as savior, 2
  use of *maiestas*, 4
Gate of Crenides, 154
gift, of Philippians to Paul, 41, 43, 58, 112, 137–43, 152
glory of God, as outcome of Christ drama, 98
god, as title in emperor cult, 1, 2
god speakers, 16
God the Father
  presence at death and exaltation of Jesus, 90, 91
  role in exaltation of Jesus, 91–93
gods/goddesses, cult of, at Philippi, 14
golden chains, of Nero, 122, 123
gospel
  advanced by Paul's chains, 62, 63–65
  use in Philippians, 55, 58
governance, of Philippi, 8, 9, 10
grace, in Pauline greeting, 53, 54
gymnasia, and emperor cult, 15

Herod Agrippa, in chains, 57
hetaeria, 27, 28

humility, exhortation to, 80

irenarchae, 8, 10, 14
Isis, 14, 53, 121
Isis and Sarapis, cult at Philippi, 53
Ius Italicum, 8

Jerusalem collection, 25
Jesus
  condemnation on grounds of *maiestas*, 89, 90
  exaltation, in every realm of creation, 94, 95
  in form of slave, 39, 129
  as ground for Paul's joy, 103
  humiliation of, 89
  as king, 129
  as Lord, 54, 108, 116, 120, 129, 130, 146
  love for slaves, 88, 89
  as savior, 129, 130
  as slave, 86–88
joy, in Philippians, 41, 42, 55, 79, 103, 113, 131, 134
Julio-Claudians
  experience of shame at exaltation of Jesus, 95, 96
  as saviors, 129
Julius Caesar
  depiction on coin, 161, 162
  as a god, 84
Jupiter, as controlling the triformed universe, 95
koinōnia, 55, 61
  of Paul with Philippians, 55, 61, 116, 139

Latin, use at Philippi, 8, 12
leschai, 26
letters, ancient, types of, 34
libertini, 19, 58

lictors, attendance on *duumviri*, 10
Livia cult, at Philippi, 12, 13
locator scaenicorum, 10
lord
  as exalted name of Jesus, 93, 94, 95, 96, 97
  as title in emperor cult, 1, 2
Lydia, 20, 110
  and Christian community at Philippi, 22, 24–26

magistrates, as agents of persecution, 27, 28, 29, 117
maiestas
  in Julio-Claudian era, 3–5
  offenses against, 3, 4, 35, 36
manumission, formal and informal, 19
map, route between Philippi and Rome, 148, 149
Marcion, on letter to the Philippians, 31
Mark Antony, 6
marriage, prohibition between slaves, 18
martyrdom, for Paul, 102, 103
military personnel, at Philippi, 6, 7, 136
money, difficulty of transporting, 141
muneriarus, 10

natal alienation, of slaves, 18
Neapolis, 8, 148, 150
Neapolis Gate, 150, 154
Nero
  as adversary of Paul in Rome, 121, 122
  as benefactor of the world, 129
  as crime lord, 135
  depiction on coins, 162–65
  as enemy of the cross, 122

Nero (continued)
  as god, 2, 84
  in golden chains, 122, 123
  as Jupiter, 84, 85
  as lord, 41, 84, 97, 135, 146, 147
  and *maiestas*, 4, 5, 36
  as savior, 3, 129
  sexual conduct of, 123, 124
  tour of Greece, 33
  use of donatives with praetorian guard, 64
Nero drama, 98, 99

obedience, of Jesus, 91, 92
Octavian. *See* Augustus
Onesimus, 51
Onesiphorus, 57, 67, 110

parousia
  of emperor, 74
  of Paul, 74
patriarchy, and slaves in Roman society, 18
Paul
  affection for the Philippians, 130, 131, 143
  allegiance to Christ while in prison, 115–17
  anticipation of death, 116, 117
  beatings at Philippi, 24
  critique of Roman authorities, 121–31
  date of arrival in Rome and martyrdom, 33
  encouragement of Philippians, 134–37
  experience with slavery, 49–51
  full name of, 47
  images on late sarcophagi, 170
  as imitator of Christ, 39, 40
  intention to go to Spain, 26, 65, 73, 107

  Jewish standing of, 114, 115, 128
  love for Christ and for the Father, 82, 83
  ministry at Philippi in Acts, 20, 21
  as model for Philippian Christians, 122, 136, 137
  and Philippian slaves, 20
  opposition to circumcisers, 114, 115
  potential for death or life, 70–74
  as prisoner in Caesarea, 31
  as prisoner in Rome, 29, 30, 31, 32, 33, 34–37, 56
  rejection of Philippians' gift, 139–43
  role in exonerating Christ, 59, 60, 68
  Roman citizenship of, 20, 21, 24, 126, 127, 129
  as slave, 47, 48, 49
  as slave of Christ, 86, 87
  as source of Christian contagion at Philippi, 24
  as subversive of imperial Rome, 20, 21
Paulus family, 47
pax Augustana, 136
peace, in Pauline greeting, 53
peace of God, and *pax Augustana*, 136, 137
persecution
  of Philippian Christian community, 26–29, 107, 117
  of Philippians and of Paul, 74, 75, 117
Perseus (king of Pynda), 6
Philemon (letter), and slavery, 51
Philip of Macedon, 6
  and theater at Philippi, 9
Philippi
  architecture of, 8
  Augustus as founder, 6, 7

Christian community at, 23–27
Christian community, gathering places, 26
Christian community, persecution of, 26–29, 107
Christian population, 23
city plan, 154, 155
commercial life of, 8, 10
emperor cult at, 12–16
forum and commercial market, 156, 157
governance, 8–10
military history of, 6–7
population, 7
Roman character of, 7–11
Roman citizenship at, 11–12, 20, 21, 126, 127
as Roman military colony, 6
three-dimensional rendering, 158
Philippians (community)
encouraged by Paul, 134, 135, 136, 137
gift to Paul, 41, 43, 58, 112, 137–43, 152
as imitators of Paul, 122
as participants in performance of letter, 124, 125
participation in Jerusalem collection, 25
Paul's affection for, 130, 131
public conduct, 75
unity in the community, 74–79, 119
Philippians (letter)
address and salutation, 46–54
concluding greeting and benediction, 144–47
as counter-imperial letter, 35
as covered speech/hidden transcript, 44, 124
date, 32, 33
historical narrative in, 42, 43
letter type, 35
outline of, 45
Paul's purposes in writing, 38–42
performance of, 37, 42, 43, 108
as prison letter, 34–37, 46
subversiveness of, 43–44
thanksgiving section, 46, 54–61
unity of letter, 34
Philippians 2:6-11
as drama, 37, 43–44, 81–99
as preexisting hymn, 81
Pliny, on contagion of the Christian cult, 23, 24, 27
pontifices, 12, 14
population
Christian, at Philippi, 23, 25, 26
slave, in Roman Empire, 17
praetorian guard, 30, 31, 32, 36, 38, 57, 62, 63, 109, 122, 125, 145
on coins, 160–65
involvement in imperial matters, 64
at Philippi, 6, 7, 8
at Rome, 30, 31
principalities and powers, involvement in death of Jesus, 90
prison letters, 34–37, 46
public venues, as sites for emperor cult, 15, 16
Publius Syrus, on slavery, 51

quaestores, 8, 9
quinquennales, 8, 9, 14

resurrection, of Jesus and of Paul, 118
Roman Empire, demise of, 95, 96
Rome
division in Christian community at, 43, 106
as place of origin of letter to the Philippians, 29, 30, 31

sacerdotes, for Livia at Philippi, 12
salvation
    in letter to Philippians, 100
    of Philippian Christians, 76, 77
sanctuaries
    and the emperor cult, 14
    and religious cult at Philippi, 14
Sarapis, 14, 53
sarcophagus
    of Junius Bassius, 170, 171
    of the Resurrection, 170, 171
savior, as title in emperor cult, 1, 2
self-emptying, of Christ, 41, 49, 78, 81, 82, 85, 90, 91
Sextius Paconianus, charge of *maiestas*, 35, 36
sexual organs, as gods of Nero, 123
shame
    of the authorities, 21, 95, 124, 125
    of chains, 66, 67, 70, 71, 130
    of Jesus Christ, 71, 86, 94, 95
    and Paul, 57, 70, 71, 77, 78, 137
Silvanus, 13, 14, 15, 17, 121
slave merchants, 17, 166
slave trade, 49, 50
slavery
    Paul's undermining of, 80
    in Roman Empire, 16–19
slaves
    as *augustales* at Philippi, 12, 13
    Christian, at Philippi, 21, 22
    Christian owners' treatment of, 49
    denial of Roman citizenship to, 126–28
    depiction as naked, 168, 169
    depiction on stele, 166, 167
    emancipated, rights of, 18, 19
    as friends of Jesus, 88
    heavenly citizenship of, 128
    labor of, 18
    lack of legal protections, 18
    manumission of, 18, 19
    and military conquest, 17
    names of, 18
    population of, at Philippi, 21, 22
    position during worship, 49
    public, role at Philippi, 10, 11, 17
    sources of, 17
    treatment of, 17, 18
    work of, 106
spies/informants, 36, 37, 76
Stoic moral exhortations, use by Paul, 136
suffering
    of Paul, 32, 40, 65, 67, 69, 78, 146
    of Philippian Christians, 26, 77, 146
Sulpicius Comerinus Pythicus, 5
syncretism, at Philippi, 14
Synteche, 41, 45, 92, 110, 131–34
    meaning of name, 132

taxation, 8
temples, in Philippi's forum, 13
theater, at Philippi, 9, 98, 108, 125, 126
Thrasea Paetus, charge of *maiestas*, 36
Three Niches sanctuary, 14
Tiberius
    as benefactor of whole world, 2
    as god, 2
    as savior, 2
    use of *maiestas*, 4
Timothy, 26, 33, 37, 38, 44, 45, 46, 47, 48, 57, 64, 67, 69, 99, 102, 104–10, 112, 124, 132, 143, 144, 147
    circumcision of, 105
    mission of, 104–8
    relationship with Paul, 106
    role as envoy of Paul, 105

travel plans, 104–7
titles, used in emperor cult, 1–3
Trajan, and persecution of Christian community, 27, 28

universe, realms of, 94, 95

Via Egnatia, 8, 22, 104, 141, 148, 150, 152, 154, 156, 172
Virgil, on the rule of Augustus, 5

www.ingramcontent.com/pod-product-compliance
Lightning Source LLC
Chambersburg PA
CBHW030110010526
44116CB00005B/188